CULT COLLECTORS

Cult Collectors examines cultures of consumption and the fans who collect cult film and TV merchandise.

Author Lincoln Geraghty argues that there has been a change in the fan convention space, where collectible merchandise and toys, rather than just the fictional text, have become objects for trade, nostalgia, and a focal point for fans' personal narratives. New technologies also add to this changing identity of cult fandom whereby popular websites such as eBay and ThinkGeek become cyber sites of memory and profit for cult fan communities.

The book opens with an analysis of the problematic representations of fans and fandom in film and television. Stereotypes of the fan and collector as portrayed in series such as *The Big Bang Theory* and films like *The 40-Year-Old Virgin* are discussed alongside changes in consumption practices and the mainstreaming of cult media. Following this, theoretical chapters consider issues of gender, representation, nostalgia and the influence of social media. Finally, extended case study chapters examine in detail the connections between the fan community and the commodities bought and sold.

Topics discussed include:

- The San Diego Comic-Con and the cult geographies of the fan convention
- Hollywood memorabilia and collecting cinema history
- The *Star Wars* franchise, merchandising and the adult collector
- Online stores and the commercialisation of cult fandom
- Mattel, Hasbro and nostalgia for animated eighties children's television.

Lincoln Geraghty is Reader in Popular Media Cultures and Director of the Centre for Cultural and Creative Research in the School of Creative Arts, Film and Media at the University of Portsmouth, UK. His research interests lie within the broad contexts of British and American popular culture and he has written extensively in these areas.

"*Cult Collectors* makes a skillful contribution to cultural and fan studies, theorizing 'second-hand fandom' whilst smartly tackling 'transformative nostalgia'. Emphasizing places and spaces of collecting – whether San Diego Comic-Con, Collectormania or Forbidden Planet – Lincoln Geraghty forcefully argues for the individualizing vitality of collectors' material and consumer practices. This is a valuable study of how fans commemorate, curate and create value in today's media culture. Definitely one to add to your collection."

Matt Hills, *Professor of Film and TV Studies, Aberystwyth University, Wales*

"As I sat down to read *Cult Collectors* in an office full of licensed toys, posters, mugs, and candy, its importance was clear: film and television studies have had too little to say about collectibles and about the huge role they play in media culture. Geraghty delivers the goods in this accessible, smart, fun, and highly perceptive book. Highly recommended."

Jonathan Gray, *Professor of Media and Cultural Studies, University of Wisconsin, Madison, USA*

CULT COLLECTORS

Nostalgia, Fandom and Collecting Popular Culture

Lincoln Geraghty

Routledge
Taylor & Francis Group

LONDON AND NEW YORK

First published 2014
by Routledge
2 Park Square, Milton Park, Abingdon, Oxon OX14 4RN

and by Routledge
711 Third Avenue, New York, NY 10017

Routledge is an imprint of the Taylor & Francis Group, an informa business

British Library Cataloguing in Publication Data
A catalogue record for this book is available from the British Library

Library of Congress Cataloging in Publication Data
Geraghty, Lincoln, 1977-
Cult collectors : nostalgia, fandom and collecting popular culture /
Lincoln Geraghty.
pages cm
Includes bibliographical references and index.
Includes filmography.
1. Fans (Persons) – Psychology. 2. Mass media – Social aspects. 3. Mass media and culture. 4. Collectors and collecting – Social aspects. 5. Motion pictures – Collectibles. 6. Television broadcasting – Collectibles. I. Title.
HM646.G48 2014
302.23 – dc23
2013027210

ISBN: 978-0-415-61764-2 (hbk)
ISBN: 978-0-415-61766-6 (pbk)
ISBN: 978-0-203-13026-1 (ebk)

Typeset in Bembo
by Taylor & Francis Books

Printed and bound in Great Britain by
TJ International Ltd, Padstow, Cornwall

I dedicate this book to my dad.

CONTENTS

LIST OF ILLUSTRATIONS

ACKNOWLEDGEMENTS

A book of this nature has inevitably required the help of a number of people who I must acknowledge. For originally having the faith to take this project on I wish to thank the editorial staff at Routledge, particularly Sheni Kruger and Natalie Foster. I can't thank those individuals enough for having the patience while this book was in progress and for allowing me those extensions as I gathered more material and needed time to develop those ideas. Much of the onsite research at the San Diego Comic-Con, Forbidden Planet and other conventions I attended would not have been possible without the financial support of the Centre for Cultural and Creative Research (CCCR) at the University of Portsmouth. Through the aid of project funding and teaching relief I was able to get this book started and do the serious research that was required – of course, being able to do some of that research in San Diego helped enormously! I must also thank CCCR and the British Association for American Studies for awarding me travel funds to gather primary material from the Special Collections Department at the University of Iowa, that it came near the completion of this book gave me that last injection of energy to see where this work needs to go next and what future projects should come off the back of it. My thanks go to Kathryn Hodson at Iowa for helping me enormously during the short time I was there. During the writing of this book I was kindly invited to join PLACIM (Platform for a Cultural History of Children's Media) a research group based at Maastricht University, led by Elisabeth Wesseling. I want to thank Lies, Gary Cross, Joshua Garrison, and all the group members for their thoughtful comments and stimulating ideas we shared at workshops on remediation and nostalgia in Maastricht and Reading. They have informed the development of this book in numerous ways. Keeping me going throughout the whole research and writing process has been the enthusiasm of the students on my two fan studies units, discussions proved very inspiring. To my friends and colleagues (past and present) in the School of Creative Arts, Film and Media – John Caro, Van Norris,

Graham Spencer, Imogen Jeffery, Justin Smith, Paul McDonald and Derek Johnston – I thank you all for your support and encouragement.

The inspiration for this book comes from the toys and memorabilia I had as a kid and now collect and display around my office and house. For this I must thank my parents; without their love and support, of course, none of that would have been possible and I would not be where I am today without it. Who else would have bought me those Transformers at Christmas? Lastly, I offer my deepest gratitude to my wife Rebecca – without her encouragement, love and patience this book would not exist at all. She deserves the biggest credit for letting me get away with the line, "I need that new Lego *Star Wars* Battle of Hoth set for my research."

Picture Acknowledgements

All images are by permission of the author.

INTRODUCTION

Cult Collectors: Nostalgia, Fandom and Collecting

In a BBC news article from December 2011 it was revealed that a copy of the first issue of *Action Comics*, featuring Superman's debut, was sold at an auction in New York for $2.16 million (£1.4 million). Not giving too much detail the article surmised that the seller was actor Nicolas Cage, a self-confessed Superman fan and well-known collector, who had originally bought the copy for $150,000 in 1997 ("Action Comics Superman"). Offering a brief suggestion that collecting high value items such as first editions of famous comic books was a more stable form of investment in "troubled economic times" the article did not discuss why collecting memorabilia from famous media franchises might be such a popular and profitable endeavour. Indeed, the reason given why high ticket items were selling well at auction does not really take into account the motivations and pleasures fans get out of collecting – apart from making money it seems. In fact, objects and ephemera from popular culture have proven for a long time to be quite lucrative money-spinners at auctions, fan conventions and online so implying that only during a recession comics are deemed valuable is rather short-sighted. However, what I think this news article about the sale of a first edition *Action Comics* does highlight is the continued fascination for and value placed on iconic and historic pieces of our cultural history, and that fans of popular media culture (in this case Superman comic fans) are always good for a story in the mainstream press.

Examples of fan collecting and collections are common news stories. Compared with extremes such as the Superman story and an article about car collector Mark Perkins who had to sell his original Batmobile car so as to create more space at his Berkshire home for his James Bond DB5, *Ghostbusters* Ecto-1, and Volkswagen Beetle from *The Love Bug* (1968), there are hundreds of other examples of collectors who simply collect for the joy of collecting (Radnedge, 2010: 37). Small items, second-hand objects, records, toys, autographs, badges, models, comics, pins, stickers, dolls, DVDs, videos, CDs, games, clothes, movie props, posters, and the list goes on. The collecting of popular culture has never been so popular, as more things are produced and the media landscape continues to grow everything becomes collectible. As a result, the collecting practices of fans become more sophisticated. The Internet becomes the first port of call for fans who want an item to start or complete that all-important collection. Sites such as eBay have revolutionised collecting and made the physical objects of popular media culture all the more available. What the web has also done is make history more accessible, our memories more tangible, thus bringing the past into the present. In that sense, collecting enables fans to connect with the histories of their favourite media texts in ways they just could not achieve twenty or thirty years ago.

This book is an attempt to understand the popularity of collecting items of popular media culture. In an age where digital culture threatens to replace older forms and formats of entertainment, the material objects that fans collect remain solid signifiers of the historical significance of previous media texts. That they do not go away suggests that they are worth more to fans than simply money; they must mean something personal for such demand to still exist. Throughout this book, I will be examining the collecting practices of fans within the contexts of the personal meanings they bring to the objects that make up their collections. In an interview for the website doctorwhotoys.net, Matt Hills suggests that while fan studies is a thriving area of academic inquiry, collecting and the physical objects that fans collect have attracted less critical attention: "Much has been written about fan fiction, and there's started to be more on costuming and pilgrimage (visiting locations linked to filming), but the fan craft of modding and creating one-offs as well as generating photographs/videos of toys, has not been studied enough" (Hills, 2009b).

At the same time I absolutely agree with Hills that collecting has been overlooked in fan studies and argue that it is devalued as a fan practice because of its basis in consumption rather than production, I would also stress that little work has been done on fandom in terms of memory and nostalgia – two driving influences on what makes fans collect and why they become fans in the first place. Again the reason for this lack of research is down to the negative critical attention nostalgia as an emotion has attracted, particularly when related to fandom. Eminent media fan scholar Henry Jenkins argues that in order "for nostalgia to operate, we must in fact forget aspects of the actual past and substitute a sentimental myth about how things might have been" (2007: 157) or the "objects we never possessed" (Jenkins, 1998a: 4). However, this cannot be true since fans utilise media archives, YouTube, eBay and other social media to discuss old and once-forgotten media texts all the time – it is the very essence that drives the daily interactions of fan culture. Nothing is ever forgotten, even intentionally, because it always exists in the present – either through the remediation of film and television online or in high street stores that sell repackaged and relaunched merchandise to eager fans. If sentimentality is the threat to established fan cultures, it is also the impetus for fans to take action when texts and objects are under threat of disappearing, being cancelled or taken off the shelves. Fans are always reassessing and re-evaluating media texts from the past; they bring them into the present and reconstitute them as part of contemporary fan culture. Indeed, this would seem to be the result of convergence culture.

Take for example the website tv.cream.org, designed to archive and catalogue media ephemera from yesteryear and celebrate popular media history that is often ignored for its cheapness, tackiness, or simple poor quality. Started in 1997, the site attracts thousands of fans of UK TV and popular culture. It has its own YouTube channel and also publishes books that list vintage objects and collectibles (see Berry, 2007). A similar website, tv-ark.org.uk, serves as a repository of old television idents, formats, logos, commercials, news programmes, genres, and TV presenters. These sites don't forget aspects of the past; they seek absolute accuracy and authenticity. Those who surf the pages of these sites might feel a sense of nostalgia for media of the past but what they are viewing are unsentimentalised remediations of actual content – these websites act as digital museums. Websites and books that can be considered nostalgic are part of a renewed cultural interest in and recycling of media history that serves to keep the past very much in the minds of contemporary audiences. Popular books on television in the 1970s and 1980s by Viner (2009) and Bromley (2010), or books on toys from yesteryear by May (2009), Novick (2006) and Berry (2007) suggest that the histories of popular culture are being constantly rewritten, re-evaluated and there is an audience out there that wants to engage with and relive that history in some form or another. Tara Brabazon contends that popular culture and memory are linked: "Popular culture is a conduit for popular memory, moving words, ideas, ideologies and narratives through time ... Popular memory, by its very nature, is a fount of consensus and a building block of 'the mainstream'" (2005: 67).

The death of former British Prime Minister Margaret Thatcher created hundreds of newspaper column inches but it also induced a national remembering and reassessment of popular culture of the 1980s. Both UK and US press were engaged in a nostalgic reappraisal of history. An article in the *USA Today* describes the results of a survey that revealed more than half of Americans polled missed leg warmers (DiBlasio, 2013: 1A) and a LoveFilm poll was reported in *The I* ("Holding out", 2013) as showing a massive surge in downloads of old 1980s and 1990s animated TV series, the top download was *Super Mario Bros. Super Show!* (1989–91). For Paul Grainge, "As a cultural style, nostalgia has developed in accordance with a series of political, cultural, and material factors that have made 'pastness' an expedient and marketable mode" (2002: 58). In this regard we might understand the nostalgia fans feel for relaunched toylines, film franchises or television series as being part of contemporary culture's marketing and remediation of the past; not necessarily a longing for what historical texts may or may not get brought back but a re-examination of the media history archive. By extension, in the physical objects that fans collect, salvage and reclaim from the past we can see how notions of nostalgia and memory are bound up in the creation of a contemporary fan identity rather than a recreation of past by substituting bits of history with myth or things that never existed. For Svetlana Boym, "nostalgia is about the relationship between individual biography and the biography of groups or nations, between personal and collective memory" (2001: xvi). Therefore, collecting objects that form a visual and physical biography of the self is an act of improvement not loss; it is not about mourning the past but about creating a reflexive and tangible identity in the present: "Nostalgia is not always about the past; it can be retrospective but also prospective" (Boym, 2001: xvi).

In the examples of collecting and collections discussed throughout this book popular culture is made meaningful through memories; fan culture is not commodified but personalised. Memories are essential to the production of subjectivity therefore the memories embedded within collections of toys, merchandise and collectibles are emblems of the self, markers of identity and symbolic of the cultural capital that fans accumulate in their life-long engagement with a media text. As Mieke Bal suggests, collecting is a form of narrative where "a subjectively focalised sequence of events is presented and communicated" through the acquisition, cataloguing and reordering of objects (Bal, 1994: 100). Nostalgia is not so much about loss but a romance of the self and a celebration of historical texts that no longer disappear thanks to new media technologies and the spaces of fan interaction like the convention or collectible store. Personal histories become embodied in the collected objects of popular culture, and archives devoted to their preservation are rebuilt through remediation.

In *The System of Objects* Jean Baudrillard proposes that the collection is personal and "what you really collect is always yourself" (2005: 97). As in fan studies, there is a clear link between identity and object of fandom – one reflects the other. In that respect, Cornel Sandvoss argues that fandom is "a symbolic resource in the formation of identity and in the positioning of one's self in the modern world … and the integration of the self into the dominant economic, social and cultural conditions of industrial modernity … it is, in every sense, a mirror of consumption" (2005: 165). In the collection, then, we see personalised depictions of history – mirrors to the self. Objects therefore embody memories of things past and inform activities and what you do with the collection in the present. They are necessary components of life as it is defined by the historical trajectory from birth to death. Baudrillard continues, "It is in this sense that the environment of private objects and their possession (collecting being the most extreme instance) is a dimension of our life which, though imaginary, is absolutely essential. Just as essential as dreams" (2005: 103). However, if fandom and collecting are about formations of the self then they are also products of the cultural environment – how we are influenced by culture and what parts of culture we take into our own lives. Jenkins defines fan culture as a "culture that is produced by fans and other amateurs for circulation through an underground economy and that draws much of its content from the commercial culture" (2006a: 325). In this way we can also understand practices of collecting as mass produced and public objects are taken into the personal collection of the individual. Once collected, these objects become talking points and allow for social exchange between individuals as they become highly valued and desirable within the wider fan community. Again Baudrillard recognises this:

As for collecting proper, it has a door open onto culture, being concerned with differentiated objects which often have exchange value, which may also be "objects" of preservation, trade, social ritual, exhibition – perhaps even generators of profit. Such objects are accompanied by projects. And though they remain interrelated, their interplay involves the social world outside, and embraces human relationships.

(2005: 111)

The following chapters examine the human relationships created by and embodied in the collection. In looking at specific examples of collecting and the types of objects collected I hope to build an understanding of how physical objects and personal memories impact on fan identity. Consideration will also be given to how environmental conditions, spaces and places influence the relationships between individuals and fan communities. This is because where those objects of fandom are collected provides enormous insight into how the past is brought through to the present.

The Book

Cult Collectors: Nostalgia, Fandom and Collecting Popular Culture examines cultures of consumption and the fans who collect cult film and TV merchandise. I focus on textual representations of cult collecting in film and TV and examine geographical sites of collecting cult media such as the convention or collector's fair (e.g. the San Diego Comic-Con, the chain store Forbidden Planet). The book is split into four parts: the first discusses the stereotypes of fans who collect merchandise; the second focuses on the actual fans who collect; the third discusses the places where this collecting takes place; and the fourth looks at the virtual spaces visited by collectors. Each part also contains a case study chapter, focusing on Hollywood cinema, *The Transformers* TV series and toys, *Star Wars* action figures, and the Lego fan club and fan videos. All examine in detail the connections between the fan community and the commodities bought and sold (from autographs to toys, DVDs to models). I argue that collectible merchandise, rather than just the fictional text, becomes an object for trade, nostalgia, and personal identity. New technologies help provide access to old media forms and collectibles and fan conventions represent a physical space where collecting and recollecting personal histories takes place.

In chapter one I discuss the various representations and stereotypes of the fan and cult collector presented in media and culture. It sets out to deconstruct the images we have of the fan (the geek, nerd, etc.) and assesses to what extent these representations have been created and perpetuated by the media, fans themselves, and academics that have sought to study their practices. In discussing a selection of popular films and television I address notions of genre, subcultural capital, nostalgia and identity. Fan collectors are not merely consumers; they are often active producers of more collectibles that assume greater value in fan communities. Therefore, it will be important to not only highlight the individual fan collector but also discuss their relationship with other collectors. How do people relate to an ever growing and diversifying media landscape? How important is technology in the development of networks for collectors? How does nostalgia act as an impetus for collecting and preserving media ephemera?

Collecting movie merchandise is not a new phenomenon. The relics of Hollywood, from star autographs to movie props and other cinema-related material are highly sought-after objects that not only remind fans and collectors of the golden age of cinema but are connectors to a past they may not have experienced in person. They allow them access to a world of celebrity, stardom and fantasy. Historically, merchandising has been part of the moviemaking industry since the beginning: freebies were handed out in the age of the Dream Palace to encourage audiences to go to the cinema and boost box office takings (Gomery, 1992). As some audiences evolved into devoted fan communities, dedicated to following a particular star or genre, these groups bought and collected Hollywood icons in a search for authenticity, to get closer to their idols and look beyond the cinematic illusion. Collecting Hollywood memorabilia today serves to recreate that illusion and break it down; fans wish to be part of Hollywood history and seek to redefine it by amassing a collection that suits their own passions and desires. Chapter two will analyse the notion of enduring fandom (Kuhn, 1999) and discuss to what extent collecting expensive movie memorabilia from Hollywood history allows contemporary fans access into a fantasy world of their own creation. Often cult fans are fans of franchises that are based in science fiction and fantasy universes, therefore memorabilia from these texts provide the only physical connections to those fantasy worlds. Those fans that collect merchandise of a bygone cinema celebrate a world that once existed in the real world but also existed in the imaginations of those who went to see movies when cinema was in its infancy.

Chapter three focuses on gender and generations of fan collecting and will theorise how practices of cult collecting create meaning for both male and female fans across different generations. Following on from the previous two chapters on stereotypes of the fan collector as predominantly middle-aged males, or "fanboys", this chapter will show how female fans engage in similar collecting practices and that specific cult texts aimed at women have become meaningful texts in their own right for female fans. Since objects are ascribed meaning by culture and those who own them, we must consider the implications such meanings have for the construction of a fan collector identity. In examining online spaces such as ThinkGeek.com, iconic collectibles such as the Barbie doll, and fan collector clubs like Mattel's Matty Collector this chapter asserts that while gender can be an important part of this process it is not the fact either men or women collect things or that the things they collect are gendered differently. It is that both men and women use the past as an arena for self-identification and recall moments from childhood through the collection and preservation of physical objects

Following on as case study, chapter four examines the rebirth and repackaging of *The Transformers* franchise, establishing to what extent the role of the adult collector has influenced the continued popularity and lifespan of a 1980s children's toy and

TV series. *The Transformers* has undergone a generic shift between children's TV and adult TV as the series and its associated brand merchandise have become part of a new form of cultural capital. Fans that once played with the toys as children now collect the originals (called Generation One) and specially marketed reproductions in order to claim ownership of *The Transformers* movie and television texts. Special DVD box sets of the original Saturday morning cartoon series are big sellers in the high street stores as fans remember their love for the show and seek to reclaim some part of their childhood. Collecting the entire range of toys from the originals up until the present day versions and having the original series on DVD becomes an important part of the competitive struggle within *Transformers* fandom. Fan debates surrounding the Spielberg produced, live-action *Transformers* movies will also be examined, highlighting the establishment of a fan canon in the children's TV fan community and how these discourses contribute to the creation and fragmentation of fan identity and culture. As a result, notions of genre and genre boundaries are becoming blurred as films, TV and toys originally aimed at children are now being collected and traded by adults keen to relive their youth.

Previous studies of popular media conventions have compared them to a religious pilgrimage (Aden, 1999), where fans travel to meet other fans, discuss their mutual love for a particular cult film or series and analyse their "sacred" text within complex debates over authenticity and subcultural capital. However, debates over authenticity and the sacred aside, what is fascinating about the convention space is how fans use it as a place for buying and selling goods. Indeed, the notion of a convention being dedicated to one specific text such as *Star Trek* has now evolved, the event has become a more adaptable and porous experience: from being held in non-specific venues such as the hotel conference room these events often take place in shopping malls or giant halls used to holding business or trade fairs. The venue has evolved to accommodate all types of fans, from those still wishing to meet other fans or their favourite star, to those simply there to buy merchandise. These goods range from factory line disposables to limited edition memorabilia. However, the accumulation of "stuff" is not only symbolic of economic status (a marker of how much fans can afford to spend on their favourite show); it is evidence of the intense relationship fans share with the fictional text and its associated fan community. According to John Fiske, the convention is a physical space where "cultural and economic capital come together" (Fiske, 1992: 43) and as such chapter five analyses the commodification of popular fandom and the geographies of the most iconic site for fan consumption: the San Diego Comic-Con. Using the work of Michel Foucault, I argue that it represents a fan heterotopia, containing real objects from real places, in which and through which fans can access new worlds, meet new people and travel through different physical spaces.

Chapter six examines the cultural impact of the *Star Wars* franchise through an analysis of the toys and the fans that collect them. It extends and reappraises arguments I made in previous work that the production and collecting of *Star Wars* toys from the first three released movies represented a return to the tradition of war "play" in American youth culture. This was in response to America's own lack of self-security after defeat in Vietnam and the effects of the "end of victory culture" as described by Tom Engelhardt (1995). Instead, I propose that the production and collecting of *Star Wars* toys today represents a new form of cultural capital as fans collect in order to possess and gain special access to the *Star Wars* movies and texts, making claims of ownership. Collecting the entire range of toys from the original movies up until the more modern releases becomes an important part of the competitive struggle within *Star Wars* fandom. *Star Wars* toy collecting can no longer be connected to debates over American national identity but rather the cultural significance of international fandom and the influence of what is now a global media franchise. Fans bring their own life contexts to the toys and merchandise they collect and so I would argue that a refocusing on the fans and their practices of collecting and remodelling existing toys inscribe new meanings. Super collectors, like Stephen J. Sansweet, are transforming the nature of *Star Wars* collectibles; making them objects of cultural history, transforming the notion of the museum and what should be preserved there.

Chapter seven extends my focus on large scale fan collecting places such as Comic-Con and turns to the various spaces of cult consumption that exist in the more mundane and functional environments of the high street and Internet. As spaces that accommodate all types of consumer, from casual shopper to fan collector, these sites for the exchange of cult commodities highlight the continued importance of physical interaction and the centrality of the physical object in the construction of fan subcultural capital. Through analyses of events such as Collectormania and Memorabilia, independent stores on the high street, and the defined spaces of Forbidden Planet's London Megastore and website, I argue that notions of space evolve depending on physical surroundings, assumed and actual audience, and the use of new media technologies. The Internet has had a profound effect on collecting film and TV merchandise – once lost and rare collectibles are now accessible to fans all over the globe. The Internet has levelled the field in terms of being able to bid for an item on sites such as eBay, whatever the time of day or where ever you may live. Collecting merchandise, once only available if you lived in the country of production, is now open to all (Hillis et al., 2006). However, this chapter will also discuss how new technologies allow fans to share and display their collections – symbols of subcultural hierarchies and their economic investment in a text – and how online networks encourage fans to feel nostalgic and share personal memories of their collections and specific collectible items. Through these collecting sites a new history of the collectible is created, it changes from mass-produced merchandise to become an artefact of personalised memory. The Internet becomes an archive, a virtual space that fans can enter whenever they like to access memories and images that contribute to meta-narratives of their favourite franchise.

As will be argued in chapter four, the remediation of classic and long-lost children's film, television, games and toys highlights the increasing importance of nostalgia within contemporary popular culture. The proliferation of official and unofficial, corporate and fan produced websites and online databases allows access to media from a pre-Internet era. Tied to this digital rebirth of children's media is a growing adult fan culture centred on the remembering and recollecting of childhood where memory forms the basis for active online communities that engage in the trading and (re)purchasing of new and old toys and games from their youth. Similarly, Lego's shift to producing product tie-ins has been supported by a very popular range of video games (e.g. *Lego Star Wars*) and the creation of online fan clubs aimed at both children and adults. This convergence of popular fandom, new media, nostalgia and contemporary toy culture suggests that the lines between past and present, technology and culture, childhood and adulthood are increasingly porous. Memory is an important component of being a fan and the remediation of childhood toys like Lego through video games and online communities helps to reconstruct memories of youth that are subsequently used to negotiate digital collaborative spaces shared by other fans. Lego, a children's toy originally based on the physicality of construction, has taken on new significance in contemporary media culture as it allows adult collectors/fans to reconnect with their past and define a fan identity through more ephemeral and digital interaction. Now that the Lego "system" incorporates global franchises like *Star Wars* it means collectors/fans of one brand crossover to become collectors/fans of the other. Therefore, I argue in chapter eight that Lego's shift from educational children's toy to transmedia adult collectible is characteristic of contemporary convergence culture. It highlights the importance of nostalgia in the influencing of what childhood media and commodities are remembered but also how nostalgia acts to expand the original potentials of those remediated texts and commodities.

PART I

Stereotypes

1

CONTESTING COMIC BOOK GUY

Stereotypes of the Nerd, Fan and Cult Collector in Film and Television

In a 2008 article called "*Wired*'s Geekster Handbook, a Field Guide to the Nerd Underground" published online and in its magazine Troy Brownfield describes six types of geek, with their characteristics and beliefs outlined in a dating profile style list. Repeating most and updating some of the common nerd/geek stereotypes, Brownfield's target audience would not find these particularly unfamiliar considering the magazine's youthful tech-savvy readership and own staff. The article came with a photo that depicted the six types of geek: the fanboy wearing a Green Lantern T-shirt; the music geek with ear phones; the gamer holding a Wii remote; the gadget guy with a jacket full of convenient pockets; the hacker sporting a hoody; and the otaku dressed in a Japanese school girl outfit. Descriptions matched with images underline the ubiquity of cultural stereotypes but also the increased attention geek culture (as it is mediated in *Wired* and on screen) is receiving in the mainstream media. Such attention is not missing within academia either. Gary Hoppenstand, in an editorial called "Revenge of the nerds" in *The Journal of Popular Culture*, champions *The Big Bang Theory* (2007–present) for having "struck a responsive chord in its audience, giving hope that nerds have become at least an interesting topic for Mr. And Mrs. Average American" (2009: 810). Similarly, J.A. McArthur argues that "the transition from geek-as-sideshow freak to geek-as-intelligent expert has moved the term from one of insult to one of endearment" citing computer software designers and the founders of Google and Facebook as having brought geeks positions of power, wealth and respect in the cultural mainstream (2009: 61). Both pieces point to a renaissance in representations of nerd and geek culture and a renewed interest in nerd and geek texts in popular mainstream media.

Perhaps equally revelatory is the 2011 article by Patton Oswalt, again in *Wired* magazine, that warns of this geek revival. Suggesting now that everyone can claim some form of connection to nerd culture, displaying their fandom of a cult or mainstream text with similar techno-savvy gusto, nothing remains unpopular – even what was once loved only by a select few. He blames this phenomenon on the Internet and the increased access people have to images and texts from the past. As I have argued in the introduction to this book, old media texts are remediated and fans are able to again celebrate their favourite shows and icons from yesteryear. Oswalt appears to believe this is a backward step in the development of popular culture, threatening the very fabric of what it means to be a fan:

> Now, with everyone more or less otaku and everything *immediately* awesome ... the old inner longing for more or better that made our present pop culture so amazing is dwindling ... Etewaf [Everything That Ever Was – Available Forever] doesn't produce a new generation of artists – just an army of sated consumers.

Not wanting to repeat some of the issues I raised regarding negative conceptions of nostalgia and fan consumption in the introduction, I quote Oswalt here because his article's whole thrust is seemingly based on the premise that the one true image of a fan/nerd/geek is that they are a minority, they should be seen as a special "other", a group with special knowledge to enjoy and unlock the potentials of obscure texts that "normal" people can't. This mirrors Brownfield's Geekster Handbook, where he suggests there are six types of people who display characteristics one would not normally find in mainstream culture. What is troubling about both these articles is that in order to defend fan culture (albeit fans as part of nerd/ geek culture) the authors are arguing for some kind of special status – or least to recognise special qualities in the character types. However, this unintentionally confirms to readers who might not ordinarily identify themselves in such ways that fans are a minority group, who value the unpopular and culturally obscure, and are solely defined by these stereotypes. Lumping fans with the nerd/geek paradigm also means the one remains entirely contingent upon, and connected to, the other.

I argue in this chapter that by separating the nerd stereotype from that of fan culture, we might get a better understanding of the personal, social, and cultural meanings involved with being a fan. Having a fan identity is important and so film and television that emphasise this, even only in part and using humour to do so, are instructive and necessary for the circulation of positive representations. They remind us that popular media texts play significant roles in the construction of said identities and therefore should be celebrated for doing so. As a consequence, I wish to examine a range of popular stereotypes of the nerd and fan circulated in the media, reappraising and reclaiming some of those that encapsulate the meaning of fandom. I contend that media representations of fan collectors are useful in that they remind viewers that fandom is a form of consumption, but consumption does not just mean consuming for the sake of it. Collecting is an active and discerning process that relies on many of the same strategies and processes fans employ in poaching and creating new texts. The collection can and should be read as a text and therefore the examples discussed in this chapter are illustrative of the productive and transformative processes that being a fan entails.

Freaky Fans

Stereotypes are often powerful mechanisms used to label and objectify people from various social, national, racial, and ethnic groups. Their dissemination through contemporary media is tied to the production of meaning and the pervasiveness of fear of the unfamiliar and the unknown in an increasingly global society. However, while stereotypes are used to construct an image of the other, they more often provide the first and most illuminating insight into how we see ourselves. Therefore, stereotypes help in the construction of identity, both the identity of the group being stereotyped and the individual or group who create and make use of the stereotype. Through language and the media we get a sense of who we are in opposition to those who we think we are not. The formulation of different *types* of people and social groups in *our* minds, or *them*, creates stereotypes that *we* use to help unify concepts about *us*. So, stereotypes may be harmful, often degrading, offensive and simplistic in their representation of the other but they are important components in the process of social identification. For Richard Jenkins, "Identity" denotes "the ways in which individuals and collectivities are distinguished in their relations with other individuals and collectivities"; "Identification" is "the systematic establishment and signification, between collectivities, and between individuals and collectivities, of relationships of similarity and difference" (2004: 5). Taken together, similarity and difference are the principles of identification, and are at the heart of the human world. Stereotypes, therefore, contribute to this since identity is our understanding of who we are and who other people are, and, reciprocally, other people's understanding of themselves and of others (which includes us).

Taking this into account, we can understand the continued creation and circulation of stereotypes of fans and fandom in the media as signs of how groups within society are continually rearticulating and reasserting what it means to be a fan. Read this way, I would suggest that while some media representations of fans and associated fan practices stereotype them as "sad", "weird", "nerdy", "freakish" and "juvenile" (or any other derogatory label fans have had applied to them) this merely highlights the fact that those who mediate such stereotypes are themselves trying to comprehend and justify their own identity as a fan. Or, more simply, we are all fans of something – and the repetition and intensity of fan stereotypes demonstrates that some people have not quite figured out what they are fans of. In many ways my argument about fan stereotypes is mirrored in Henry Jenkins's recent appraisal of fan studies in the updated anniversary edition of *Textual Poachers* (1992, 2013). He asserts that, "Fan studies offers us some important glimpses into the ways that everyday people are adjusting to changes in the media landscape … As such, fan studies could be a key for understanding current debates about globalization, offering a somewhat more optimistic picture than generalized accounts of cultural imperialism" (Jenkins in Scott, 2013: xl–xli). Alongside our changing conceptions of fan studies, then, we should also reassess the representation and remediation of fan stereotypes to reappraise that shifting and ever-changing sense of the self in the media world.

Taking a holistic view of the past twenty years in fan studies we can appreciate the continued significance of fan stereotypes in that Jenkins uses the most famous, the William Shatner "Get a life" sketch on *Saturday Night Live* in 1986, as the platform to begin his seminal work on fans as poachers. The stereotype of the nerdy, basement dwelling *Star Trek* fan – unable to discern real life from what appears on the television screen – has not only permeated popular culture for nearly as long as the history of the series, it has become the ultimate stereotype from which all fan studies scholarship post-Jenkins has tried to distance itself. Subsequently, any and all recent media texts that have depicted fans and fan practices (whether well meaning and popular, fan-made or Hollywood) have been discussed in ways that proclaim their negativity and harmfulness. These discussions thus try to correct the stereotype rather than understand the necessary actions that have brought about those representations in the first place. So, for example, in Suzanne Scott's interview with Henry Jenkins there is an assumptive connection made between the "Get a life" fan stereotype from 1986 and more recent media that depict fans, such as *The 40-Year-Old Virgin* (2005) and *The Big Bang Theory*. In one of Scott's questions to Jenkins, she suggests that there is little difference between said representations and Jenkins's answer implies that both examples still display and reinforce old stereotypes to the detriment of creating "an alternative conception of what it might mean to be a fan" (Jenkins in Scott, 2013: xv). Yet, what this exchange ignores is that both media texts (as I shall go on to explore later in this chapter) do conceptualise what being a fan means and what constitutes having a fan identity. That these films "trade in stereotypes" points to the fact that they are engaging with and depicting elements of how individuals are adapting to a changing multimedia society.

The popularity of media texts like *The Big Bang Theory* has reignited debate over the pathologising of fan behaviour. Joli Jenson describes how excessive fandom has been seen "as a form of psychological compensation, an attempt to make up for all that modern life lacks" (1992: 16). Negative stereotypes of adult fans as pathological others, who have not grown out of childhood, still form the bedrock for scholarship on contemporary fan representations. Fans, critics and academics alike have viewed the representation of Sheldon Cooper in particular as problematic since much of the comedy that stems from his character is based on his total lack of social skills and over-obsession with fan texts. For Monika Bednarek, Sheldon is "styled as someone who fulfils all the stereotypical character traits of a nerd/geek as well as some others that are shared with particular psychological conditions", ranging from "arrogance, obsessive-compulsive and Asperger-like behaviour" (2012: 223). Indeed, the other characters on the show, also depicted as "geeks" or "nerds", often deride Sheldon for the extreme behaviour he displays above and beyond their own circumstances. So, while *The Big Bang Theory* is seen as a positive show in that it creates a space in mainstream popular entertainment for fannish celebration, it negates that by reasserting stereotypes that audiences will recognise from the history of fans in film and television – namely, the antisocial "nerdish" fan. However, since *The Big Bang Theory* is a result of the popular media entertainment industry, should it be a surprise that those stereotypes are recirculated and rearticulated for a contemporary audience? Indeed, Bednarek does recognise this in her linguistic study of the series: "Like other media texts it thus both shapes audience stereotypes and is shaped by mainstream stereotypes in a reflexive relationship ... The stereotypical styling of others is clearly tied to the production of entertainment" (2012: 223–4). This point perhaps helps to contextualise Larry Gross's argument that "representation in the mediated 'reality' of our mass culture is in itself power" (1989: 131).

Such an evaluation of the series is clearly related to wider considerations of the fan stereotype and its relationship to how we understand ourselves compared to others and the social world we live in, as I have already outlined. For psychologists Martha Augoustinos and Iain Walker, stereotypes underlie the basic form of social representations and thus, I would argue, are important components in how fans communicate with other fans and interact with the social world around them.

> Stereotypes are social representations: they are objectified cognitive and affective structures about social groups within society which are extensively shared and which emerge and proliferate within the particular social and political milieu of a given historical moment ... They are social and discursively constructed in the course of everyday communication, and, once objectified, assume an independent and sometimes prescriptive reality.
>
> *(Augoustinos and Walker, 1995: 222)*

One of the redeeming features of *The Big Bang Theory* for some critics is that it does have a dual address; that much of its humour lies in an in-joke that only the fans of particular media texts might recognise. Yet, what this admission of praise highlights is that there is recognition of social representations and therefore stereotypes are important in communicating that piece of knowledge or in-joke to those fans that will understand and appreciate it. *The Big Bang Theory* should then be considered a fan text that demonstrates what it means to be a fan and what being a fan in a world where "nerd" or "freak" stereotypes exist is really like. This concept applies to any of the fan representations discussed by Jenkins and others but I would stress that with each example there will be variations in the accuracy of the textual practices on display and differences between the levels of fan devotion exemplified by each character.

Academic literature that has focused specifically on the stereotyping of fans in film and television almost all evaluate representations of fan behaviour through the lens of the "nerd" or "geek", but none really separate the actions and practices of the "nerd" or "geek" from that of being a fan. Thus the two social groupings become conflated and the stereotype of the "nerd" as that which inevitably entails an obsessive and enthusiastic appreciation of a media text like *Star Wars* or *Star Trek* becomes endemic. Indeed, Bednarek argues in her analysis of *The Big Bang Theory* that "Identities such as nerdiness are constructed through semiotic practices that include more than language but may also encompass hairstyles, clothes and accessories, activities, musical performances and other values" (2012: 224). However, her assertions exclude the word fan in this instance (in fact her entire article minimises the term fan in preference to "nerd") and thus also lack recognition of the fact that being a fan of something means all of the above and more. Perhaps one step on the road to deconstructing the fan stereotype, while also recognising its importance and positive value in constructing a fan identity, is to detach it from the various and, I would argue, inherently different representations of the "nerd" found in popular media.

Nerds as Fans

Stereotypes accentuate elements of what it means to be a fan that correspond to the multiple and varied definitions of fandom offered by scholars. Those definitions also contribute to how we might understand and critique depictions on screen. For Nicholas Abercrombie and Brian Longhurst, media audiences can be categorised in one of three ways: "fan, cultist (or subcultist) and enthusiast, who are members of fandoms, cults (or subcultures) and enthusiasms" (1998: 138). These types are part of the same continuum and involve production and consumption. The authors describe "fans" as heavy media users, "particularly attached to certain programmes or stars … individuals who are not yet in contact with other people who share their attachments" (1998: 138). If a connection exists, it does so only on the level of consuming "fannish literature" or within "day-to-day contact with peers". I find this description troubling in that it appears to be the very definition of fandom displayed in certain representations of fans ("Get a life" for example) and appears to emphasise, at the simplest of levels, that fandom is simply a mode of lone consumption. The term fan is thus diminished in favour of the next one on their continuum, the cultist.

Abercrombie and Longhurst view cultists as more the typical fan than the word fan actually involves, specialising in particular types of media and focusing their efforts on creating networks of other cultists who share their passion for a text: "Cultists are more organized than fans. They meet each other and circulate specialized materials that constitute the nodes of a *network*" (1998: 139). Whilst clearly seeing value in the nature of the cultist as a social person, the authors are by association denigrating the work of the previously defined fan because it is carried out in isolation – thereby again confirming the stereotype that fans in isolation are somehow not doing it right and are thus deviant in their detachment from the wider cultist community. Here, we might read the problems typically ascribed to the representation of Andy Stitzer as a 40-year-old toy collector living on his own in *The 40-Year-Old Virgin* as being framed by the notion that audience consumption has to happen in a cultist community or else the fan is a mere lone consumer, not actively engaged in sharing materials within a network. A point perhaps visualised in that the only group he seems to feel comfortable in the presence of is his toy collection which he displays all about his house. The celebration of "arrested development" in middle-aged fans is played up in this movie according to Henry

Jenkins (Jenkins in Scott, 2013: xv), but what is more worrying is that Abercrombie and Longhurst appear to locate being a fan as part of childhood (1998: 138) – associating mere fannish consumption with pre-adolescence and immaturity. So, in effect, the stereotype of the fan as childish, underdeveloped and living in isolation is embedded in a scholarly definition which other media merely replicate in their depictions of fandom.

Prejudices against fans as consumers working in isolation continue in descriptions of Abercrombie and Longhurst's "enthusiast". Those audience members that share enthusiasms do so "based predominantly on activities rather than media or stars" and being located within a community means activities are typically focused on the production of new media texts intended for circulation amongst other enthusiasts (1998: 139). Consumption only exists for the benefit of the community, and the production of alternative texts in opposition to those made by the entertainment media industry is perceived as having more value. Here we see the definition of the fan enthusiast merge with that of the textual poacher, as outlined by Henry Jenkins, who is engaged in the organisation of their enthusiasm via a struggle against those who might take it away or change it. Fans, in this sense, "draw strength and courage from the ability to identify themselves as members of a group of other fans who shared common interests and confronted common problems" as well as speaking "from a position of collective identity, to forge an alliance with a common community of others in defense of tastes which, as a result, cannot be read as totally aberrant and idiosyncratic" (Jenkins, 1992: 23). However, in today's media landscape is it possible to distinguish "totally aberrant and idiosyncratic" tastes and unique methods of circulation when it appears fandom is more mainstream than ever? The popularity of *The Big Bang Theory*, Sheldon T-shirts and made-up games based on fictional characters ("rock, paper, scissors, lizard, Spock") suggests that idiosyncratic is now the norm. As I discussed in the introduction to this book, it is now cool to be seen as a fan – with shops on the high street selling "geek chic" T-shirts of your favourite show. Therefore, the stereotypes once employed for derogatory comic effect now only work because they have become signifiers of a fan identity circulated through the media and in wider popular culture.

Fandom has been viewed through the lens of religious devotion, with many studies equating fan dedication to a media text – and travelling to and gathering at convention spaces – akin to religious pilgrimage. Indeed, this scholarship has been useful in understanding the relationship between space, place and fandom as will be discussed in chapters five and seven. Jenkins surveys some of the early work on *Star Trek* fans which draws on religious themes and sees these as more harmful in that they position fans as fanatical and obsessive: with "connotations of religious and political zealotry, false beliefs, orgiastic excess, possession, and madness" (1992: 12). Arguments for fandom as a form of secular faith abound in early work. Susan Sackett likens fans' need to share experiences with others to those newly converted to a religion who become "its most fervent proselytes" (1977: 15). Similarly, William B. Tyrrell, argues *Star Trek* not only "offers the comfort of religion" but for its fans it represents a world where they belong (1977: 717). Much to Jenkins's dislike,

Robert Jewett and John Shelton Lawrence argue that the series and its fans constitute "a strange, electronic religion … in the making" (1977: 24). Alternatively, for Michael Jindra, *Star Trek* "does not have the thoroughgoing seriousness of established religions, but it is also not mere entertainment". The combination and interplay of the two facets is a sign of its unique "vitality" (1994: 50).

A more recent piece of scholarship that ties fandom together with religion, specifically the more fringe religions and cult groups, is David Scott Diffrient's work on what he calls "the cult imaginary" (2010: 463). Outlining a thesis that contends representations of fans and cult religions on screen have drawn on existing stereotypes that depict loners and losers getting caught up in the more controlled life of being in a cult, he argues that as "cultic representations on the small screen, fiction-based television programs have contributed to many of the prejudicial attitudes and misperceptions people have about alternative religions in the United States" (2010: 476). However, the examples he draws upon to support his argument are solely those that concern actual or fictional religious groups or cults, primarily depicted in sitcoms, police or detective series, and science fiction. Nowhere does he actually discuss a textual example of a fan (media, sport or otherwise) but in his connecting of fringe religions with fan cultures in the title of the article he follows earlier scholars in their description of fans as religious fanatics. This is more than somewhat problematic since, despite the fact that his work promised an analysis of fan cultures on screen and failed to deliver, the omission means fans are yet again demonised and it is intimated that being a fan makes you automatically part of a socially ostracised group.

Either defining active fans and fan communities in opposition to fan consumption, or paralleling secular faith movements, the previous works discussed omit references to another socially excluded group, namely that of the "nerd". Yet, it is perhaps more troubling that the stereotypes of the fan (loner, childish, obsessive) and nerd (techie, predominantly white, effeminate) have become enmeshed in more recent scholarship, again problematising what it means to be a fan of a media franchise, text or star. In effect, nerd stereotypes are circulated, taking on new negative connotations and stigmatising legitimate fan activities such as collecting, costuming, making, blogging, convention attending, and watching. In his well-meaning critique of the nerd/geek stereotype in American culture, psychologist David Anderegg wastes little time in condemning *The Big Bang Theory*'s depiction of scientists as nerds – merely there to be laughed at by audiences who assume that people "gifted in science and math also love comic books, have no social skills and no sense of humor, and cannot get a girl no matter what" (2011: 6). In repeating the mistake of Diffrient's understanding of fan culture and omission of fan examples, Anderegg ignores the fact that while Sheldon, Raj, Leonard and Howard are scientists they are first and foremost shown as fans – in where they socialise, what they wear, talk about and consume – and therefore it is no surprise that they are seen to love comic books, enjoy gaming and watch TV shows like *Star Trek*. As I have already argued, the show's humour stems from its dual address, speaking to fans and depicting what it means to be one while also playing on stereotypes for the mainstream audience. By only arguing the show portrays scientists as nerds, Anderegg does it a much bigger disservice by ignoring the fact that it portrays scientists as fans – celebrating fan cultures and speaking to a fan audience.

One could argue that that the popular media representation of the nerd started on the nostalgic 1970s TV series, *Happy Days* (1974–84). Used as a stock phrase, most often by Fonzie, it was aimed at characters seen as smart but inept or at those unsuccessful with women. This also drew upon the diner setting and teenage group dynamic, with jocks, cool kids, and shy types competing for the attention of girls. There has been considerable work done on representations of nerds in popular culture by authors investigating the relationships between race, gender and technology. Lori Kendall, in particular, has stressed that "cultural expectations regarding technology usage converge with stereotypes concerning race and gender, resulting in a white nerd masculine identity congruent with related forms of masculinity found in computing and engineering fields" (2000: 271). In recent films and television series revolving around computers and computer technology, nerds are seen as experts with powers to control financial and political spheres that rely on computers. The association between technology and nerds is made so as to deflect fears of computers taking over our lives – they represent our ambivalence towards computers and the fact they are becoming increasingly like us in their responses to human interaction. For Kendall, the figure of the nerd keeps these fears at bay – at a cost: "Representing nerds as lacking social and sartorial skills, obsessed with trivia, and interested in fringe cultural activities, allays fears of the nerd's power, and by extension, the power of the computer" (2011: 521).

In her analysis of *Revenge of the Nerds* (1984) and its sequels, she argues that representations can "either challenge or reinforce hegemonic masculinity … displacing bids for equality by African Americans and gay men, but also broadening the definition of masculinity to better include those groups" (Kendall, 1999a: 279). The first film tells the story of Lewis and Gilbert, stereotypical white nerds with a fascination for technology, and their college campus based quest to outsmart the fraternity jocks who have kicked them out of their dorm. A typical rise to heroism sees the nerds defeat their foes and gain acceptance in the college community. As well as representing a "persistent uneasiness with computer use and computer users" (Kendall, 1999a: 280) the film positions white nerds within the usually marked off territory of hegemonic masculinity, with them acting as a buffer against other versions of non-hegemonic masculinity depicted as black or homosexual. The repositioning of the nerd stereotype during the 1980s, Kendall argues, "relates both to changes in economic and job prospects for middle-class white males, and to the growing pervasiveness of computers in work and leisure activities" (1999a: 261). As the American economy was becoming increasingly reliant on computers those men who were seen as technologically proficient, entrepreneurial, and successful at business were labelled "nerds"; reclaiming the term while at the same time locating it within a particular type of white masculinity that was perceived to be under threat in the popular media:

> The timing of the increased prevalence of nerd references in the culture, especially in mainstream media, synchronizes with a backlash against Affirmative Action and other civil rights efforts. Nerds become an oppressed straight white male identity that then stands in for other oppressed groups, waylaying critiques of hegemonic masculinity while only expanding its definition.
>
> *(Kendall, 1999b: 368)*

Ron Eglash continues this focus on race and the representation of nerds in his analysis of popular film and television such as the *Star Wars* prequels, *Star Trek: The Next Generation* (1987–94), and the sitcom *Family Matters* (1989–98). He argues that Samuel L. Jackson's roles as scientist in *Jurassic Park* (1993) and *Sphere* (1998) depict him as a black nerd, with his casting as Mace Windu in *The Phantom Menace* (1999) also confirming the actor's geekier side as a *Star Wars* fan. The Steve Urkel character in *Family Matters*, although nerdy, proved more of a "signature" while other "technology-associated black television figures remained less nerd-identified" (Eglash, 2002: 55). In *Star Trek*, for example, Geordi LaForge is technologically gifted but displays none of the trappings of being a nerd – I would argue these are transferred onto his overtly "robotic" and socially awkward friend, Data. Still, for Eglash, in popular representations of the nerd character we see African American actors play more "cool" than nerd, and Asian American men conform to the asexual role stereotyped in the media. Indeed, race is used in such a way as to position whiteness "as the perfect balance between these two extremes" (Eglash, 2002: 52). This argument is developed in May Bucholtz's study of language use by California high school students. She argues that terms and phrases used by white students that marked them out as "nerds" in opposition to other white social groups within the school environment was a strategy to reject the cultural norm of coolness. Yet, this "also caused them to be racially marked with respect to blacks and whites", making them whiter than white and reinforcing "racial ideologies of difference and division" (Bucholtz, 2001: 96).

Updating this literature on the nerd stereotype Christine Quail argues that popular media texts such as the film *Napoleon Dynamite* (2004) "pushed nerd identity into the realm of mass merchandising and the nerd identity into cult status" (2011: 465). Yet, on the other hand, reality TV series like *Beauty and the Geek* (2005–8) highlight how texts that depict a nerd character alongside a more masculine figure – something she terms "the hip/square dialectic" – continue to "cast serious doubt on actual cultural acceptance of the nerd as the new hipster" (2011: 479). In the pairing up of a stereotyped geek (usually a science fiction fan, techno enthusiast, and socially inept male) with an overtly sexualised young woman (more interested in her looks and potential career as a model) the series followed a "rags to riches" format that rewarded couples who could show signs of change and self-improvement. The geek manages to come out of his shell, talk to women and drop his uncool persona while the sexy female learns more about social acceptance, science, and the importance of science fiction trivia. Even in later series when these roles are reversed, with female "nerd" contestants paired up with male models, Quail argues that "both imprints require the male and female nerd to conform to gendered social and aesthetic standards that lend themselves to consumptive practices and hegemonic genders" (2011: 479).

In *Beauty and the Geek* we see the "nerd" stereotype again conflated with being a fan of texts like *Star Trek* which are thus coded as "nerd" – but we do not get a sense of what being a fan means. In Quail's analysis there is also this intuitive acceptance that somehow being a nerd and fan is the same thing, and thus in her critique of the reality show she does not point out that the two are mutually exclusive. This, in effect, extends the problematic representation of the fan within popular culture and, more significantly, within the very scholarship that is written with the intention of breaking those stereotypes down. The more recent *King of the Nerds* (2013–present) continues in this tradition of conflating being a fan of popular media culture with being a stereotypical nerd (high IQ, not good at sports, technical ability) but also merges some of the geek characteristics described in Troy Browfield's Geekster Handbook discussed at the start of this chapter. A reality show based on pitting contestants against each other to determine who could be called "King of the Nerds" the tasks revolved around typically fannish activities, like debating who is the best superhero and creating a cosplay character. So-called "nerd" credentials were enhanced by the fact the presenters were original actors from *Revenge of the Nerds* and celebrity judges included George Takei and Kevin Smith. Perhaps the only progressive thing about the show is that a woman won the first series – providing an interesting challenge to the typical gender bias in stereotypes of the fan/nerd identity.

Fans on Film, Films on Fans

Current debates within fan scholarship are focusing more on the differences between gendered conceptions of the fanboy and fangirl: with the former perceived as being more affirmational and celebratory of the mediated text while the latter is more likely to transform it and reconstitute it for the needs of the wider fan community. I explore this dichotomy further in relation to fan collectors in chapter three. However, it is important to note here how modern representations of fans and fandom in film and television have remained firmly focused on the fanboy stereotype as seen in movies like *Paul* (2011), *Fanboys* (2008) and *Free Enterprise* (1999), or television such as *The Simpsons* (1989–present), *Spaced* (1999–2001), and *Community* (2009–present). Historically, for Matthew Pustz, the term "fanboy" originated in the world of comic books, specifically in the accumulation and preservation of original and rare issues of famous titles by men still devoted to the comics from their youth. Pustz argues that the term has become more derisive within the comic book fan community as younger readers buy titles in the often vain hope that they are preserving a potentially rare issue that will be worth something to collectors in the future. Still a controversial term within the community, some "readers have recaptured the term *fanboy*, using it to describe reading comics of any kind with a sense of fun and fascination" (Pustz, 1999: xii).

In keeping with its comic book roots, the figure of the fanboy is most often associated with Comic Book Guy from *The Simpsons*. Encompassing all the stereotypes of the middle-age male fan – awkward around women, sarcastic, intelligent, obsessive and protective of his collection – he is an iconic representation of the comic book fanboy. Kurt Fawver identifies him as "something of an American archetype" (2012: 4). In many ways I would agree with this assessment since the continued presence of the fanboy stereotype in American culture coincides with the contemporary nostalgia for childhood and the collecting of one's youth as discussed in the introduction. Conversely, Peter Chvany analyses the community fundraising activities of a Klingon fan group on the Internet. Rather than being fanboys, he asserts that they have become "American ethnics": a community of people whose investment in convention performances and the fictional history of the Klingon culture "gives way to belief in their reality, to conviction, to 'identity'" (2003: 106–7). Both assessments of fan cultural stereotypes highlight key issues related to consumption, community, identity and what it means to be a fan that require further investigation in the remainder of this chapter. Despite Henry Jenkins's claim that fanboys "have been, by and large, better served by literary representations" (Jenkins in Scott, 2013: xv), I will continue to explore the fanboy stereotype recycled in popular media. Both film and television representations tend to locate fandom within a masculine culture, as did those texts that centred on the nerd stereotype, thus, the following examples I discuss substantiate the fanboy figure as the norm. However, unlike Jenkins, I see valuable articulations of fan identity in contemporary media, which do highlight a general acceptance of otherness in mainstream culture. As I will now show, the texts discussed in both this and the last section offer insight (for fans and non-fans) into legitimate fan practices, current debates, the importance of cultural objects, and the changing relationship they have with the media industry.

Spaced is clearly on the one hand a traditional sitcom yet its positioning of fandom and fan culture, particularly relating to the *Star Wars* franchise, lends it a certain intertextuality that references both the George Lucas text and the enormous fan base surrounding it. Will Brooker discusses Simon Pegg's role as Tim, the archetypal middle-age *Star Wars* fanboy, in conjunction with the release of *The Phantom Menace* and the mass backlash against the film from those fans who saw it as childish and hollow. Scenes between Tim and his flatmate Daisy, where they talk about how bad the film was, are interwoven with fantasy scenes that depict Tim dressed up as Luke Skywalker burning his *Star Wars* collectibles in a form of silent protest towards Lucas. Brooker calls this an example of the series' "dual address" whereby it speaks to the popular audience of the time and offers a more subversive reading to those fans who are able to understand the reference within the joke and sympathise with Tim, and also Pegg as self-confessed *Star Wars* fan (Brooker, 2002: 79–85). Pegg as intertextual referent also appears in *Shaun of the Dead* (2004) as he reprises the archetypal role of middle-age cult fan and uses his knowledge of zombie horror films to help him and his friends escape hordes of the walking dead in the streets of London.

It is interesting to note the role Simon Pegg has in constructing the image of the contemporary fanboy, both in his performances as Tim and Shaun in British examples as well as in the American-based comedy, *Paul*. Along with Nick Frost, his co-star in all three examples and writing partner for *Paul*, Pegg represents the stereotype of the young British male – predominantly interested in drinking, popular media entertainment and avoiding hard work. In *Spaced*, Pegg as Tim is seen to avoid hard labour at all costs – either living off the dole or working within the laid back and familiar environment of the comic book store. Tim's real dream is to be a successful comic book artist, yet he does not have the conviction to follow that dream as it might result in rejection. Frost's character, Mike, follows Tim's lead – leading a largely transient life shifting between part time jobs and unemployment. Both enjoy sitting on the couch playing computer games and watching cult movies. Likewise, in *Shaun of the Dead*, Pegg as Shaun and Frost as Ed are best friends who prefer rewatching old horror films and testing each other's knowledge rather than pursuing any defined career goals. The interest in horror movie trivia proves essential, however, as they are called into action to fight off a horde of zombies. Fan knowledge is legitimated within the contexts of the apocalyptic events to befall England. In *Paul*, Pegg and Frost play Graeme and Clive, aspiring fantasy artist and writer respectively, who travel to Comic-Con (which they describe as "home" at the opening of the movie) on a fan pilgrimage to meet their favourite author. As they take a road trip through the desert they meet the eponymous Paul (voiced by American "fanboy" actor Seth Rogen), an escaped alien from Area 51, who gives them the confidence to pursue their dreams and publish their own fantasy work. At the end of the film Graeme and Clive are seen returning to Comic-Con, not as attendees but as headlining speakers with their own auditorium full of adoring fans. In all three examples we see the merging of real and fictional identities through the figure of the fanboy: Pegg as star and writer together with his roles as slacker and aspiring artist. Therefore, Pegg's own experience and self-proclaimed fandom contributes to, even enabled, his career as a writer of media texts that promote a fanboy identity.

Pegg's shift from fan to fanboy producer follows in the tradition of what Roberta Pearson described as the rise of the "writer/producer" in US network television during the 1990s. Writers such as J. Michael Straczynski (*Babylon 5*), Chris Carter (*The X-Files*), Joss Whedon (*Buffy the Vampire Slayer*), and latterly J.J. Abrams (*Lost*) and Tim Kring (*Heroes*), assumed tremendous power over the creative directions their series took and their names were used strategically by the networks to attract new and younger audiences to their schedules. What characterised the newer auteurs in the late nineties is the relationship they had with the networks and the freedom the networks gave them in order to increase ratings and audience share. For Roberta Pearson (2005: 17), "The networks granted this creative control because in the post-classical network system era the names of important hyphenates, the hyphenate brand as it were, proved more attractive to demographically desirable audiences than did the network brand". Similarly, with Pegg being used as a brand to advertise and market specific "fanboy" texts like

Shaun of the Dead and *Paul*, we can see him assuming greater creative control and acting more like a "gamekeeper" within their associated fan communities. "Textual Gamekeeping" is explained by Matt Hills as the process through which "poacher" fans become legitimate producers and owners of cult texts, storywriters for example, within the "cultural parameters of niche marketing" and an "interpretive community" of fans (2002: 40). This idea is something I will be exploring further in connection with *Star Wars* toy collecting and "celebrity" fan collectors in chapter six.

Pegg's fanboy credentials have been enhanced again by the fact he now plays Scotty in the rebooted *Star Trek* films. The influence of that franchise in depictions of fan culture is clear to see in other comedy films. In *Free Enterprise* characters Robert and Mark are thirty-something friends that value their love of popular media franchises like *Star Wars* and *Star Trek*, taking regular trips to comic stores and Toys R Us to add to their cult collections. Always living for the next big idea Robert typifies the fanboy stereotype while Mark, who works in Hollywood, feels trapped – both use their fandom as a form of personal expression to their peer group. In meeting William Shatner, playing an embarrassingly parodic version of himself, Mark and Robert undergo a cathartic process of self-examination – re-evaluating their lives and where they want to go before they hit 40. What is perhaps interesting with this film is its marketing, using other cult fan texts to advertise it to a presumed audience: "[T]he two friends must face their fears about the future in this contemporary comedy that combines the hip, L.A. romantics milieu of *Swingers*, with the knowing pop culture sophistication of *Clerks*." The DVD box is replete with promotional puns: "Love Long and Party"; "The first movie by the *Star Wars* generation, for the *Star Wars* generation"; "William Shatner. Only one man in the universe can get them on the right trek ... "

Similarly, in *Fanboys* we see four die-hard *Star Wars* fans take a cross-country road trip across America to see *The Phantom Menace* at Lucas's Skywalker Ranch before it is released in cinemas. Having grown up together the four friends live and breathe cult media texts, particularly *Star Wars*, and interpret their daily life and work experiences through their fandom. One of the friends, Eric, is an aspiring artist who by the end of the film has managed to get his own comic book published. The repetition of this character arc, similar to the roles played by Simon Pegg, suggests that fans are inherently creative and use their childhood love of a media text as inspiration to continue it through adulthood. However, it also seems to imply that there has to be some legitimate end result for all that time, money and effort invested in their fandom when they were young otherwise it is proven to be a waste. For one of the other four friends, Linus, the trip to see *The Phantom Menace* before release takes on a literal life or death significance as he has a terminal illness that ultimately prevents him from attending the premiere with the group. In *Fanboys* the emotional investment in the *Star Wars* universe is depicted as transformational; not for Linus but for his friends who use the premiere to honour him and promise they will make something of their lives after he is gone.

As a film directly targeted at a fan audience it plays on the communal affection shown towards the franchise and specific knowledge of the fictional text to provide the humour. Cameos by Carrie Fisher, William Shatner and Kevin Smith also add to its fan credentials. It also contributes to the stereotyping of *Star Trek* fans as "nerds" and "geeks" by having the four friends take a detour on their trip to California and visit Riverside, Iowa (fictional birthplace of Captain Kirk or "enemy territory" as they call it) to pick a fight and trash talk a group of Trekkies. While clearly targeting *Star Trek* fans there is evidence of the dual address here that suggests the film is taking fan rivalry quite seriously. The main Trekkie is played by Seth Rogen, making another fanboy appearance, and while it mocks *Star Trek* the textual knowledge it uses to do so is symptomatic of what Jonathan Gray terms "anti-fandom". For Gray, the "anti-fan" demonstrates an "anti" view of perceived pop-ular texts; often based on a well-informed, knowledgeable understanding of the fan text they dislike or actively rail against. Such scenes in *Fanboys* display a sense of "affective involvement" typical of anti-fans "who strongly dislike a given chosen text or genre, considering it inane, stupid, morally bankrupt and/or aesthetic drivel" (Gray, 2003: 70). Therefore, this film can be read as both a fan and anti-fan text – employing conventional stereotypes to feed both fan and anti-fan readings yet encapsulating what it means to be a *Star Wars* fan and have an identity constructed, in part, out of a hatred for *Star Trek* and its fan community.

In *Galaxy Quest* (1999), a parody of the *Star Trek* franchise and mythos, fans are portrayed as strong and competent individuals who are part of a supportive and culturally integrated group. This of course plays in stark contrast to the media ste-reotype of the "geeky" or "nerdy" fan, so often associated with the science fiction genre. As a film about a once-popular science fiction TV series that is brought back for a new generation of fans (mirroring the death and rebirth of *Star Trek* in the late eighties), *Galaxy Quest* examines perceptions of the frontier as a both physical and personal boundary. In previous work on the film I argued that the "fans are portrayed as functional agents who both watch and enjoy the show and are rewarded for their devotion by being incorporated into the very narrative that feeds their passion for the series" (Geraghty, 2007: 146). We see this in the film when a group of fans are scolded early on for not realising the TV show is fake, their time questioning the technical specifications of the fictional spaceship seen as a waste, but called into action at the film's conclusion to help save the real ship, using their knowledge and guile to save the crew and the aliens trapped on board. Borrowing generic elements from science fiction and the western, the film emphasises notions of self-improvement within a frontier setting. Fans are depicted as active, using the fictional show as "a template" (Geraghty, 2007: 147) that means something positive within the contexts of the social world in which they live.

In the case of *Galaxy Quest*, science fiction film was promoting its television counterpart – using familiar fan stereotypes, generic tropes and parody to highlight the personal and cultural importance of the genre to contemporary fan audiences. As science fiction television series continue to be popular commissions on main-stream network and cable channels the representation of fandom in *Galaxy Quest* stands as an interesting gauge of how the genre is perceived by Hollywood. While media fans are clearly able to recognise and laugh at the stereotypes lovingly played within the film, it more than anything communicates a sense of what it means to be a fan. Using the usual stereotypes to construct a narrative that places fans and associated fan practices (costuming, making models, blogging, conventions, watching, actively engaging with a fictional universe) at the heart of the film's positive resolution shows that you cannot separate the stereotypes from reality. In fact, to do so would mean that the very things that make being a fan such an affirmative and rewarding social and personal experience would be lost.

The more positive examples of media texts discussed so far depict fandom as a complex activity, detached from problematic stereotypes of the "nerd", which encapsulates a number of important processes based on defining an identity and displaying that identity to a peer group or the wider fan community. What you do as a fan often relies on being with, or at least contacting, another fan group and many of the issues and ideas that real fans feel are important to being a fan are represented as such. Indeed, being a fan is seen as an integral part of achieving one's dreams, either becoming a famous comic artist or author, or using the knowledge accrued over years about a show to make a difference and be a hero. However, in the contexts of this book and the importance of collecting as a fan practice, for the remainder of this chapter I want to focus on specific media texts that depict fans as collectors; examining how collecting merchandise, objects and ephemera, and the physical collection itself, are positioned as both positive and negative aspects of what it means to be a fan.

Fans as Collectors

As well as being considered the personification of the American fanboy "archetype" *The Simpson*'s Comic Book Guy is a collector. As seen in numerous episodes his shop, The Android's Dungeon, is home to a vast array of comics, toys and other media merchandise that are, more often than not, objects from his own personal collection. They are on display but not for sale. In the 1999 "Treehouse of Horror X" story, "Desperately Xeeking Xena", Comic Book Guy plays the role of super villain, The Collector. He raids a *Xena: Warrior Princess* (1995–2001) convention attended by various "nerd" characters, including Professor Frink, to kidnap Lucy Lawless and add her to his collection of favourite cult television characters. As one of the Halloween specials, the story clearly plays fast and loose with the established continuity of the series: making Comic Book Guy a super villain and having Bart and Lisa as superheroes, Stretch Dude and Clobber Girl, trying to prevent him completing his evil plan. After returning to his lair, the basement of The Android's Dungeon, The Collector sets about displaying Xena/Lawless in a Mylar pouch alongside other "collectibles": Tom Baker as The Doctor, Mr Spock, Seven of Nine, the Robot from *Lost in Space* (1965–8), *Baywatch* (1989–99) star Yasmine Bleeth, Gilligan from *Gilligan's Island* (1964–7), and Matt Groening (metatextual reference to the series). Following a fight with Clobber Girl and Stretch Dude, The Collector is captured and Lawless is set free. Proving to be a popular "fantasy" storyline, The Collector returned in a special edition comic book published as a

San Diego Comic-Con exclusive – the collecting theme clearly linking with what Comic-Con is best known for, comics and collectible merchandise.

This story might, on the one level, be seen as continuing the fan stereotype: Comic Book Guy as The Collector having to kidnap the object of his fantasies because he has no luck with women. The fact he refuses to believe Lawless's declaration that she is not Xena also underlines the stereotype of fans not being able to discern reality from fiction. However, on a deeper level, the story tries to encapsulate and sympathise with many of the common practicalities, joys and frustrations of being a collector. The joy of completing a collection, putting it on display, is enhanced by the visual gag of seeing Lawless and other fictional characters all preserved in Mylar pouches – standard practice for comic book fans who store their rare issues in protective Mylar sleeves for storage. The Collector's pleasure in completing his collection is ultimately curtailed by the fact he is tricked into ruining the economic value of one of his other collectibles by Stretch Dude. In the final battle The Collector takes out a dual lightsabre from its packaging but is reminded that doing so erases its mint-in-box condition. He is distracted and falls to his end into a giant pot of boiling acrylic. Emphasising the importance fans place on collectible objects such as the piece of *Star Wars* merchandise, the story uses humour to communicate what it means and takes to be a serious fan collector: the lengths people go to pursue rare and wanted items; the effort put into preserving their collectibles; and the value placed on objects often seen as throw-away and useless in mainstream consumer culture.

With *The 40-Year-Old Virgin*, already discussed in this chapter, the stereotype of the loner fan is in many ways a distraction from the more positive representation of the fan collector. Andy Stitzer may not have luck with women but it is his collection of toys and merchandise that brings him into contact with his future girlfriend and ultimately brings him happiness in that he is able to start his own online business and quit his dead-end salesman job that only brought him ridicule and monotony. Thus, while critics have argued that having to sell his collectibles to get the girl shows he must disavow his fandom and geekier side, I would argue that his collection and attention to preserving that collection gives him access to a career path that brings him joy and offers him an equal partnership with Trish, his girlfriend. She handles the selling of items on eBay to other collectors and his knowledge of the collectible market allows him to pick the right items to put up for sale – and what items he wants to keep in his personal collection. It must be pointed out that he does not get rid of all his toys and collectibles, the ones he considers special are kept and thus remain as markers of personal identity – a fan collector identity.

So, like the examples from *Paul* and *Fanboys*, where fan labour and talent is turned into a career, *The 40-Year-Old Virgin* again stresses that there is real worth in the collecting activities that fans carry out and in which they invest heavily. Reflective of the popular media industry and the recycling of popular texts through physical ephemera and collectible objects, the film paints an accurate picture of the contemporary fan experience of building, keeping and living with a collection. It emphasises that being a fan is not just about making and doing but also about preserving and celebrating favourite media texts through modes of consumption such as collecting, e-commerce and making connections with fellow collectors. Collecting is in many ways, as shall be discussed throughout this book, a social and competitive fan practice that employs specific skills, strategies and knowledge to get the best bargain, acquire the rarest item and negotiate with those who see equal and greater value in the same objects. While Stitzer starts out a loner, confirming the fan stereotype, his transformation to professional collector and businessman suggests that being a fan is about capital consumption and defining an identity and social life with others through the popular culture texts on offer in contemporary society. This is also emphasised in the film *High Fidelity* (2000), adapted from Nick Hornby's 1995 novel of the same name, by the Rob Gordon character whose encyclopaedic knowledge of music structures his professional and personal life. His vinyl music collection is at first a barrier to, but then a way of, understanding how he can create and sustain relationships with the people he loves and cares for in his life.

Conclusion

The nerd/fan stereotype is not restricted to fiction. A recent article in *The Times* discusses the renewed popularity of science programming on mainstream UK television, with seasonal shows like the BBC's *Stargazing Live* (2011–present) proving particularly relevant in the current times. Oliver Moody writes in his article, "Nerds don't care that cool kids like them at last", that thanks to celebrity academics like Professor Brian Cox and the success of the *Star Trek* reboots in cinemas "science has rarely been more at home in popular culture" (2013: 7). The association with a "nerd" audience and the mention of *Star Trek*, however, continues to conflate fan cultures with a presumed nerd culture that propagates the same stereotypes discussed throughout this chapter.

However, as I have also argued, representations of fans that do separate the nerd stereotype from characteristics attributed to media fandom are important examples that require and deserve further study – they should not be dismissed as being derogatory but rather seen as celebratory of what it means to be a fan in a net-worked and socially connected community. Indeed, films and television that play up and focus on the multiple practices that make being a fan so attractive are instructive in the processes that fans go through to create, build and maintain their fan identity. For Kath Woodward, "identity involves the interrelationship between the personal and the social; between what I feel inside and what is known about me from the outside" (2002: 16). Therefore, the stereotypes discussed throughout this chapter are important indicators of what is "known" in the wider social community about fandom and how much fans "feel" their fandom is being accurately represented. But also, "identity is marked by difference and the ways in which we distinguish between ourselves and others" (Woodward, 2002: 167), thus stereotypes that focus on differences between a marked fan identity and that of the perceived mainstream are important clues as to where fans might lie in the wider contexts of society and the power relations between individuals and groups within that culture.

For the purposes of the next chapter, the examples of fan collectors discussed here offer insight into how a collection provides fans with a stable and fixed identity represented in the physical objects displayed and preserved. Collecting is not about mere consumption but is a reflective and strategic process, just like other legitimated fan practices such as fan fiction writing and costuming, that articulates notions of identity, provides social connections and offers multiple experiences as fans acquire, expand and catalogue their collections. These ideas, expressed in fictional films about fan collectors, will be further explored in relation to film and television documentaries and real life collectors of popular media entertainment ephemera. It will be shown that the physical objects, toys and merchandise produced by Hollywood, an industry based entirely on the production, circulation and consumption of popular media texts, are important components in the mediation of fan identity and the collection is fundamental to the understanding of what it means to be a fan.

2

MOVIE MAGIC

Collecting, Authenticity and the Enduring Fandom of Hollywood Memorabilia

Those media texts that emphasise a "dual address" as discussed in the previous chapter are examples of where issues of similarity and difference are fundamental to the construction of a fan identity. The codes and conventions of what makes up a fan identity are continually being contested within and by the media; how fans interact and transform media texts so often come to define fan stereotypes and how fan stereotypes are critiqued by scholars help construct an ideological narrative of what constitutes being a particular type of fan. However, by focusing on the processes and conventions associated with one type of fan practice, it is possible to discern the fundamental characteristics of what being a fan means to an individual and how it shapes their personal and social life within a community. With this in mind, chapter two will pay particular attention to the collecting practices of fans. It will analyse the significance of the collection in the production of fan identities, the importance of physical objects in the display and communication of those identities, and in understanding the relationship between both it will evaluate their mediation through documentaries, lifestyle television and press articles.

However, the concept of a "dual address" in certain media texts for and about fans is somewhat limiting in that it does not fully provide a rationale for what it means to be a fan of a particular film, TV show or star. Rather, it points to the fact that one might recognise it in their own habits, activities and clothes they wear yet does that count the same for another fan watching the same programme that considers themselves a fan of the same things. Measures of being a fan are based on accumulated knowledge and invested cultural capital, but of course that will vary depending on the circumstances of the individual. Instead of thinking about practices, objects and the visual signs of being a fan on their own terms it is worth conceptualising these processes of fandom through the lens of enchantment and enthrallment. Both of these concepts have been discussed in relation to popular media texts and their associated fan groups before but neither has been applied to any particular fan practices outside of those routinely highlighted as important, expressive and creative. Therefore, I want to apply these terms to fan collectors, their collections and collecting practices to help provide a framework for how and why fans collect, what they do with their collections, and where their collecting takes place.

The following analyses of documentaries and reality television about fans and their collecting practices suggest that fandom is about the search for authenticity, the establishment of meaning and the construction of identity. The physical objects that make up a collection are semiotic signifiers of self, and how fans use, display and exchange them is determined by processes similar to those defined by subcultural distinction and the accumulation of fan cultural capital. However, fandom often develops over a long period of time and the texts that fans hold dear can create a bond that lasts a lifetime. Therefore, this chapter will also consider the importance of "enduring fandom" (Kuhn, 1999) in shaping how fans interact with and build collections. Over the years, Hollywood has made thousands of movies and many of them have attracted devoted fan communities. Moreover, the industry itself attracts fans and collectors who feel that the history of Hollywood needs to be promoted, protected and preserved. Fans that collect Hollywood memorabilia do so to both recreate the illusion and break it down; they wish to be part of Hollywood history and seek to redefine it by amassing a collection that represents considerable financial investment and signifies their own cultural capital.

Enchanting Texts and Enthralling Collections

Michael Saler's article, "Modernity, disenchantment, and the ironic imagination", offers us a useful way of understanding the relationship fans have with the popular media texts they watch and consume, the practices and activities in which they participate, and the things they collect and keep. For Saler, the history of modernity is a history of disenchantment, the distancing from wonder, delight and enchantment with aspects of the world around us, and therefore ideologies of the modern encompass "the ongoing diffusion of rationality, secularism, democracy, urbanization, industrialization, and bureaucratization" (Saler, 2004: 137). However, there is a way in which we can balance the tenants of modernity and that of enchantment in order to better understand how we interact with an increasingly rationalised and technologically driven society. Saler argues that both worlds, of wonder and disillusion, fiction and reality, can be drawn together through what he calls the "ironic imagination": "Ideally, the ironic imagination promises a way to experience wonders and marvels while avoiding enchantment's potential to beguile" (Saler, 2004: 139). If we apply this to fan culture, we might argue that while fans are clearly enchanted by the texts they watch, transform, and claim ownership of, they do so knowing that the text is a fiction – it is a text that operates as inspiration within the world of work, family, and other social relations. How we view, play and consume popular texts is done so at an ironic distance, we understand ourselves within such texts and how they relate to the wider world around us. In terms of the "dual address" which fans experience when confronted with images and narratives that speak to their fandom the idea of the "ironic imagination" provides a useful contrast.

Saler goes further and states that "irony provides a ludic space in which reason and imagination cavort, neither succumbing to the other, a utopic ideal" (2004: 139). The ironic imagination is in itself "a form of the modernist 'double consciousness' that is found not only in the high modernist works of late nineteenth and early twentieth centuries, but also in the mass culture of the same period" (139–40). Expressions of ironic imagination are self-conscious and reflexive, as well as liberating and engrossing. Therefore, they allow for "imaginative immersion" as well as critical distance (140). It "emphasizes the provisional, the contingent, and the artificial" and it "is comfortable with the artifices of mass culture, and the phantasmagoria of symbols and representations that accompany a capitalist economic order" (140). Saler provides examples of popular texts that are consistent with providing space for ironic imagination; no surprise that some of the biggest pop culture franchises are top of his list: *Star Wars, Star Trek, The Lord of the Rings*. Through their depictions of fantasy worlds they offer people opportunities for play that we have come to expect from all popular media texts. The ironic imagination is a compelling way for understanding why fans gravitate to such franchises and enjoy being immersed in the narratives that sustain them. Using the ironic imagination to frame the contexts for why fans do what they do, make what they make, collect what they collect helps us understand what it means to be a fan. Saler argues that it provides "critical distance" while keeping "potential delusions in abeyance" and it promotes, quoting Arjun Appadurai, "fantasy as social practice" (2004: 147).

However, while the ironic imagination goes some way in helping us to understand how fans interact with popular culture it does not fully account for the affective relationship fans have with the objects and ephemera produced by and for their favourite texts. Peter Stromberg's "The 'I' of Enthrallment" offers further means to explore fans' engagement. "Enthrallment", he argues, "is a term of art here, referring to the immersion in culturally available fictions" (Stromberg, 1999: 491). A similar assertion to that of Saler but different in one important aspect; for Stromberg, enthrallment is "an intense involvement in fictional narratives that is a source both of pleasure and of moral guidance" (1999: 501). Thus, the text becomes part of a fan's identity inasmuch as it creates meaning that is internalised and utilised for various purposes: "Contemporary readers operate within a tradition of narratives that define universes of meaning for fictional subjects with whom those readers identify" (Stromberg, 1999: 500). He further elucidates his argument by saying that when fans identify themselves in the process of enthrallment, communicating to others in conversation or online for example, they are often positioning themselves within the narrative of the fictional world – it provides a framework for understanding their relationship with the text and the community of fans.

Stromberg's concept is based on his research drawn from fans that play *Star Trek* video games, specifically first-person shooters. Again, like Saler, his interpretation of an audience's relationship and interaction with popular media includes an understanding of the social contexts in which the audience is located. Fans do not practise their fandom on their own, they are part of a larger community that shares in the same affective relationship, but in articulating their affiliation with a favourite film or television series individual fans are able to express their own identities and fantasies in ways that differ from the social group:

> The *I* of enthrallment becomes visible through pragmatic features of communicative behavior because such features constitute social realities. Careful attention to pragmatics reveals that role-players construct a complex social situation in which persons are at once fully aware of their surroundings, as conventionally defined, and closely identified with characters in a collectively defined narrative. Although it is in once sense accurate to refer to this as a "blending of fantasy and reality", such language does not do credit to the complexity of the communicative processes whereby both reality and fantasy are constructed and maintained.
>
> *(Stromberg, 1999: 500)*

With such emphasis placed on the individual's role in bridging the gap between fantasy and reality, the fictional narrative and the social world in which it sits, I wish to now turn to an analysis of the fan collector and apply both the ironic imagination and the notion of enthrallment to the practices of collecting and building a collection. However, in applying such work it is important to acknowledge that the creation of a fan identity through an emotional connection with a text is also influenced by the physical contexts of immersion. Therefore, it is necessary to take into account the spaces in which such connections are made; specifically, where and how fan collections are put together and displayed.

Trekkies and *Starwoids*

As chapter one outlined, stereotypes of fans have abounded in the media. *Star Trek*, as one might expect, has received more than its fair share of attention. In an attempt to counter some of those familiar stereotypes the 1999 documentary *Trekkies* (and its 2004 sequel) was marketed as a truth laid bare story of Trekkies, supposedly aimed at reversing the stereotypes and showing fans as "normal" people. Despite its noble intentions the film tended to dwell on the more excessive fan practices, going to work dressed in costume or tattooing insignia on one's skin. A number of well-known fans and fan stories featured heavily, thus making the documentary appear more like a psychological analysis of extreme behaviour rather than a feature about what it means to be a fan. However, it is interesting to note how collecting and the value of building a *Star Trek* collection are depicted and discussed in the film. Several of the fans talk about their collecting habits, the processes of picking out rare items and the financial value of their collections. These practices highlight interesting aspects of fandom that perhaps recede into the background as the film focuses on the more colourful fan activities.

Gabriel Köerner and his father, Richard, are interviewed several times through-out the documentary. They discuss their *Star Trek* fan club membership, handmade costumes and their converted pick-up truck that looks like a space shuttle. But Gabriel is a collector, particularly of action figures, and how he chooses which to buy and which to trade reveal a lot about the levels of enthrallment he experiences when consuming *Star Trek* – which, for him, clearly happens on a regular basis at either a convention or a club meeting or when he drops by the collectible store to view the latest memorabilia for sale. He talks about the numerous self-made rules or processes involved in collecting. The collection includes examples of toy action figures of all the captains, both in and out of box. Those still in boxes are often signed by the actor who played the particular character contained in plastic packaging. These figures are on display in his bedroom and suggest an ordering of his own personal world through the arrangement of physical objects.

Susan Pearce argues that the ordering of personal objects and collections dates back to medieval times, where they were used to furnish a room and indicate status or wealth. In Gabriel's case we can read his display of signed figures and those taken out of their packaging to be displayed in a pose as similar in that they both furnish his room but also signal his status as fully invested *Star Trek* fan. Pearce points out that "the emotional satisfaction taken in the spatial arrangement of col-lections comes in many different guises: aesthetic and intellectual satisfactions have their emotional sides" (1995: 259). How objects are spaced in the room and in relation to each other depend on two interrelated things. For Pearce, the first is that every arrangement is "an act of imagination" and the second is that "collec-tions are the fruit of a selecting process in which both the collector and the objects themselves enter into a symbiotic relationship" (1995: 255). This means that Gabriel's collection represents him, how he relates to the space in which his collection sits and his relationship with the imagined subjectivity of the *Star Trek* universe depicted by those action figures.

In addition to the signed figures and the captains, Gabriel displays a series of Data figures – one from each TV and film incarnation. Thus, he has created a set which defines the timeline of *Star Trek: The Next Generation* through the changing face and uniform of Data. The collecting of sets is about filling in the blanks, get-ting one of everything related to the set in order to complete it. The satisfaction of chasing down individual items that make up the set is the driving force behind the set collector. For Pearce, "the collector may know supporting information about the individual objects, but the sense of their collection rests in its truly collective nature, and in the investment of time and effort which have gone to make it so" (1995: 260). The chronological ordering to Gabriel's display of Datas is significant also in that such temporal progression implies an inevitable end (of course, by 1999 several more incarnations of Data were yet to appear on screen) and with an end comes completion: "The point of such collections is the finite conclusion which they offer, for the sets are genuinely delimited and completion is a possibility, where generally it is not. These collections, *par excellence*, demonstrate the joys of possession and control, and of opening and closure in closely defined context of spatial layout" (Pearce, 1995: 260). Perhaps then the potential enthrallment in *Star Trek* for Gabriel comes in the form of control and being able to order the progressive changes in appearance of Data's action figure through his collection.

Other fan collectors appear in *Trekkies*, including a die-hard Klingon costumer who bids at convention auctions for authentic Klingon props and screen-worn prosthetics in order to preserve them and Erik Larson who collects all sorts of *Star Trek* memorabilia with the goal of one day putting them on display for future and fellow fans. What both fan collectors are alluding to in their personal missions is that which has gone on in public museums for decades: the preservation of commonly assumed valuable items for the social good. Again, Pearce acknowledges that even in the smallest collections collectors are seeking such a thing so as to bring some kind of order and reason to their endeavours. As museums are examples of the "community manifestation of the sacred set-aside, an emotional response which we all share and which we all attribute to our individual collections, it follows that deposition in a museum, through which sacredness and significance are guaranteed, is the goal to which many collectors aspire for their material" (Pearce, 1995: 390). Fan collectors who reclaim the objects of their youth that represent their emotional investment and enthrallment in a media text are also blurring the lines between official and non-official versions of the cultural museum. "Consumable goods are displayed as if they were in a museum, just as some museums displays become increasingly like department stores" (Pearce, 1995: 382), therefore even the humblest of fan attempts to display, store and preserve bring their collections more attention as cultural artefacts rather than mass produced consumables.

The bridge between private and public as seen in the collections and collecting activities discussed so far is brought into particular focus with the example of Starbase Dental in another segment from the documentary. A dentist decided to decorate his surgery with all manner of *Star Trek* memorabilia, toys, posters and life size cardboard cut outs to bring a little pizzazz to his business and mark himself out from his competitors. While this clearly intimates a level of enthrallment that emphasises the pre-eminence of the individual within the social space of a dental surgery we might also view it as another attempt at ordering space through the collecting of fan objects. New objects are added every time the owner comes back from a convention, the space is enlivened with new posters and props that have some financial value but greater personal value. Most of the employees who work in the surgery don't have any fan knowledge nor share a close affinity with *Star Trek* yet they recognise the space as an enjoyable one to work in – thus the collection of objects on display creates the emotional attachment and in itself becomes the subject of enthrallment experienced by those who enter the space. Here again, we might use the work of Susan Pearce to understand the creation of a material identity through the objects collected and put on display:

> Collections are psychic ordering, of individuality, of public and private relationships, and of time and space. They live in the minds and hearts of their collectors, for whom they act as material autobiographies, chronicling the

cycle of a life, from the first moment an object strikes a particular personal chord, to specialised accumulation, to constructing the dimensions of life, to a final measure of immortality.

(Pearce, 1995: 279)

So, viewing *Trekkies* as evidence of the enthrallment fans feel and experience when interacting with *Star Trek* is perhaps more helpful in its deconstruction as a documentary than is a mere focus on the repetition of extreme fan stereotypes. Moreover, by analysing fan collecting practices as depicted on screen – talking through their collections, buying and preserving rare pieces, getting to see their collections displayed in personal spaces – we can get a better sense of who they really are and what collecting *Star Trek* memorabilia really offers them as fans. These objects have meanings ascribed to them and thus fulfil roles within a fan's life above and beyond the show itself. They are markers of personal identity and their display and ordering within domestic space closes down the gap between the fiction of the series and the reality of their social situation. Collections are the physical artefacts of fan enthrallment with texts of popular culture.

Starwoids (2001), like *Trekkies*, is a documentary that plays on the name of the fan community that inspired it. Mainly devoted to following *Star Wars* fans that spent over a month waiting in line to see the first screening of *The Phantom Menace* in 1999, the documentary tries to encapsulate what it means to be a fan and draws connections between fandom and religious devotion, obsession and worship. Interspersed between interviews with fans waiting in line outside Mann's Chinese Theater in Hollywood and another cinema in Westwood are several short spots that highlight the other kinds of activities in which *Star Wars* fans participate: musicals, conventions, costuming and collecting. The fan collectors filmed are quite candid in their discussions of what it means to be a collector, as compared to a *Star Wars* collectible dealer, and they display several characteristics of what scholar Russell Belk defines as collecting in a consumer society.

Guy Klender, self-confessed toy collector, started his collection of *Star Wars* memorabilia in 1996 with new action figures made following the release of the digitally remastered original trilogy. Following a strict routine that sees him travel to all the local toy stores in his neighbourhood on the morning a new delivery is shipped out, he targets figures that are both rare and widespread – buying two of the more common ones (one to open, one to keep in box) and preserving rarer items in extra plastic display packaging. A strategy is outlined as he jumps in his car to reach the stores before opening and before rivals beat him to the newest toys. He makes it clear in the interview that he could make it easy for himself by purchasing harder to find items from the collectible store in the mall but he wants to pay less and not give the dealer the satisfaction of buying from him. Belk argues that collecting is not done in isolation, even though collectors are most often individuals. It is a competitive activity and therefore collectors go to great lengths in securing the desired object or objects that fit their collection (Belk, 1995: 68). Collecting is also about discrimination, in that collectors can discriminate between worthwhile and valuable objects and decide what new things require collecting before they become popular (Belk, 1995: 88). However, that *Star Wars* action figures are worthwhile collectibles is not something Klender tries to defend or argue. He discriminates between the right and wrong ways people should be collecting the toys and is very discriminating in where he chooses to go to find the best figures. Indeed, while it is obvious that he is enthralled by the *Star Wars* franchise – including all its textual and paratextual elements – he is clearly more enthralled by the chase and the potentially fulfilling experience it offers when he finds that bargain or rare item.

Later in the film Klender is filmed taking some of his toys to the filming locations of the original film. A road trip through California's Death Valley allows him some physical connection with the fictional text as well as a connection with his memories of watching it for the first time as a child. The past is brought into the present through the process of fan pilgrimage, something I explore further in chapter five, but it is made tangible by the fact that his toys become physical representations of the characters seen on screen. At Dante's View, where Luke and Obi-Wan are filmed overlooking the Mos Eisley spaceport in *Star Wars* (1977), Klender places Luke and Obi-Wan action figures on the cliff's edge posed as if they were in the movie. Similarly, at the Dunes he recreates the scene where R2-D2 leaves C-3PO just after crash landing on Tatooine by using a R2 figure perched on a ridge of sand. Finally, he completes his *Star Wars* road trip at the Artists Palette – a colourful rock formation in the valley – which was the location for R2-D2's capture at the hands of the Jawas. Using his R2 action figure along with several small Jawas he attempts to recreate the tension of the original scene by acting as R2, walking through the space and looking around warily, intercut with shots of his toy R2 surrounded by the Jawa figures positioned in crevices.

Using his toy collection to connect with both his personal past, in the memories of seeing the film for the first time, and the actual past of the film, represented by the physical locations, Klender's actions contribute to his "sense of extended self" (Belk, 1995: 91). Collections are markers of personal history and thus they contribute to the collector's sense of past as well as present. For Belk, "collectors see the items in their collections not as objects occupying a cell in a taxonomy, but as packages of memories" (1995: 92), therefore we can indeed recognise in Klender's collection a sense of his packaged memories. However, it is the fact that the figures are placed in a specific space, thus transforming their original use value as objects of play in childhood, that makes this all the more significant and emblematic of what it means being a fan collector of *Star Wars* memorabilia. Klender is justifying his collecting efforts, discussed earlier in the film, by taking his toys out and making use of them beyond displaying them in a domestic setting. The toy objects are given more meaning than that of being static parts of a collection; they become active parts of the film itself by occupying the spaces in which it was originally brought to life. This rendering of the film through immersion of the collection into the fictional narrative is akin to how fans attempt to exercise control over mass-reproduced objects. Taking the toys out of the box, playing with them in spaces connected to the movie, makes them more than just mass-produced commodities: "By decommoditizing and sacralizing items that enter the collection, the collector also transcends the profane commodity market" (Belk, 1995: 151). What is more, the toys become symbols of Klender's "ironic imagination" in that they allow him to be self-conscious and reflexive, both immersed in and standing outside of, the fictional text. His collection represents a celebration of the history of *Star Wars* and can thus be seen also as part of his enduring fandom for the franchise.

Enduring Fandom and the Celebration of Cinema History

It is not just the fans that can be seen to be in a state of enthrallment for bygone films. As I argued in the introduction to this book, there is a deeply entrenched sense of nostalgia for the past that permeates contemporary media. That fans choose to celebrate now-classic texts like *Star Wars* by re-enacting scenes using toy collectibles suggests that memories and spaces are merging in order to provide a tangible and reliveable cinematic experience. The production of merchandise, once considered a purely moneymaking exercise to extend the shelf life of a film, is now integral to the fans' continued memorialisation of the text. Collectibles are important physical reminders of the visual experience on screen and as such can be just as important in the processes of celebration and meaning making fans go through when returning to and rewatching their favourite films. They become part of the long-term personal memories associated with the film, paratextual signifiers of the original viewing experience.

As well as nostalgic fans, we can see the industry itself is becoming more aware and celebratory of its own movie history. The recent award-winning films, like *The Artist* (2011) and *Hugo* (2011), highlight Hollywood's return to its cinematic past, using the latest special effects technology to represent an age where cinema audiences were enthralled with the spectacle and wonder of the moving image. This in turn encourages contemporary audiences to become enthralled once more with the magic of cinema, viewing history through the lens of nostalgia. An article in the *Sunday Express* published just before *The Artist's* success at the 2012 Oscars outlines the contemporary appeal of nostalgic cinema. Henry Fitzherbert argued that the "Academy Awards are all about one thing, the past, and it's a place we all seem to want to be" (2012: 7). *The Artist* is described as being "bathed in nostalgia … reaching back into the past both in subject and form" with *Hugo* seen as "another exercise in nostalgia" (7). Both films are set in cinema's past, the golden age of silent film, and reflect a period that Tom Gunning would call the "The Cinema of Attractions". For Gunning, early cinema presented audiences a series of views, and they were fascinated by the "power" of "magical illusion" (1990: 57). Film was not used merely to tell a story, but to show off the creative, scientific and artistic talents of the filmmaker: "The cinema of attractions directly solicits spectator attention, inciting visual curiosity, and supplying pleasure through an exciting spectacle – a unique event, whether fictional or documentary" (Gunning, 1990: 58).

Fitzherbert's article suggests that while both films celebrate the past they also "look as if they were made then too", celebrating that fact and emphasising that "Change is a bad thing" (2012: 7). The silent movie star in *The Artist* is threatened by technological change and the coming of sound, while George Méliès in *Hugo* is consigned to obscurity when his films and filmmaking techniques are seen as too simplistic. While Fitzherbert's argument is compelling, his ambiguous set of reasons for the renewed popularity in Hollywood for nostalgia films is less so:

> Like Oscar voters audiences are in the mood for escapism, comfort and reassurance. There is quite enough wretched reality on the news, it seems, while the disorientating pace of modern life, with all its attendant technological advances, is leaving many of us yearning for calmer, more straightforward times.
>
> *(2012: 7)*

I would argue that fans reliving personal film memories through collectibles and Hollywood celebrating its own past through cinematic nostalgia are both contemporary examples of what Annette Kuhn calls "enduring fandom". In her work on cinema memory and fandom Kuhn argues that the act of fans staying with a film, rewatching it and following its star through their own lifetime is a mode of reception: enduring fandom is "loyalty to a star which continues throughout the fan's life, and even beyond the star's death" (Kuhn, 1999: 135). In the cases I have outlined so far a star is not particularly the object of a fan's attention – although in *Hugo* we see the reclamation of Méliès's creative work and his role as a director that in many respects would count as a more exact example of Kuhn's definition of "enduring fandom". However, as Kuhn goes on to outline using the work of John Fiske, "enduring fandom adds something of its own to the usual repertoire of fan productivity" (1999: 136). It is not an interior form of film reception like "semiotic productivity" which "consists of the making of meanings of social identity and of social experience from the semiotic resources of the cultural commodity" (Fiske, 1992: 37), but is "enacted in fans' discourses and practices" (Kuhn, 1999: 136). "Enduring fandom embodies distinctive modes of remembering" and "is ongoingly produced as a vital part of daily life in the present" (Kuhn, 2002: 197).

Fans who are members of clubs that watch classic films together, meet to discuss their passion for cinema, and relive early cinema-going by organising vintage cinema events are displaying their enduring fandom for historic texts in the present. Likewise, *Star Wars* fans that insert collectibles into the physical spaces of film locations and audiences who go to watch films that celebrate cinema history are enacting their sense of enduring fandom – while also highlighting the connection they share with the past. Both activities hint at the search for authenticity, somehow trying to recreate an authentic version of the past through physical re-enactment or special effects wizardry. Samantha Barbas, in her study of early Hollywood fan clubs, conceives fandom as a quest for authenticity and that fans who become actively involved in their entertainment are "attempting to make more real and immediate the simulated reality presented by the movies, television, and other mass media" (2001: 6). Perhaps it was the search for an authentic movie experience that made audiences flock to see *The Artist* and continues to inspire fan collectors to hunt for rare and iconic items from Hollywood's past:

> After nearly 100 years of motion pictures, Americans are still fascinated by the cinema. Although most of us feel quite sure about the way the movies work – that the camera depicts a distorted, constructed version of reality – we still engage in acts of verification. Although most of us accept that we cannot take part directly in the filmmaking process, we still want to feel a part of the movies … As long as we go to the movies, we will probably always be fascinated by questions of authenticity and involvement.
>
> *(Barbas, 2001: 7)*

As such, the following analysis of reality programmes about the collecting and preservation of Hollywood memorabilia and collectibles should be read as mediated searches for authenticity. Representing our continued fascination for movie history and the search for a tangible connection with the past, these shows are evidence of the fan collector's enduring fandom and eternal desire to own what is valuable, real, and authentic.

Hollywood Treasure and the Collector's Search for the Authentic

Our love of movies is such that the film itself is not enough, we want more from Hollywood and Hollywood is quite prepared to give us more, for a price. Multiplex cinemas, theme parks and rides extend movies into real spaces where we can feel immersed in the fictional text, visiting filming locations (as discussed above) allows for a connection to the realities of production, DVD and cable TV have made our homes into private spaces of film spectatorship, merchandise provides an extended shelf life for films and gives them broad appeal, and finally, collecting the props and costumes bestows upon fans a sense of ownership of the text. Through the purchasing of movie memorabilia fan collectors achieve closeness with the film text that increases their sense of identity as fans, as preservers of film history, and as discerners of authenticity. In her study of three Hollywood photograph collectors Janet Staiger argues that their collections "display self-fashioning and authorship" and that "each collector used the objects to attempt to come close to their objects of desire" (2005). Therefore, it is not enough to have a replica for Hollywood memorabilia collectors – that would be like just owning the DVD and rewatching the film. Owning an authentic piece from a film or the movie industry (whether it be prop, costume, car, poster, animation cell, original script) adds meaning and significance to a film beyond spectatorship – its collectors achieve a level of authority, it distinguishes them from ordinary film fans.

The popularity of reality series like *Hollywood Treasure* (2010–present), *Pawn Stars* (2009–present), and *Toy Hunter* (2012–present) suggests that not only do collectors continually search for authentic pieces of social and cultural history but also that audiences enjoy watching the processes of collecting such as the hunt and acquisition. In addition to this is the fascination for value, how much is an object worth, and will it reach that figure at final auction. Series about the collecting and auctioning of memorabilia are embedded in a tradition of history as a hobby and the antique programme, the most famous of which is the BBC's *Antiques Roadshow* (1979–present). With imitations across the globe in North America and Europe the format clearly has a universal appeal. The show involves ordinary people taking their antique artefacts to experts to be valued – most go away disappointed that their item is deemed to be worth a few hundred pounds, a select few leave delighted with the news that their favourite object could fetch hundreds of thousands of pounds at auction. For Jerome de Groot, antiques "demonstrate a complex commodification of the past – the fetishisation of the object due in main to its age and historical context as well as any innate value or craftsmanship" (2009: 67). On series like *Antiques Roadshow*, unique and significant pieces are at the high end of value, with the majority of items such as second hand goods, memorabilia and vintage clothing occupying the middle and lower end. Antiques are representative of both the owner's economic and cultural capital, they are worth a sum of money or cost something to buy and they enhance the owner's sense of worth and establish their position in a hierarchy of collectors. Like fandom, the collecting community is built in hierarchies of taste defined by cultural capital, however, economic capital plays a much bigger part in the distinction between individuals as objects are bought and sold and rarity increases both financial value and esteem.

Another feature of the antique programme is that they are presented by an expert or group of experts that assert their knowledge over those that bring items for valuation. They add colour to the televisual presentation, telling jokes and anecdotes, as well as showing off their expertise by filling in the historical blanks and predicting the value of an object and what it might make at auction. They induce suspense in both the owner of the piece and the television audience by narrating the history of the object, revealing its flaws and casting doubt on its authenticity, before finally passing judgement on value. They help construct a narrative of authenticity by establishing provenance, retelling history and qualifying taste. The expert presenter is someone who evidently works in the field and is a collector themselves but they also make the journey into the past for the audience an enjoyable one, we trust their expertise and authority. They make the history on show accessible and of contemporary significance to the collector and viewer at home:

> These shows demonstrate that the past can provide a subject for leisure-driven daytime television programming, but only if yoked to elements of competition and financial worth. They communicate to the viewer that the past might be valuable, that the expert can guide you, and that anyone can undertake it … such shows contribute to a democratisation of the historical, with knowledge and ability moving from the elite – as represented by

> antique experts, connoisseurship and collectors perhaps – and an emphasis on
> the intervention of "ordinary" people into previously fenced off arenas.
>
> *(de Groot, 2009: 71–2)*

American series, *Hollywood Treasure*, *Pawn Stars*, and *Toy Hunter*, do most of the
above, and then some. Allowing access into previously closed-off areas of history is,
I would argue, their primary appeal for participants and viewers. All three shows
give collectors the opportunity to legitimise their hobby and have an expert affirm
not just the financial value of their collection but also its cultural and historical
worth. This is because the objects at the centre of all three series are usually the
ones that are deemed too popular and towards the lower end of the scales of value
and taste. So, in *Pawn Stars* for example, ordinary people come to the World
Famous Gold & Silver Pawn Shop in Las Vegas to get their items valued for sale
(to raise extra cash for another project or dire financial need) but after consultation
with an expert their object is usually deemed of more historical significance than
originally thought. The owner's attitude towards the piece changes and the viewer
is encouraged to see the object as historically significant rather than something
which was to be sacrificed and sold at a pawn shop. Collectible objects screened on
each episode are mixed and thus lines between what is considered as worthy are
blurred: so a Revolutionary war musket will be shown alongside a rare first edition
of *Dracula* and a Betty Boop statue.

The fencing off of what is valuable and worthy of preservation is broken down
further in *Toy Hunter*. Jordan Hembrough, presenter and toy dealer, travels the US
to pick collectible toy items for auction through his Hollywood Heroes company.
Literally rummaging through boxes in attics, garages, abandoned storage lock ups
and even other dealers' stores, Hembrough is on a mission to uncover lost items
that people think are worthless. The fact that he assigns value to throwaway items
subverts the typical scale of taste promoted in a show like *Antiques Roadshow* and
redraws the line between high and low culture. Items from film and television,
toys and games, become the contemporary antiques of popular culture. The hunt
for that rare and valuable piece of popular culture is important for him as a dealer
but also for the owner who wants to make a profit. The set up for the series on the
show's website reads like a film plot:

> In this season of the Travel Channel's *Toy Hunter*, Jordan finds the picks of a
> lifetime for struggling businesses owners, annual toy events and even a few
> celebrity collectors. He's out of his comfort zone, so he has to set his search into
> high gear. The stakes are higher, the haggles are tougher and the payoffs are
> much greater than before, because he's hunting for more than just himself – this
> time, people's livelihoods are on the line if he doesn't deliver! It's a high stakes
> toy game with demanding players that could potentially set him up for life!

Toy Hunter is pitched like a movie; with Hembrough described more like Indiana Jones than a toy dealer. Old toys, collectibles and pieces of pop culture are thus

portrayed as authentic objects of historical significance – worthy of the hunt. The dealer may make a profit from their sale but ordinary people will also benefit, either financially or culturally. Objects of popular culture are reclaimed and extolled as valuable – in need of preservation. As Dr Jones might say, they "belong in a museum!" The Indy metaphor is most obviously played out in *Hollywood Treasure*, where the hunt for valuable items takes on a practically life or death significance. Joe Maddalena is the host and owner of Profiles in History, a company that tracks down, appraises, and auctions valuable film, television and pop culture memorabilia. Shown on the SyFy Channel, which locates the series within the contexts of science fiction and fantasy, its range of items goes from the smallest prop pistols as seen in *Lara Croft: Tomb Raider* (2001) to cars, planes and the largest, a 72-acre piece of real estate used as District 12 in *The Hunger Games* (2011). Maddalena's mission is stated at the beginning of every episode:

> My name is Joe Maddalena. I hunt for iconic treasures from the movies and TV shows you loved and auction them for prices you wouldn't believe. Together, with my team of talented investigators, I will scour the globe to uncover Hollywood treasure.

There have been two seasons to date, episodes from the first lasting 30 minutes and 60 minutes in the second. The format of episodes in both seasons sees Maddalena and his team search for items to sell in an upcoming auction, investigate their authenticity, and then reveal how much they made at the end. Often items are brought in by collectors to be valued and they end up going to auction; sometimes members of the team follow up leads, competing with each other to see who finds the most prestigious item. Maddalena is their leader and purveyor of Hollywood knowledge. Objects he finds are researched and viewers get to see where or when a particular piece showed up in a movie or TV show. Getting the best price at auction is all important; therefore authenticity is central to the narrative of each object included in an episode. Indeed, much more time is devoted to the hunt and investigation than the final auction – the credits roll when the hammer falls on the last lot. Episodes are also structured around themes. Maddalena either searches for a big item in another part of the country or travels to an established collection looking for items the collector might want to part with. The titles of each episode also communicate the theme and the items found each week through references to Hollywood history and classic movies: for example, "Demons and Spacesuits and Slippers, Oh My" (*Hollywood Treasure*, 2010–present: season 1, episode 117) featured Dorothy's ruby slippers from *The Wizard of Oz* (1939), a demon costume from *Hellboy* (2004), and a spacesuit chest pack from *2001: A Space Odyssey* (1968). Episodes are genre specific: one week science fiction, fantasy or horror items or another week classical Hollywood and vintage collectibles. Maddalena also travels to events like Comic-Con to talk with industry experts and celebrities, thus adding a dimension of cult distinction to the items purchased and sold.

In "Endoskeletons in the Closet" (*Hollywood Treasure*, 2010–present: season 1, episode 114) Maddalena is given access to the Stan Winston warehouse to find potentially valuable items to go into auction and raise money for the School of Character Arts that trains would-be special effects artists for Hollywood. One of his team follows a lead to a bar that has what looks like James Bond's plane from *Octopussy* (1983) on its roof, and a long-time collector comes to Maddalena for a valuation on some title cards from RKO Studios. In the Winston archives Maddalena finds a number of items that could be attractive purchases for collectors. The biggest piece is a full *Terminator 2* (1991) T-800 animatronic endoskeleton which Maddalena estimates might make $100,000 at auction – but only if they can decipher which scene in the movie it comes from. The search for what is termed a "hero" piece is important as it adds value and assures authenticity – if it can be proven that it was used on screen then dealers and collectors deem the piece to have greater historical significance and therefore more worthy of being in a collection. For Susan Pearce, "the word 'authentic' … carries with it not only the notion of 'real' in the forensic sense, but also the feeling of 'genuine' in the emotional sense, of sincerity, honesty and truthfulness after its own kind" (1995: 291). Therefore, the props, costumes and other items of memorabilia seen on *Hollywood Treasure* embody real and emotional meaning as they connect collectors to the past.

For Walter Benjamin (2008), the aura of authenticity is bound up with originality and is therefore "jeopardized by modern reproductive technologies" that turn an original into just one of many (Appadurai, 1986: 45). However, in the case of the T-800 found in the warehouse it is an original prop, thus embodying the aura of authenticity; it is one of a kind and can be fixed to its historical contexts when watching the movie. Indeed, Maddalena's team uses a DVD to authenticate the prop, locating the scene in which it appears. Authentication is a crucial component of the show and much time is devoted to that process. Interestingly, the way the team decides on the T-800's authenticity as a high value collectible depends not on the word of the creator (Winston is of course dead) or next of kin, nor does it come from a certificate or letter. Instead, the team have to do the work of a typical fan; sit down and watch the movie, pay close attention to detail, freeze frame and look close up. Therefore, in this case, authenticity is quite subjective but it is a fan subjectivity based on years of watching and rewatching the film text, becoming expert in all of its visual elements. In this regard, the authenticity of the collection comes from the fan whose respect for the sanctity of the text places it in a canon. The matching up of a scene with the prop is an important part of the dealer's process of verification and valuation, with the hope of increased profit at the end, but it also parallels the same process of validation that fans use when discriminating between texts they deem to be cult. As Fiske argues, authenticity "is a criterion of discrimination normally used to accumulate official cultural capital but which is readily appropriated by fans in their moonlighting cultural economy" (1992: 36). The fan collectors working on *Hollywood Treasure* use their high cultural capital as fans of the movies to help achieve higher economic capital as dealers of Hollywood memorabilia.

The success in authenticating the T-800 endoskeleton (it made $180,000 at auction) is tempered by the fact that the plane suspected to be from *Octopussy* is a fake. Using the same method of watching the film, taking close-up screen grabs of the plane to compare with the real life object, proves that they are not the same. On finding this out Maddalena uses a baseball metaphor to inspire his team to continue their search for the authentic: they "struck out" this time, but next time they might "hit a home run". Collecting is thus compared to a sport, with its own rules and practices, and with the same highs and lows: sometimes you win and a loss will always spur you on to try again. The series often focuses on the failures, finding out the fakes, so as if to show the audience that collecting Hollywood memorabilia is not simply about buying what looks attractive; there is great skill involved in researching the validity of objects and thus the rewards when right are far greater. In "Hunger for District 12" (*Hollywood Treasure*, 2010–present: season 2, episode 203) a collector comes to the showroom with a puzzle box supposedly from the horror film *Hellraiser* (1987). The team are not so convinced and therefore go to the film text to check the details of the box. After close inspection it is found to be a replica, the design and workmanship not matching the quality of the real box represented on screen. I would argue that the importance of showing how fakes and replicas can be spotted when collecting and auctioning Hollywood memorabilia is linked to how the collectors and dealers attempt to legitimate their hobby and profession through discourses of authenticity and historical preservation. If "fakes are a way of subverting the established order of object value through the arts of deception", as Mark Jones would argue (1994: 92), then the methods used to spot them in *Hollywood Treasure* are highlighted as a way of proving the worthiness of collecting authentic pieces of Hollywood history and the inherent value in the real objects that come from the entertainment industry. Indeed, fakes "provide unrivalled evidence of the values and perceptions of those who made them, and of those for whom they were made" (Jones, 1994: 92).

In "Trek to the Future" (*Hollywood Treasure* 2010–present: season 1, episode 115) Maddalena helps a fan collector get his hands on a real hoverboard with handles from *Back to the Future II* (1989). In order to find the $20,000 that the item would eventually sell for at auction, the fan collector, Desi Dos Santos, has to sell a Green Goblin mask from *Spider-Man* (2002). Telling Maddalena that he is prepared to part with the mask because he is more of a fan of the *Back to the Future* films than he is of comic book adaptations is a demonstration of his cultural capital: distinguishing between the two pop culture texts and assigning value to one over the other using taste and knowledge. The mask fetches $27,500 at auction so Dos Santos has more than enough to cover the cost of the hoverboard and earn a tidy profit – although, the fact that the mask makes more money suggests that his capital investment in *Back to the Future* is not equivalent to fans who bid for comic book collectibles. Dos Santos's house is like a museum, with display cases dotted around the living room, hallway and dining room containing all manner of items including helmets from *Top Gun* (1986), Deckard's pistol from *Blade Runner* (1982) and set miniatures of the Death Star Trench from *Star Wars*. In displaying these items they become different objects, not the original but transformed: "For an object to become part of a collection it has to be *reframed* as a collectable, that is, as a potential member of a category of objects that can be treated as aesthetic objects" (Danet and Katriel, 1994: 225).

Hollywood Treasure provides an insight into the cultural and economic value placed on the physical objects produced by the movie industry. It highlights the fan collector's desire to find valuable and significant items that will bring higher status to their collection as well as the importance of authenticity and cultural capital in promoting and preserving objects from Hollywood history. The length to which collectors go to prove something is authentic, a replica, or even fake signals the personal meaning attached to the processes of collecting. It is a struggle, with high financial potential, but nonetheless a difficult journey on the road between finding an object and finally putting it into a collection or selling it at auction. Maddalena's role as expert, protector of Hollywood history, is very much at the forefront of every trip he makes or collector he talks to. After selling the T-800 at auction he says on camera that "he had a hand" in future filmmaking now that he helped raise $180,000 for the Stan Winston school. Maddalena is portrayed as expert, presenter, and the ultimate collector; legitimating what many would see as just a hobby and elevating the practices of fan collecting beyond mere consumption. Collecting Hollywood memorabilia is about connecting with the past and preserving it in the present for the future. Props, costumes, posters and cars from the movies offer collectors a chance to insert themselves into the history of the movies, if not the movies themselves.

Conclusion

In all the examples discussed throughout this chapter there is an element of play: playing within the ludic spaces of popular media texts provided by the "ironic imagination"; play associated with how individual fans are able to express their own identities and fantasies through "enthrallment" with a favourite film or television series; the "enduring fandom" of life-long play within the fictional world provided by a global franchise like *Star Wars* or *Star Trek*; literally playing with the toy objects from childhood, making them new again; or collecting rare and authentic Hollywood memorabilia, playfully displaying them to distinguish accrued cultural capital:

> The collection is a form of art as play, a form of involving the reframing of objects within a world of attention and manipulation of context. Like other forms of art, its function is not the restoration of context of origin but rather the creation of a new context, a context standing in a metaphorical, rather than a contiguous, relation to the world of everyday life.
>
> *(Stewart, 1993: 151–2)*

The physical objects and ephemera that make up a fan's collection go through a transformation and in similar ways so does the fan that uses objects and collectibles to transform and create new identities. In the examples from *Trekkies*, *Starwoids* and *Hollywood Treasure* we see how collections can come to define a fan collector, often leading to those stereotypes repeated in the media, and how collectors can redefine the meaning of physical objects depending on their uses and place within the physical environment. Toys taken to Death Valley to recreate scenes from a film or props displayed in plastic cases in a fan's living room are transformed, meant to mean something different, and take on new historical and cultural significance within the community that recognise their importance.

While both chapters one and two have sought to highlight and critique the negative stereotypes of the fan and fan collector, emphasising the transformational qualities of being a fan and discussing the active practices involved with collecting, many of the examples examined suggest that fans and collectors are predominantly male. This would indeed seem to strengthen the stereotypes rather than break them down. Therefore, in the next chapter, I want to turn to issues of gender and show how female fans engage in similar collecting practices and that specific cult texts aimed at women have become meaningful texts in their own right for female fans. Chapter three focuses on gender and generations of fan collecting, theorising how practices of cult collecting create meaning for both male and female fans and across different generations of collectors.

PART II
People

3

MASCULINE PURSUITS?

Gender, Generation and the Fan Collector

The previous chapter highlighted notions of authenticity and enduring fandom in the collecting practices of Hollywood memorabilia collectors. What was inherently distinctive about this was that movie fans seemed to have a personal connection to Hollywood's history that made them want to collect, preserve and authenticate objects in order to legitimate the industry – justifying its worthiness and significance through the creation, display and organisation of a physical collection. In this we can identify the importance of memory and nostalgia in getting close to and feeling connected with the physical objects that collectors hunt down and put on show in their homes. Collecting memorabilia today serves to recreate the illusion of Hollywood as dream factory, where the magic happens; fans wishing to be part of that history seek to shape it by amassing a collection that reflects their own passions and desires.

In this chapter I want to continue my investigation of nostalgia, fandom and the cult collector. However, in order to fully appreciate the diversity of collecting practices, objects collected and the collectors themselves, it is important to understand the role gender plays in the choice of things fans collect or how they go about collecting them. Additionally, if objects are ascribed meaning by culture and those who own them then we must consider the implications such inscribed meanings have on the construction of a fan collector identity. Undertaking this process will help us ascertain whether an identity stems from the ideologically problematic images of gender or particular memories an individual uses to identify with their objects from the past in the present. We must remember, as Susan Pearce argues, "gender patterning can be destructive because individual temperaments do not fit into prescribed forms" (1995: 200). Therefore, this chapter is not intended as a discussion of what particular collectibles are gendered objects, nor will it try to dissect different collecting practices between men and women. Rather I think it is more instructive to look at the importance of nostalgia in collecting and the identities all collectors construct through the preservation of objects from the past. Indeed, as John Windsor asserts, "Identity-creating through collecting has become a selfconscious [sic] game, with objects being collected partly as a joke, partly as a demonstration of the collector's wry view of social history" (1994: 64). Therefore, we need to recognise a collector's agency in how they represent themselves through their collections and that ideological preconceptions of gender do not necessarily impact on what they collect.

Fanboys versus Fangirls

As I allude to in chapter one, recent fan scholarship has focused on the differences between gendered conceptions of the fanboy and fangirl, with the former perceived as being more affirmational and celebratory of media texts while the latter is more likely to transform them and reconstitute them for the needs of the wider fan community. Suzanne Scott (2013: xxx–xxxi) says that the gendered division in fandom is based on the dichotomy of professional activity or amateur hobby, with men seemingly more able to profit from their fandom (going into a career based upon it) and women remaining just fans (unwilling to exploit the community of which they are members). Evaluations of transmedia narratives and media franchises that utilise transmedia texts to expand their fan audience have also highlighted a gendered division between affirmational and transformational fan groups. Narrative "extensions reward historically 'masculine' interests (including those of mastering the complexity of program content) while marginalizing historically 'feminine' interests (especially those related to exploring the emotional and erotic relations between characters)" (Jenkins, Ford, and Green, 2013: 151).

This academic interest in what counts as male and female fandom is mirrored in the enthusiasm from the press to specifically identify female fans and draw gendered distinctions between levels of fan devotion in popular media culture. In a 2010 article for *USA Today* on the San Diego Comic-Con, Scott Bowles declares, "Brace yourselves, fanboys. Real Women are here … the wonder women of Comic-Con speak geek. They quote *Star Wars*. They read graphic novels, watch *Futurama* and don't sit back in a debate over the best *Star Trek* series. They don't miss a Comic-Con" (2010: 3D). Similarly, in articles about the 2012 GeekGirlCon held in Seattle journalists were espousing the unique qualities of community and sharing in female fandom over the more competitive and goal-orientated activities promoted within male fan groups: "McGillivray [founder of GeekGirlCon], has gone to a number of other conventions and she's noticed a difference at Geek-GirlCon … 'People are as excited about meeting each other as they are about meeting our guests. At San Diego Comic-Con or Emerald City Comicon, people are like "I want to meet Leonard Nimoy" … Well, I want to meet Leonard Nimoy too. But I also want to meet this person I met online and I've talked to for years on Twitter'" (Conner, 2012: D9).

Within both articles about two very big gatherings of fans there is a sense of surprise and lack of awareness about the female fan community and both journalists use the fanboy stereotype as a point of comparison. Bowles, in interviewing the

Twilight films screenwriter Melissa Rosenberg, points to the fact that women are increasingly more vocal about their favourite texts and demand more from them in terms of quality storylines. In such ways they are just like the typical fanboy in that they get caught up in unpicking the narrative and learning everything they need to know to understand the fictional world better. Still, when it comes to attending panels at Comic-Con, Rosenberg is quoted as saying they still "tend to ask questions in the vein of how it feels to be that hot a vampire" (cited in Bowles, 2010: 3D). For attendees at GeekGirlCon the differences between male and females fans take on a deeper significance in that the organisation was established because Erica McGillivray felt that prejudice against women was preventing them from fully exploring and expressing their fan identities. In Lisa Richwine's interview with McGillivray she highlights the types of panels at GeekGirlCon, including one aimed at tackling "the hostility and harassment women face from some male geeks" called "Go Make Me a Sandwich" and a panel on a documentary about female stereotypes in computer games (Richwine, 2012: D7). In the press articles about female fans and convention attendance we see in microcosm the debate within current fan scholarship: that there is an inherent difference between male and female fans and these differences often serve to diminish the creative fan practices of the fangirl in favour of the perceived legitimate activities of fanboys. As Shawn Conner goes on to discuss in his article:

> McGillivray, 28, said that society's bias toward men sets up female geeks for ridicule. It's acceptable for two men to argue over whether Superman or Batman would win a fight, she said. But when a woman says she writes fan fiction about Harry Potter "they spend the next 30 minutes making fun of her – when they've just spent 30 minutes writing their own fan fiction".
>
> *(Conner, 2012: D9)*

One could argue that the history of fandom is very much a history of gendered discourses around production, consumption, participation and celebration. Scholarship on long-established fan practices such as slash fiction writing and costuming tend to focus on examples drawn from female fan communities. Other work on subcultural distinction and fan hierarchies has discussed typically male-orientated texts and associated fan practices such as collecting and learning trivia. Cornel Sandvoss identifies in the introduction to his book *Fans: The Mirror of Consumption* that "fandom has been identified as both a distinctly masculine and a distinctly feminine space", listing stars, romance novels, science fiction television and pop music as examples that have attracted large female followings and citing sports, films, and comics as having predominantly male fans. However, such division of interest cannot be ascribed to different gender positions as he argues that "the different socio-historic development of male and female fan cultures, the variations in chosen fan texts, and the usage of different media are indicators of the different power positions articulated in fandom" (Sandvoss, 2005: 16). Similarly, in *Spreadable Media* the authors point out that "Fan communities are often enormously heterogeneous, with values and assumptions that fragment along axes of class, age, gender, race, sexuality, and nationality, to name just a few" (Jenkins, Ford and Green, 2013: 54).

Perhaps, then, the perceived differences between male and female fans and the practices associated with both is more a matter of what gets written about and by whom. With more studies being published on specific fan groups, gender plays a much bigger role in assessing the impact of a particular media text and how fans interact with it, change it and disseminate their productivity. Yet, in focusing on trying to discern what is more of a female practice compared to a male practice we might lose sight of our broader remit to highlight what it means to be a fan in contemporary media culture and how this differs from a more general audience's use of social media and different viewing platforms. In other words, what makes being a fan of *Glee* (2009–present) different to watching it as a casual viewer? Or, in what ways does daily use of Twitter or Facebook mark you out as a social media user or a fan? In terms of this book's focus we might ask similar questions about the practice of collecting. What makes a collector a fan or a fan a collector? Do fans always collect things? If so, what things do they collect? How do space, place and technology impact on the practice of collecting?

I would agree with Jenkins, Ford and Green in their assertion that fans are not always "resisting consumer capitalism" in their "various processes and practices" of being a fan (2013: 35). There are myriad reasons for why fans do what they do and so we must not get caught up in promoting one activity over another. Indeed, a focus on collecting will uncover numerous reasons why fans collect and the fact that some of them do should not be a reason for dismissing their fandom as somehow of lesser status than other examples of fan activity. The remainder of this chapter will concentrate more on collecting as a fan practice, and highlight some of the existing scholarship on gender and the collector. However, it must be stated here that I am not trying to establish a distinction between male and female fan collectors. The examples discussed throughout this chapter and rest of the book have been chosen for what they reveal being a fan collector means and what that suggests about contemporary popular media culture. Therefore, while I raise a number of points about gender and collecting this does not mean I wish to make a case for separate treatment of either male or female collectors. What is of more interest to me is that collecting still contributes a major part to the creation of a fan identity and various fan communities. Within those, we see both male and female fans having an input and contributing to the ongoing and changing discourses around fandom as forms of cultural capital, distinction, fan ownership and material consumption. This also leads us to consider how notions of history and nostalgia impact on fandom since physical objects – which are so often drawn and preserved from the past – are integral to what it means to be a fan.

The Masculinity of Cult Collecting

The ideas of trivia, ownership and affirmation coded as that of the fanboy are clearly relatable to the new and developing technologies associated with video recording, collecting, and the DVD box set. Fans who want to enjoy the repeated pleasures of their favourite television series, without waiting for it to be repeated at the behest of a network, can either record the episodes they want to keep or collect the entire series on DVD to watch whenever they want. Watching television episodes out of order, favourite episodes that bear no relation to the over-arching chronological timeline or meta-narrative, or listening to directors' commentary upsets the flow of regular television – keeping a series located within the fan's present: "This physical and cultural connection between television and home video enables people to use their sets to create or access programming on their own terms rather than stay locked to the fare and schedule dictated by the broadcasting industry" (Kompare, 2006: 339). As a result, the viewing contexts are changed in that the flow of adverts and network logos associated with the original screening are withdrawn and the series becomes a fixed text that can be accessed whenever desired. The primacy of the box set is revealed in its physicality – it literally holds all that a fan could wish for, all in one container. As an object the DVD box set becomes a part of a collection, the ephemerality of screen media transformed into a tangible product that can be owned: "The flow of television is not only measured in time but in physical commodities, as cultural objects placed in the permanent media collection alongside similarly mass-produced media artifacts" (Kompare, 2006: 353).

However, the DVD box set also situates the media contained within in the past; the box set is an archive with added extras that locates the film or TV series in an altogether new history, a personal history: "[DVD], as a hybrid medium dedicated to reproducing an experience alien to it, standardizes, fragments, commodifies, objectifies, and segments that experience" (Tashiro, 1991: 16). As I argued in the previous chapter, collections represent personal histories – they tell a story about the fan collector and how they have interacted with a particular media text. Similarly, the repeated pleasures of watching recorded or bought episodes in box sets creates another historical and narrative space detached from that seen on screen for the first time. The collecting of associated merchandise like the DVD box set becomes part of the commodification and historicisation of popular culture. The episodic nature of cult television and the expanded narratives of franchise films with multiple prequels and sequels make them attractive and ideal forms of cultural capital in which fans can invest their viewing time, money and collecting efforts. Before home cinema and DVD, the only way a fan could own a movie would be to buy the music soundtrack or the novelisation. Owning television series was harder in that you had to rely on the broadcaster to make it available to record. In her study of the home cinephile and video/DVD collector Barbara Klinger (2006) intimates that the growth of home film cultures has had a positive effect on the once antagonistic relationship between the cinephile (a person who has a passion for film in its original exhibition contexts: projection in a dark theatre) and domestic viewing (the VCR/DVD on TV). New technologies that improve the quality and range of film and television texts that can be watched domestically have meant that it is possible for cinephiles to enjoy the object of their affection at home.

Collecting has become even more important to fans of film and television as more and more of their favourite texts can be bought, traded, and collected on formats that do not deteriorate. As chapter four will explore, long-lost or hard-to-come-by series from childhood can reappear on DVD to be enjoyed again in adulthood. Or, as Kate Egan's *Trash or Treasure?* outlines, previously banned or censored material like the 1980s video nasties can be re-circulated on newer formats, attracting younger fan audiences, while at the same time the original video tapes become collectible and are preserved as authentic artefacts of British horror censorship history by older fans (2007: 175). In addition, collections of DVD box sets "have become decorative additions to the chairs, tables, and carpets which form the familiar backdrop to their unfolding" (Tashiro, 1996: 17). The domestic space becomes an archive of film and television that represents the accumulated cultural capital of a collector and acts as a historic signifier of the impact and influence of popular media culture: "Ardent TV/video collectors are in many ways self-styled media historians, archivists dedicated to discovering and preserving remnants of television past and present" (Bjarkman, 2004: 239). Peter Hutchings expands this argument further in his analysis of the shifting definitions of the horror genre:

> DVD, in its technical superiority over video, in its compactness and sleekness and its sheer collectability, is the most intimate audio-visual format to date. The ways in which it articulates genre histories and invokes memories of genre films can help to inform an intimate bond with the consumer, a bond through which the consumer can engage with and reflect upon his or her own historical experience of the genre in question.
>
> *(Hutchings, 2008: 227)*

Collecting cult films and television on DVD and video, plus the protectionism and established hierarchies associated with the acquisition of such media artefacts in fan communities, alludes to the "masculinity of cult" as defined by Joanne Hollows (2003: 37) as the ways in which "many of the key consumption practices that constitute cult fandom" (collecting, viewing, reading fanzines, etc.) are naturalised as masculine in opposition to the gendered femininity of the cultural mainstream (popular film and television such as the romantic comedy and the soap opera). In distancing themselves from the "feminine shopper" and adopting more "assertively masculine" attitudes to consumption, those fans who collect box sets and interact with related visual products are participating in a collecting ritual that has historically been "imagined as masculine" in comparison to the idea that women merely bought objects as part of routine and domesticated consumerism (46). This can be read within the contexts of changes in consumer culture more widely, which for Hollows have "increasingly been concerned with consumption as 'heroic' activity" in comparison to the "consumption practices of the 'happy housewife heroine'" (2000: 129). Indeed, "The hero of the new consumer culture", Hollows argues, "is usually both masculine and middle class" (130). Both Hollows and Klinger do make the case that "the collector is [not] an 'essentially' masculine figure"

(Hollows, 2003: 47), film and television collectors "do not constitute a homogenous community" (Klinger, 2006: 63). However, as I outlined in chapter one, the stereotype of the socially maladjusted male fan collector still persists in popular culture.

Gendered Collections

Following the previous assertions that collecting creates an identity, allowing collectors to construct a sense of self and display that to others, it is not surprising that Susan Pearce argues "the whole of this creative process, in which both individuals and objects are both active and passive, will be shot through with emotions about sexuality and gender" (1995: 197). Pearce's history of gendered collecting records how women were seen as obsessive collectors, consuming for the sake of consuming with little or no regard for cataloguing or organisation. The stuff that women consumed consisted mainly of clothing, jewellery and items that underscored their femininity: "A great deal of feminine collecting unites around the warm material images that cluster about the persona of mature wife and mother" (Pearce, 1995: 206). Objects intended for the home were by their very nature decorative as the home was seen as the domain of women and therefore it was a woman's job to keep it looking smart and attractive. The domestic contexts of consumption and the female collector are further explored by Russell Belk and Melanie Wallendorf who argue that women were not seen as serious collectors. They were merely buyers, looking for the latest bargain whilst out shopping for the home. Extending this they propose three ways in which gender is implicated in the collecting process: "Through the gendered meaning of essential collecting activities" (as intimated in the previous example of buying for the domestic sphere); "the gender associations of the objects collected" (again, like the more decorative and feminine pieces represented in jewellery and art); "and the gendered uses of collections" (1994: 241). Through this last way suggested by Belk and Wallendorf we are able to "examine collections not just statically in terms of the objects contained in the collection, but also dynamically in terms of the collector's interaction with these objects" (1994: 246).

In this regard, Belk and Wallendorf discuss two examples of Barbie collecting. In the first, the collecting of the iconic female doll is about nurturing and achieving a sense of completeness. The woman in their case study "uses her collecting activities to enact the feminine quality of generosity", sharing tips with fellow Barbie collectors at conventions and giving them gifts (1994: 245). The same woman, after having her breasts removed following cancer, develops a renewed focus on acquiring at least one of each type of Barbie ever produced: "Through owning a full set of authentic Barbies, she is able to restore a sense of completeness. Not only does Barbie possess the kind of figure [she] no longer has, but collecting allows [her] to possess a complete set of these voluptuous dolls" (Belk and Wallendorf, 1994: 246). The second case study of a male Barbie collector suggests that the dolls come to represent particular people or types of people the collector knew or met in his own life. The Barbies were categorised so as to mediate three different types of gendered images: real-life images that exist in the collector's everyday life; real-world images that originate from his childhood, former life as an exotic dancer, male prostitute, and current career as hairdresser; other worldly images are based on mythic characters that the collector compares to images from everyday life. Both case studies reveal that,

> The feminine and masculine worldly images contained within a collection can be used to connect otherworldly meanings to real-world experiences. They do so by direct representation as well as by filling in what is otherwise missing in a person's life. Through these meanings, collections are used to mediate real-world experience with otherworldly images in a way that attempts to reconstruct and resolve personal issues concerning gender.
>
> *(Belk and Wallendorf, 1994: 250)*

In the examples of collecting considered in the previous two chapters, particularly toys and Hollywood memorabilia, we can identify the gendered character traits of collecting: "'masculine' means aggressiveness, competitiveness, and desire for mastery, and 'feminine' preservationism, creativity, and nurturance" (Belk, 1995: 97). However, these collector traits are not mutually exclusive. So, for example, when a male *Star Wars* fan takes his toy collectibles out into Death Valley to recreate scenes from the film there are clear signs of "creativity" within real spaces. When the experts in *Hollywood Treasure* (2010–present) go to extreme lengths to authenticate props and cars they are doing so in order to help preserve Hollywood for future generations, to root out the fake and promote the authentic. Both examples display "feminine" traits within the collecting practices of male collectors. Similarly, in Sarah Butler's collection of more than a thousand My Little Pony toys we can identify the more "masculine" trait of the "desire for mastery" as she spends £20,000 turning her bedroom into a "shrine" for the objects ("My little collection"). Married couple, Mr and Mrs Harvey, in attending a *Doctor Who* auction at Bonhams to look for interesting props to put in their garden, exhibit the trait of "competitiveness" when they suggest buying a Cyberman suit to just stand in the corner would inspire jealousy in the neighbours (Smyth, 2010: 11).

The "association of the female collection with consumption and the male collection with production" (Belk 1995: 99) as outlined in this and the previous section is distinctly opposite to that of the relationship between fanboy and fangirl discussed at the beginning of this chapter: where females fans are seen as more productive and transformative in practices such as fan fiction writing and male fans affirm their fandom through the buying and collecting of memorabilia. Therefore, I would argue that an appreciation of gender and fandom cannot be fully realised without taking into account the consumption practices of both male and female fans. Likewise, to understand the similarities and difference between male and female collectors we cannot assume that either group acts or displays their fandom in separately gendered ways. Since male collectors can exhibit traits formerly considered female, and vice versa, we cannot assume that all collectors are men and that all women collect to consume. There are strategies to collecting, just as there are to being a fan, that are employed by both men and women so as to help define their identities and enhance the status of their collections within a social community of collectors. Collections can make visible "the gender distinctions governing social life" but also "collecting permits experimentation with androgyny as an individual participates in the masculine hunt for additions to the collection, as well as feminine nurturance in curating the collection" (Belk and Wallendorf, 1994: 251). It is in this spirit we might look to other attributes of fandom and collecting to better understand the relationship between gender, identity and the processes of becoming a fan over time.

Generations of Nostalgia

Critiques of nostalgia outlined in the introduction to this book have coded it as a thoroughly male preserve. From collecting old vinyl records to customising an old car, those who relive their childhood through consumption and nostalgia for a previous generation are predominantly men. The increase in this yearning for things past is, according to historian Gary Cross, down to a change in attitude to male maturity. These "boy-men" are "frustrated and confused about what maturity is and whether they can or want to achieve it" (Cross, 2008: 1). For Cross, this leads to the affirmation that those men who might have been brought up in a generation that expected them to grow up immediately after childhood now act more as if they were teenagers: playing video games, collecting toys, driving fast cars, not settling down to have a family. Thus, the "boy-man" is an inevitable reflection of contemporary nostalgia in that he does not want to grow old and therefore surrounds himself with things that signify the past, both personal and public:

> Nostalgia is a relatively new phenomenon. It emerged fully only when people found an accelerating rate of change in many things so frustrating and alienating that they tried to capture the fleeting past in their "ephemeral" culture and goods. It may seem strange that we seek "stability" in what lasted only briefly when we were young, but, as we age, our experiences as children and teens seem to be "timeless" even if they were only songs by the Rolling Stones, while the latest thing today seems merely fleeting and confusing.
>
> *(Cross, 2008: 158)*

Traditional notions of maturity tied to masculinity have been transformed alongside an attractive return to the pleasures of youth. Contemporary consumer culture is defined by "Fast Capitalism", where selfhood is threatened by the fast pace of life, loss of childhood innocence, and the continued consumption of new products. Cross builds on this and argues that "while earlier forms of nostalgia might lead to intolerant tribalism or narrow-cast familialism, consumed and child-centred nostalgia leads to a mostly exuberant individualism in possession of the things of a personal past" (Cross, 2012). In terms of technology, we are encouraged to renew our phones, computers and cars every year – keeping up with technological innovation and maintaining a fashionable persona with the latest gadget. These sorts of goods become significant parts of our personal identities and reflect the ever-changing social media environment. Interestingly, however, as new devices allow for greater communication and freedom to learn all there is to learn about the world around us, new technologies give us greater access to things from our past. As I have already mentioned, DVD technologies allow collectors to create archives of films and TV once presumed lost. Similarly, the Internet as repository of information, visual media and forgotten fragments of popular culture gives users almost unlimited connections to the cultures of previous generations – all the while distracting us, according to Cross, from the roles and responsibilities we have in this current generation.

Cross again recounts examples of contemporary nostalgia that are male orientated: hot rod car culture, rock music, toys, model railroads and even beer commercials (2008: 158). They are peculiar to that time of growing up so their memories stick with the individual through to adulthood. But also, these have particular resonance in that they are/were hobbies that boys shared with their fathers. Thus, the cross-generational appeal of nostalgia is handed down from father to son, with boys inheriting their love of fast cars from their dads and rebelling against more modern examples deemed inferior to older models. It is not surprising that Cross identifies in the automobile a high level of male nostalgia for youth and the liberating potentials of technology. As Dan Fleming and Damion Sturm argue in the foreword to their book on media, masculinity and the machine, "today masculinity is also shaped in relation to another overall structure of power – the subordination of technology to men – and in relation to another general symbolism of difference – the opposition of human and machine" (2011: x). The gadgets used to communicate in today's networked society present "more specifically usable resources for masculine image self-maintenance than the more varied choices afforded to a popular feminism" (Fleming and Sturm, 2011: 176) and so technology is linked with masculinity and technological objects are coded as male rather than female. Similar arguments could be made about toys that emphasise technology and develop skills in construction and engineering. The so-called "boys' toys" (e.g. Meccano, Airfix models, Scalextric, Lego, Hornby model railways) "are a mirror of the technological developments and social aspirations of their eras" (May, 2009: 6) and thus inevitably connect masculinity, childhood and technology through the physicality of play. If they provide a nostalgic "thread connecting us to the joy of childhood" (May, 2009: 8) then that means childhood is inevitably almost always imagined as a male domain, with generations of boys looking back on their toys with fond memories. The collection of said objects also implies collecting is a thoroughly male endeavour.

Record collecting and the nostalgia for the musical ephemera of previous generations have been discussed in a similar vein. Roy Shuker's analysis of record collecting as social practice articulates that popular representations of the record collector depict them as predominantly male. Like the mediated stereotypes discussed in chapter one, Shuker argues that both the book (Hornby, 1995) and the film *High Fidelity* (2000) suggest "considerable empathy" for the lone male collector (Shuker, 2010: 34). Websites, shops and magazines perceive record collecting as male dominated. The Canadian documentary *Vinyl* (2000), which presents a picture of the local record collecting community in Toronto, is based on one hundred interviews of which only five are with women. As with the masculinity of cult and DVD collecting discussed above, vinyl record collecting can be seen as part of the music fan's mission to protect their object of affection from the perceived threat of mainstream music, commercialisation and new formats of musical recording. The record collection "not only embodies personal history, it also represents the original historical artefact: how the vinyl single, EP, LP was originally recorded, and therefore the form in which it should be listened to" (Shuker, 2010: 65). Vinyl is also handed down from generation to generation and the practices associated with collecting vinyl records become the established traditions that new collectors follow in order to be recognised as authentic record collectors in particular and music fans in general. For Shuker, "the valorizing of the obscure is linked to trash fandoms generally, and the subsequent discourse surrounding these is a feature of the homosocial world of young men" (2010: 35). This follows Will Straw's argument that:

> Record collections, like sports statistics, provide the raw materials around which the rituals of homosocial interaction take shape. Just as ongoing conversation between men shapes the composition and extension of each man's collection, so each man finds, in the similarity of his points of reference to his peers, confirmation of a shared universe of critical judgement.
>
> *(Straw, 1997: 5)*

However, we must not eliminate the role women play in these so-called nostalgic times. Female collectors, as discussed by Pearce, Belk and others, display characteristics of nurturing, creativity and preservation that help define their collections. But the very act of keeping and collecting items from childhood, defined by Gary Cross as solely that of the "boy-man" in contemporary culture, is one increasingly being copied by women. Barbie has become the iconic toy that allows women to return to an imaginary past. Collectible boutiques in department stores, limited edition Barbies only available through the collector's club, and vintage dolls bought and sold at conventions and fairs all highlight what Christopher Noxon identifies as "the aging of the Baby Boomers" (2006: 114). Like Cross, he sees those adults with a fixation for the trappings of youth, perennially trying to retain and regain their youth through surgery, buying vintage products and listening to older music, as seeking out the sensation of nostalgia. The texts that are brought back and re-circulated might be different for men and women but both do it nonetheless. As a result, corporations that had a hit on their hands long ago find that they are able to again tap into that enthusiasm a generation later as men and women seek out those old products once more:

> The secret to what toymakers reverently call "the bi-modal brand" was revealed in 2001 to American Greetings, which owns the rights to Care Bears, Strawberry Shortcake, and Holly Hobbie … icons of the eighties that had long since passed out of the public eye. In a poll of more than one thousand American women, however, American Greetings learned that not only were these supposedly washed-up characters fondly remembered, "purchase interest" was identical among women who wanted to buy a doll for their child and those women who wanted to rekindle a love affair of their own.
>
> *(Noxon, 2006: 118)*

In the guise of the "rejuvenile", a person who cultivate "tastes and mind-sets traditionally associated with those younger than themselves" (Noxon, 2006: 4), both men and women look to the past for familiar and encouraging objects that bring with them nostalgic memories. From one generation to the next, nostalgia becomes a means through which people can communicate what it was like growing up and share experiences of different forms of popular culture. As a consequence, new media technologies and platforms for media entertainment become sites for nostalgic recollection and aid in the transmission of one generation's childhood memory to become that of another.

ThinkGeek as Gendered Nostalgia Archive

ThinkGeek is an American online retailer that caters for all manner of so-called "geek" cultures. Merchandise spans a range of items, from clothes and electronics to toys and drinks, and most are intimately related to well-known brands and media texts from popular culture. Founded in 1999 it continues to sell items that attract big fan communities, with franchise merchandise from the likes of *Star Wars*, *Star Trek*, *Harry Potter*, *Doctor Who*, *The Big Bang Theory* and *The Hunger Games* repeatedly being top-sellers. Technology and gadgets also form core product lines, with accessories for Apple iPhones, iPods, and iPads proving to be particularly popular with a "geek" online clientele: "For its target audience – sci-fi addicts, practical jokers, anyone who has ever worn a calculator watch – ThinkGeek inspires an Apple-like level of cultish adoration" (Honan, 2010). The company's motto is "Stuff for Smart Masses" and their website promotes the brand ethos:

> ThinkGeek started as an idea. A simple idea to create and sell stuff that would appeal to the thousands of people out there who were on the front line and in the trenches as the Internet was forged. ThinkGeek started as a way to serve a market that was passionate about technology, from programmers, engineers, students, lovers of open source, to masses that helped create the behind-the-scenes Internet culture.

In citing a connection between geek culture, technology and popular media texts, the stereotype of the fan as geek discussed in chapter one is again circulated here.

However, there is a strong ethos of consumption (as one might expect from an online retailer) filtered through the company webpages: "For over half of the square root of a century, we here at ThinkGeek have tried to build the sort of site that we'd like to shop at. We put every product we sell through a gauntlet of tests (even if it means eating candy or playing with toys) to make sure it's just right for our customers." There is in an implication in this statement that the creators, employees and customers think the same (made overt in the name), and that the work they do to ensure quality is not really work at all – this is similar to fandom in that the "work" fans do in making, doing and producing is not seen as work but part of what it means to be a fan. The website goes on to explain that ThinkGeek is a small company, run more like a family than a corporate business: "ThinkGeek is run from a small office with dogs and bare feet at every turn. We're geeks and we're proud. We think of our customers as our friends, and want to do everything we can to make you happy." Again, the marketing is suggestive of the communal nature of fandom – everyone sharing in the celebration of "geek" culture. However, as the work on fans and collecting cultures already outlined in this chapter indicates, there are differences within fan and collecting communities, many of which are divided along generational and gender lines. ThinkGeek as purveyor of fan ephemera and collectibles is no different in this regard. Its assortment of merchandise and seasonal promotions suggests that the genderfication of fans and collectors continues online, alongside a continued interest in the recycling of popular culture concomitant with our nostalgic fascination with media texts from the past.

ThinkGeek promotes seasonal lines and takes advantage of significant dates in the calendar to create a buzz for its products. Even when products are not real, fan demand on the site encourages the company to reconsider. On 1 April 2009 ThinkGeek listed a fake item under its *Star Wars* line: a sleeping bag in the shape of a tauntaun from *The Empire Strikes Back* (1980). Fitted with printed internal intestines and a lightsaber for a zipper pull, it was the ultimate fan accessory, despite being an April Fool's Day joke. However, after thousands of fans tried to order it ThinkGeek got permission from Lucasfilm to make it and they started retailing at $99.99. The following year the website advertised tinned unicorn meat, with the label "the new white meat". Instead of fan demand ThinkGeek received complaints from the American National Pork Board who clearly felt this created unfair competition. Unusual items abound on the site, all intended to attract a specific buyer – male or female: a Tiki Cthulhu Mug, *Game of Thrones* House Sigil Wine Charms, Adventure Time Tank Dress, *Star Trek* Pizza Cutter, USB Snowbot, Bluetooth Retro Handset, and the list goes on. As Mathew Honan points out in his article in *Wired* magazine, "ThinkGeek has begun selling in bulk and designing its own increasingly sophisticated products" (2010). This means more time, money and effort has been put into creating new products to sell online. In 2010 the company had created around 30 new products, on the back of increasing its R&D budget from $240,000 in 2007 to $869,000 in 2008 (Honan, 2010). It also acts as a wholesaler to independent stores that buy items in bulk to sell to their own "geek" clientele.

Depending on the season some items are recoded as either male or female in their combinations as part of a gift pack. For Father's Day in 2013 customers could buy gift packs to send to their dads that came in particular themed combinations: one for *Star Wars*, *The Big Bang Theory*, *Doctor Who*, and even a DIY version which included a screwdriver kit, a project mat, conductive glue and a handbook for geek dads. Most likely insufficient to help dad to actually put up a shelf, the items in the DIY gift pack emphasised a "geek within" persona – the gadgets included can help him tinker and play at being the genius inventor he had dreamed of when he was a child. This sense of nostalgia is common to all the Father's Day gift packs. *The Big Bang Theory* box included "Bazinga" and "Soft Kitty" shot glasses, a Soft Kitty plush toy, a Friendship Flow Chart and a set of "Rock, Paper, Scissors, Lizard, Spock" dice. These items, inspired by the series, link the recipient to the fictional text – letting them enter into its narrative through the means of performance. The *Doctor Who* gift pack included a TARDIS beach towel, TARDIS coasters, travel mugs and sonic screwdriver pens. In addition, customers could buy a TARDIS bathrobe to add to their father's leisure attire. Clearly in this pack, items are gendered through the idea of leisure and travel, the towel and the drinking devices, but also the pens suggest play and performance as the online description says they are for "timey-wimey adventuring". The equivalent Mother's Day gift pack contained the same except for the sonic screwdrivers – mums received a replica of River Song's TARDIS journal instead. Interestingly, in spin-off series *The Sarah Jane Adventures* (2007–11) Sarah is equipped with a sonic lipstick rather than a sonic screwdriver. The distinction between screwdrivers for men and journal for women is obvious but it is also calls attention to the perceived difference between male fans as affirmational (playing within the text) and female fans as creative (writing in a journal).

As I will explore further in chapter seven, the Internet has expanded what items are now seen as collectible and allowed collectors to acquire things they want from anywhere in the world. The Internet now provides an almost limitless visual digital space for fans and collectors to search and gain access to their favourite popular culture texts. Defining the search terms can present the collector with a list of potential outlets to trade and purchase objects from past and present. Websites like ThinkGeek are a repository for fans and collectors looking to expand their collection or simply buy a quirky gift for a fellow enthusiast. It offers collectors a visual archive of what collectible objects are available and which ones might add cult status and value to their own collections. Access is not dependent on purchase so fan collectors can browse and collate images and information for future reference, or share images with others through social media. The company has its own Twitter, Facebook and YouTube pages so that its own brand fans can get information on the next product and suggest things they want to see made and sold. It has its own video library of adverts for some of its more quirky and popular products. Customers can then post comments, most of which celebrate the ingenious and cultish nature of the gadget and ThinkGeek as provider of such cult ephemera. In joining up with the social media landscape ThinkGeek has become part of what

José van Dijck terms the "culture of connectivity", in which "perspectives, expressions, experiences and productions are increasingly mediated by social media sites ... [Manifested] through platforms such as YouTube, MySpace, Facebook, Twitter, and others" (2011: 402). Of course, ThinkGeek is using these platforms to market its wares but having that connection with web users makes them inter-active participants in the construction of a geek subculture and gives them space to share stories about their favourite gadget, collectible and media text. Accordingly, we can read ThinkGeek's use of social media sites, which themselves act as archives for user generated content, as part of the "'continuous present' of the World-Wide-Web" and the "constant connectivity of people and digital networks" (van Dijck, 2011: 404). Social media and ThinkGeek provide content, products and images and become searchable archives for the preservation of such material. However, it is the connection between users and content that creates the memories – the interaction between objects online and the collectors who search for new items to add to their collections.

The success of ThinkGeek in creating an image of cult distinction is due in part to what the Internet allows users to do online: "Whereas television and print transmit and push goods and services into the home to audiences via a one-way line of communication, the Internet enables individuals to access information at their own pace, build their own Web pages, and ultimately become producers and promoters of their own popular culture artifacts" (Smith Feranec, 2008: 10). In the commodification of popular film texts, as seen in the demand for a real tauntaun sleeping bag and the gendered seasonal gift packs, we can identify an increasing array of fan identities – partly defined by what people collect and partly determined by what media texts are brought back from the past. ThinkGeek as nostalgia archive provides fans and collectors of all ages, both male and female, with the space to explore what was once popular for the previous generation and what might yet be for the next.

Barbie and Matty Collector

As already discussed in this chapter, one of the most iconic toy collectibles is the Barbie doll. Collectors of various ages go to great lengths to collect every doll, both old and new. Clubs bring people together to swap accessories and tell stories about their latest find. Barbie is Mattel's biggest seller, it may be a girl's toy but it has dwarfed the toys Mattel has made for boys: "Today Barbie is sold in 140 countries, with sales totalling more than $1.5 billion a year" (Noxon, 2006: 113). According to Lynn Spigel, "In the early 1990s, Mattel estimated that two Barbie dolls are sold every second somewhere in the world, and when placed head to toe there are enough Barbies to circle the earth more than three-and-a-half times" (2001: 310). Taking advantage of this popularity and the cross-generational appeal of the doll for women, Mattel has incorporated Barbie into its very successful online com-munity of collectors. The Barbie Collector Club caters for all collector tastes, pro-ducing limited edition dolls, replica vintage dolls, and Barbies for a range of popular film and television franchises that attract a strong female following. At the 2010 San Diego Comic-Con, fans could catch a glimpse of the new range of collectible dolls, including *Mad Men* Barbie, *Twilight* Barbie, a retro *I Dream of Jeannie* Barbie, and a range of dolls encompassing every Bond girl.

As a gendered object Barbie has been condemned by many and received negative criticism in the media. In an early episode of *The Simpsons* (1989–present), "Lisa vs. Malibu Stacey" (season 5, episode 14), Lisa is appalled that her new talking Malibu Stacey doll (an obvious Barbie imitation) spouts misogynistic catchphrases like "Don't ask me, I'm just a girl". Determined to take her complaint all the way to the top she meets the doll's original creator and gets her help to design a new doll that will act as a positive role model for girls. Her plans are eventually thwarted by toy executives who release a Stacey doll with new hat that pushes Lisa's doll out of the market. In light of this, much work has been done on the Barbie doll in terms of the representation of women, the commodification of femininity, and the toy's influence on the identities of young girls. For example, Judy Attfield's work on Barbie and Action Man proposes that the difference in body design (Barbie has fewer body joints than Action Man, prioritising the female form over poseability) "illustrates how the cliché of 'feminine' as passive and 'masculine' as active is literally embodied in the design of the toys" (1996: 85). In addition, A.F. Robertson points out that "Modern feminists have consistently attacked children's dolls as embodying the worst sorts of conservative, patriarchal ideal" (2004: 147). Other girl's toys have also come under scrutiny. Strawberry Shortcake, a cute doll with a strawberry odour, became very popular in the 1980s. First launched as a character in greetings cards in 1977 she was expanded to toys, clothing, food products and other merchandise the following decade. The cartoon series *Strawberry Shortcake* (1980–5) helped create a market for the character but, like other 1980s children's toy series on TV I discuss in chapter four, was criticised by parenting groups and cultural critics for contributing to the commodification of childhood. Heather Hendershot analyses the doll in terms of odour and femininity and argues that, "Strongly gender-coded toys, such as Strawberry Shortcake, were particularly successful in the 1980s because of the Reagan-era backlash against the questioning of attitudes towards toys and sex roles that took place in the 1970s. [The] dolls are both symptomatic of and contributors to a post-1970s conservative construction of femininity" (1996: 96).

However, despite these problematic issues revolving around representation and female consumption, Barbie is for many collectors a symbol of pride and gives collectors a sense of identity through a collecting community. Spigel argues that Barbie dolls "are assigned values by the collectors" and various collecting groups "ascribe meanings" to the doll "not originally intended by corporate giants such as Mattel" (2001: 312). Similarly, Attfield concludes her study of Barbie and Action Man by reminding us that "Toys cannot fully determine actions or thoughts, they are themselves the focus of play – a dynamic activity used to rehearse, interpret and try out new meanings as well as products of complex social relations" (1996: 88). Furthermore, in the introduction to their edited collection *The Gendered Object*, Pat

Kirkham and Judy Attfield argue that to study gendered objects "it is necessary to locate them both historically and within the sphere of consumption in which the appropriation of goods into people's lives is part of the cultural process of making meanings with and through things" (1996: 2). Therefore, while the image of Barbie is seen as problematic by many we should look more closely at what collectors are doing with the dolls as new meanings and readings are inscribed once the toy becomes a collectible, an object of distinction and value.

The longevity and collectible appeal of Barbie gave Mattel a model to repeat its success in sustaining a collector's market for other toys in its catalogue. In order to exploit its corporate image as an historic American toy manufacturer it brought back one of its brand logos and refigured it to launch a new club called Matty Collector. Originally, Matty Mattell was the boy mascot for the company, used in advertising from the late 1950s up to 1970. Drawn as a small white boy wearing black shorts, red and white striped shirt and a crown, he was used in TV spots, on toy packaging and even hosted his own cartoon anthology show on Saturday mornings during the 1960s. In 2008 Mattel relaunched Matty and introduced him as Master Toy Collector, mascot for Matty Collector and figurehead for Matty-collector.com – the online space for Mattel's collectible toy brands. Now grown up, Matty still sporting a crown wears a black sports jacket over his red and white striped shirt and long trousers instead of shorts. He represents the more sophisticated collector, adult and highly knowledgeable about Mattel's history and toy range.

Matty Collector has thus become the focal point for Mattel toy collectors. The club supports a number of toylines including Masters of the Universe, She-Ra, DC Comic Superheroes, Ghostbusters and WWE wrestling. Having launched in 2008 Matty Collector has been an annual presence at the San Diego Comic-Con ever since. A giant shop takes up floor space in the main exhibition hall and a massive display booth promotes new action figures in glass cases. This is where we see Barbie, He-Man and Batman come together as doll and figure stand side-by-side as objects of fan curiosity. In creating an online space for Mattel toy collectors to buy new and limited edition action figures, as well as providing a physical space to connect with fellow collectors and toy designers at Comic-Con, Matty Collector Club represents the convergence of once-distinct collecting practices of male and female collectors. Under the Matty brand men and women are clubbed together as collectors. Matty may be depicted as a man but he represents a markedly genderless group of collectors that share a passion for Mattel's products that exist as collectibles, for adults and children alike.

In Matty Mattel we can see an example of where nostalgia and corporate needs come together. In bringing back an icon from the 1960s Mattel is nostalgically looking back to its own past, when its position as toy manufacturer for children was stable and defined. In an age where toys are produced on a global scale and traditional companies compete with other forms of children's entertainment, adult toy collecting has become an increasingly large component of their marketing strategy. As a result, Matty provides a link to the image of a childhood past that Mattel was instrumental in creating but he also becomes a figure to which collectors can also respond. Moreover, Mattel's online spaces help to make collectors feel connected – as nostalgia is so often that sense of feeling reunited with the comfortable and the familiar. On Mattycollector.com members are encouraged to see it as "a place to call home" and at Comic-Con members are asked to feedback to designers on what toys they would like to see made. Because of these attempts to connect with collectors a sense of brand loyalty develops. Michele White, in her study of eBay fans, argues that brands have fans: "Brand community members tend to be active fans of particular companies, products, logos, virtual communities, and media texts" (White, 2012: 55). In Matty Collector there is clearly a brand which collectors can actively follow, products they can collect, and a virtual community with which they can engage. White goes on to argue that "Internet settings have methods to tap into and control members' attachments" (2012: 83), thus in Mattycollector.com we see a website designed so that collectors can add to their collections but also promote their attachment to the brand through competitions, newsfeed and web chats with toy designers. Matty Collector is both a symbol of nostalgia for the Mattel brand of the past and a transmitter of personal nostalgia for the thousands of collectors that sign up to the website every year and attend conventions to see and hear what new collectibles are forthcoming. For male and female collectors it represents a connection to their childhood at the same time as it remains a dependable and nostalgic commercial brand with which to identify in the present.

Conclusion

Simon Reynolds argues in his book *Retromania*, "nostalgia is now thoroughly entwined with the consumer-entertainment complex: we feel pangs for the products of yesteryear, the novelties and distractions that filled up our youth" (2011: xxix). With all the examples discussed in this chapter we can understand nostalgia to be a genderless emotion; while immature "boy-men" revert to their childhood in a technological society women also look to the objects of their youth to build a sense of community and comfort through Barbie collector clubs. Therefore, what appears to be important in this process is not the fact either men or women collect things or that the things they collect are different depending on their gendered identity. It is that both men and women use the past as an arena for self-identification and recall moments from childhood through the collection and preservation of physical objects. This has become more prevalent because of the Internet and its ability to act as an archive of stored memories: photos, websites, videos, blogs, and so on. Nothing dies or goes away, therefore nostalgia for things once thought lost is fulfilled by simply searching for sites that preserve and sell the past like Mattycollector.com.

The next chapter extends this discussion about nostalgia, media memories and the adult fan collector by focusing on the generations of Transformer fans who continue to buy DVDs and toys. Through the remediation of a 1980s television series fans are able to reconnect with their past as well as create and share new memories as collectors. These toy objects don't just signify a childhood past, they represent a contemporary fan's cultural capital. Remediation keeps old media forms, images and icons alive in the electronic world and the physical objects that are kept, recollected and redistributed embody a sense of identity in the present. While issues of gender are important in the consideration of what makes a fan a fan, this chapter has argued that we must acknowledge the impact of technology and memory on the construction of identity and what it means to be a fan. As a consequence, the following case study of Transformer toy collectors will necessarily take into account the impact of remediation and contemporary convergence culture on the practices of fan collecting.

4

REPACKAGING GENERATION ONE

Genre, Memory and the Remediation of *The Transformers* in Contemporary Fan Culture

Following chapter three's focus on gender, nostalgia and the fan collector this chapter examines the rebirth and repackaging of *The Transformers* (1984–7) and related toy franchise, establishing the extent to which the role of the adult collector has influenced the continued popularity and lifespan of a 1980s children's toy and television series in the early years of the twenty-first century. *The Transformers* has undergone a generic shift between children's TV and adult TV. Fans that once played with the toys as children now collect the originals (retroactively called Generation One and first released in 1984) and their specially marketed reproductions; in so doing, their memories of *The Transformers* as a multimedia text become integral to the creation and perpetuation of an active online and convention attending fan community. In addition, special DVD box sets of the original American Saturday morning cartoon series are big sellers in US and UK high street stores as fans remember their love for the show and seek to reclaim some part of their childhood. Collecting the entire range of toys from Generation One up until more modern versions such as the CGI animated series *Transformers: Prime* (2010–present), and having the original episodes on DVD, becomes an important part of Transformers fandom. In highlighting the establishment of a fan canon in the children's television fan community, and how those discourses contribute to the creation and fragmentation of fan identity and culture, I argue that the series has become a sight of experimentation for individual and personal exploration. Fan affection and memory join the more familiar visual characteristics of the series – poor animation, poor dubbing, obvious commercialisation – and become additional generic signifiers of a well-loved, but not atypical, children's animated television series. My analysis ultimately suggests that notions of genre and genre boundaries are becoming blurred as films, television and toys originally aimed at children are now being remediated, collected and traded by adults keen to resurrect a once loved toy from their youth.

The fictional worlds of science fiction and fantasy seen in 1980s toy franchises like *The Transformers* and global brands such as *Star Wars* and *Star Trek*, that have kept children and adults alike engrossed for years, also have underlying marketing advantages: they can grow as new characters and therefore new toys are added to fit in with the mythology surrounding the overall franchise narrative (Wyatt, 1994: 153). The infinite potential for expansion keeps the toys popular as children continue to watch and rewatch the movies and play within their own "mythological" make-believe worlds. Similarly, other 1980s children's animated television such as *Teenage Mutant Ninja Turtles* (1987–96 & 2003–9), *He-Man and the Masters of the Universe* (1983–5), *She-Ra: Princess of Power* (1985–7), *My Little Pony* (1984–7), *The Care Bears* (1985–8) and *M.A.S.K* (1985–6) – with their relentless potential for remarketing and rebirth discussed in the previous chapter – have shown, through market diversification into areas such as live action film, animated series, associated toy lines and online fan clubs, that they are capable of offering adults (men and women as highlighted in chapter three) their own make-believe worlds where "affective play" and narrative are combined in a sustainable two-way relationship. However, as I shall outline in the next section, the fictional worlds that animated series originally offered children in the 1980s have also been heavily criticised for their banal storylines and overt commercialisation as part of the global toy industry.

The Banality of Children's Television

For several cultural critics, "most animated programs were little more than poorly drawn, glorified half-hour commercials for action figures and video games" flooding the children's toy market in the early part of the 1980s (Hilton-Morrow and McMahan, 2003: 78). Widely regarded as one of the poorer cartoon imports in the Saturday morning TV schedule, itself "characterised by animation which was uninspired and aesthetically redundant" (Wells, 2002: 81), critics of *The Transformers* saw it as an obvious attempt by toy manufactures to take advantage of an already open global market by producing "the big hit with a promotional toy" (Kline, 1993: 221). Timothy Burke and Kevin Burke, in their nostalgic look back at the cartoons and Saturday morning TV shows they watched when growing up, see the series as just one out of a myriad of cartoons that tried to cash in on the merchandising market. For them toy companies like Mattel and Hasbro were merely trying to copy the success of Kenner's *Star Wars* action figures by establishing and sustaining a market where the TV show acted as an extended commercial for the range of figures, robots, plush dolls and toy sets that were being produced cheaply in Asia and being sold in America (Burke and Burke, 1999: 57–8). Although I wish only to highlight the view that *The Transformers* was a banal by-product of the wider market concerns of the global toy industry, it is important to stress that despite the series' unpopularity in some academic circles the series was extremely popular with children. So much so that, as I will be looking at in closer detail in later sections, those children who grew up watching and collecting the transforming robots in the 1980s continue to watch and collect them as adults in the 2000s. In fact, even though the series has been continually blamed for contributing to the increased commercialisation of childhood, it can be asserted that many of the adults who deride the series are actually fans and enjoy poking fun at the toys and characters that used to keep them entertained as children. The defining characteristics of the children's animated television genre – the badly dubbed and drawn animation, the blatant commodity tie-ins, the poor stories – become an essential part of what it means to be a fan of the series; in effect, those who remember the series in such ways see themselves as fans because of and not in spite of them.

Part of the success of *The Transformers* can be ascribed to the fact that it was a joint project, where American Sunbow Productions and Marvel Productions were able to take advantage of the cheaper production costs in Japan and then flood the television market back in the US with dozens of cheaply made cartoons that could be endlessly rerun in syndication (Hubka, 2002: 242). David Hubka sees the co-produced success of series like *The Transformers* as evidence of the new developments in the production and distribution of animated television in the 1980s and 1990s where global markets had to be reached and networks had to find suitable material to fill air time (251). However, these developments were largely seen as negative since, as Stephen Kline notes about the genre, critics continually saw the problems associated with "letting businessmen decide the fate of children's culture … not only in the banality and violence in the programming but also in the growing commercialisation of the children's cultural industries, wherein artistically sophisticated, intellectually demanding and socially relevant" kid's TV competed for audiences "with cheaply produced low-quality entertainment" (Kline, 1995: 151). Furthermore, American children's television as a genre was slowly transformed from a period where cheap entertainment was important to one where its sole purpose was "to serve the marketer's promotional needs and not those of the children" (154). As part of a calculated success story *The Transformers* phenomenon in the mid- to late 1980s, just like the more modern animated series *Pokémon* in the late 1990s, created a "false need" that could only be satisfied through consumption; in the process it prevented other forms of children's culture – that might have been more dangerous or subversive – from existing (Buckingham and Sefton-Green, 2003: 384). Bob Dixon sees this "false need" most evident in the example of *The Transformers'* Optimus Prime:

> Optimus Prime, a leading figure in the Transformer concept, was so much in demand for Christmas 1985 that supplies ran short. Nevertheless, by early 1986 it had already been decided to replace the figure by Ultra Magnus, in accordance with the tactic of killing off toys when they reach a sales peak. This, it can be said, is catering for children's *wants* (which are created by advertising and publicity). But then these wants are displaced by other wants (artificially created again) the whole operation being designed to set up a puppet-like consumerism, and a condition of endless dissatisfaction.
>
> *(Dixon, 1990: 265)*

Clearly then, the successes of both *The Transformers* and *Pokémon*, being made in Japan and transferred to the American market, epitomizes the continued consumerism and dumbing-down of American youth culture (where cartoons are merely adverts) and the over-simplification of narrative in the genre of children's animated television (the only memorable thing being a catchphrase, e.g. "Robots in Disguise" or "Gotta Catch'em all"). Parental concern over the commercialised nature of children's toys has even been the basis for the *South Park* (1997–present) episode "Chinpokomon" (season 3, episode10), where contemporary fears of a widespread degradation of American culture due to Japanese imports are lampooned. In this episode the children of South Park are brainwashed into buying Chinpokomon toys (with the catchphrase being "Buy them all"), and the video game emphasizes the message that in order to be the master you must buy every one so that you have the power to defeat evil. Unbeknownst to the children the toys are actually miniature antennas that help Japan launch an invasion of Pearl Harbor and the evil force that the children must defeat is America.

Despite the quality of animation as a result of the genre's emphasis on low cost production, audiences were increasingly exposed to homogenised global products made in Japan and shipped to the US (see also Tobin, 2004). *The Transformers* was inspired by an original toy line of transforming robots produced by the Japanese Takara Corp., which was sold in the US and Britain by Hasbro. Kline intimates that children's television is important since it serves as potential space for child growth and development. Unfortunately, arguments from critics so far outlined, about the quality and industry of Saturday morning television, often overshadow the important debates surrounding the genre as latent narrative storyteller – in fact, for Kline the medium "has become the great storyteller of post-modern culture" (1995: 162). The problem lies with those companies who place profit over story and the risk they run in upsetting the potential for children's television to act as a social guide during a child's formative years. Children "internalise and use the social knowledge conveyed in these cartoons", therefore critics should be aware of not just how they were produced and marketed but also how they are used and adapted by their key demographic (Kline, 1995: 163–4).

The Transformers should not be singled out as the first children's cartoon to be used as the focus of a merchandising campaign; Stefan Kanfer's *Serious Business* rightly points out the historical links that Disney's Mickey had with early retailers such as Woolworth's and how "the spinach industry credited Popeye for increasing its sales some 33 percent" (1997: 96). Also, in previous work on 1980s animation series and public service announcements I argue that *The Transformers* and *G.I. Joe: A Real American Hero* (1983–7) were used by the US government to serve the public interest. "Viewers were treated as both consumers and active participants", empowered by axiomatic messages "telling a generation of American children how to be good citizens – you did not have to just buy these toys but through the narrativisation of play and social interaction you had to perform your civic duty: 'think before you act', 'don't judge people', and 'work in a team'" (Geraghty, 2010: 298). Furthermore, as Hubka also maintains, to get a full understanding of these programs' cultural impact we must examine the audiences at which they were aimed and acknowledge that although they may simply be children's cartoons, part of an industry, children, like adults, "consume television programs in ways that articulate their own social relationships and identities" (2002: 252).

Transforming Genres of Animated Television

On the one hand the concept of genre in television studies is a useful one; it is clear from some programs – comedy, soap opera, quiz shows, news – that generic conventions are easily identifiable and that networks are keen to capitalize on the potential audiences that watch these shows. Yet, on the other, critics are keenly aware of the difficulty in trying to apply genre theory to television since networks also organize viewing patterns around time slots and "a traditional division between 'fiction' and 'faction'" (Casey et al., 2002: 110). This means that while some viewers will specifically choose to watch science fiction shows or solely factual programming such as documentary and the news, others will "channel-hop" across a whole range of material: "They may watch a range of different genres as an evening's package on one channel, or they may pick out specific programs or genres (including feature films previously shown in cinemas) across channels" (110). However, this does not mean we cannot try to define Saturday morning children's television as a genre with an associated audience; as discussed in the previous section, criticism of animated series centred on their banality, commercialisation and poor quality have themselves highlighted a series of codes and conventions that can be used to help define the genre. As well as being located within a specific time period, when the growth of the cable networks and their industrial relationships with toy manufacturers helped create a market for cheap toys and associated spin-offs, children's animated television was distinguished by its precise location in the Saturday morning schedules.

In creating a time and a place for viewing (usually the lounge before parents woke up), children were given the opportunity to pick and choose (channel-hop) between their favourite programs – depending on their favourite toys, etc. – thereby establishing a particular cultural and historical timeframe in which the specific programs were interpreted by their audiences. As well as studying the obvious visual and audio markers that help discriminate between good quality animation and cheap imports – the dubbing, stories, artwork, one-dimensional characterisation – it is important to remember that all genres, including animated television, can also be studied "as socio-historical actualities, as thematic and *ideological* constructions deriving from history" (Casey et al., 2002: 109). As I begin to address the fan culture surrounding *The Transformers* in the rest of the chapter it is important to keep in mind the flexible generic qualities of the series and its relationship with the freedom offered by television schedules. Also, as new forms of recording and viewing technology enter today's market, it is possible for fans to recreate the specific conditions of the original Saturday morning schedule (watching the episodes on DVD) on Saturdays, or any other day of the week for that matter.

Although the historical conditions may have changed since childhood, the physical location and form in which audiences now watch the series may not have changed at all since the 1980s. However, while the visible generic "qualities" of the animated Saturday morning series may still be enjoyed again and again, the cultural contexts in which they were watched have changed – *The Transformers* has changed and evolved alongside its historical contexts and the personal contexts of the fans that continue to watch it.

According to Rick Altman genres "serve what we might call a *memorial* purpose; that is, they recall a society's collective experience, by rehearsing the stories, characters and topics that the culture deems important". Failing to "serve as a memorial both to a collective past and to a current collectivity" means the genre is not fulfilling its role (Altman, 1999: 188). In terms of series like *The Transformers*, part of the animated Saturday morning television genre, the historically specific experiences that are required for it to act as a memorial are things like its use of familiar cultural narratives, its animation, the contexts of viewing and the associated merchandise. Traditionally, for Altman, "in order to provide the mutual reinforcement on which genres depend, social and generic structures" such as those outlined above had to be "carefully aligned" so that unified audiences could recognize the genre (188). Now that genres are routinely aimed at diverse and disunited audiences, Altman sees them as being unable to act as "collective memorials" and instead act as "pseudo-memorials" where certain genres evoke familiar practices or force audiences to recollect specific experiences. This new reliance on the memory and intertextual experience of the audience means that genres no longer act as communal historical markers but as personal indicators of "the experience of the culture and its assumptions, rules and myths, as well as experience of other genre texts" (189). I would maintain, with regard to *The Transformers*, that those fans that now collect the toys and rewatch the cartoons are doing so because they are taking part in the pseudo-memorialisation of their youth. The series, and therefore the genre from which it originates, is now no longer historically specific, to the extent that it recalls the 1980s, but rather it has shifted to become a genre of universal narrative intertexts and personal fan contexts.

It is particularly significant for the purposes of the last section, and the chapter overall, that Altman suggests "the rise of consumerism and the mass media, along with the extraordinary proliferation of narrative entertainment that they have brought, have tilted the typical generic mix of life experience/textual experience radically towards the experience of previous texts" (189–90). The experience of *The Transformers* and other childhood series of the 1980s as previous texts is an integral component of what it means to be a fan in today's Transformer collecting community. Memories of watching the series on Saturday mornings, getting that all too rare and expensive Optimus Prime for Christmas, or trading stickers in the playground to complete your sticker album, are important experiences and memories that are both shared and unique experiences which individual fans confess as part of their membership within the Transformer community. Just as Altman sees genres today performing "a pseudo-memorial function" counting on "spectator memory to work their magic", the continued popularity and affection that fans show towards series like *The Transformers* is part of the same trend in contemporary popular culture (191). In what P. David Marshall calls an "intertextual matrix", the result of various media such as film, music, video, websites, television, and licensed products being "elaborately cross-referenced in the contemporary entertainment industry" through magazines, papers, and news programs, *The Transformers* as television show and Transformers as objects of adult play have also become "new intertextual commodities" that can be learned about and understood by audiences through their relationships with other cultural forms (Marshall, 2002: 69).

"Robots in Disguise": Adult Toy Collecting and Fan Memory

On the reverse of the episode guide booklet, supplied with *The Transformers* Season 2 Part 1 DVD box set released in 2003, Daz Jamieson – a self-confessed lifelong fan and collector – reminisces about the series. Along with his own personal opinions on a range of episodes in the set, Jamieson paints a picture for readers of the world that he inhabited as a child when the series was new and the toys were at the centre of his universe. The two booklets from subsequent box sets follow this pattern, reminding fans that they were once part of an important cultural phenomenon and still are members of a unique family where Generation One Transformers are intrinsic objects of affection and value. I quote at length from the first booklet to show how important nostalgia and community are both within *The Transformer* fandom and the creation of adult-orientated, repackaged media merchandising:

> The Transformers cartoon takes us all back to that special time, when life was simpler, pop bands were funkier and jeans were tighter. Timmy Mallet would introduce each episode on Wac-A-Day with an infectious smile that just wouldn't fade. Thankfully we don't have to watch the episodes in five parts, over the period of a week anymore, or sit through another round of Mallet's Mallet just to find out whether Grimlock betrayed the Autobots or not. No, now we we've got DVD, and the first twenty-four episodes from season two are here in all of their unedited glory …
>
> The Transformers cartoon stands out today as a classic of animation, and features one of the finest collections of voice talent ever assembled for a series, headed up by the legends Frank Welker and Peter Cullen. With complex characters, great action sequences and a bad guy who turns into a gun, The Transformers remains one of the coolest cartoons of all time. Now let us all play that game where we try to transform our Transformers as they transform in the episodes, you know you want to.
> 'til all are one!
>
> *(Jamieson, 2003)*

Jamieson weaves an attractive path through a mosaic of media memories that are designed to enthuse fans and reintroduce them to a world that they have long forgotten. Not only do we see that the DVD set is aimed at fans specifically located in the UK through the region 2 packaging, but also by Jamieson's recollection of his own viewing practices. As I previously mentioned, regarding the importance of television schedules and child viewing habits, Jamieson recollects how he (therefore the audience) watched the series as part of Timmy Mallet's own television show and how one episode was cut into five so that it could be spread across five days (part of TV-am's half-term or summer holiday morning entertainment schedule for children). Fans are given a nostalgic frame of reference to begin re-imagining their own viewing practices and episode memories. Jamieson, both as a fan and fan/producer, seemingly contextualizes *The Transformers* by describing the decade as a "special time" personified by funkier pop bands and tighter jeans. This not only sets the series within a specific timeframe but also highlights his own personal memories of Britain in the 1980s.

Referring to criticism the series received for its lack of quality and commercial links with the toy industry, Jamieson appears to counter these claims by describing the series as a "classic of animation". Not only are its Japanese production roots missed out, the series is located as an original through Jamieson's description of the voice artists Frank Welker (Megatron) and Peter Cullen (Optimus Prime). Their voices in particular make the series legendary and are aspects of fan experience that should be emphasized and remembered – a point further underscored by talk before the first live action film in 2007 where producers assured fans that all living original voice cast members would reprise their roles (retaining voices does not make a difference to new fans of the film but would certainly attract original fans). Notions of community, friendship and shared experience are important themes in most Transformer fan output: From Jamieson's booklet sign off "'til all are one!" which comes from the 1986 movie, to his own weblog on the TheTransformers. net website. Nostalgia clearly plays a key role in Jamieson's personal blogs: on his page he starts by confessing his first experiences as a kid collecting the toys, "My first Transformer was Inferno … I thought he was so cool, he led to my being driven away from the road that was *Star Wars* and down the Transformers path", then he moves on to describe key moments in his childhood when he remembers the toys giving him joy and pleasure, "One of my favourite Transformer moments was playing with Jetfire on the coach on the way to swimming in school." As well as the emotional attachment he had with the toys, Jamieson expands upon the other important part of being a modern collector by describing valuable and rare toys in a collection:

> The rarest tf I ever had was probably the find of all time, for £4 in a pokey news agents. It was the unbranded Shockwave released in the UK. The same mould as the original shockers, and the same quality but without the tf brand or stickers, and for some reason a dark grey. Very nice though.

In this blog extract we can see how collecting rare examples from childhood, even better if you had them when they were first released, is important to fans and their position within the online community – previous studies have highlighted how degrees of cult fandom and subcultural capital can be gauged through levels of consumption, knowledge and esteem within a particular fan community (see Jancovich, 2002; Jancovich and Hunt, 2004) – however, it is also clear that personal experience shared with the group is also integral to the memorialisation of *The Transformers* as adult/child television. This form of collecting, where fans get just as much enjoyment than financial gain from things they collect, corresponds to the type of consumption known as "curatorial consumption" (see McCracken, 1988). Each piece in a person's collection conveyed a sense of personal and social history and it was curatorial "in that possession, preservation, and orderly succession of ownership superseded the immediate use dictated by industrial production" (Tankel and Murphy, 1998: 59). The memories attached to the toy and its collection distinguishes the fan experience as a form of nostalgia rather than a process of consumer capitalism. Furthermore, since "the collection may provide its owner with an omnipotent sense of mastery" (Belk, 1995: 70) we can also see how Jamieson's knowledge and ownership of the rare toy set his revelation in the contexts of subcultural hierarchies that "operate to establish the ownership" and exclusivity of cult texts within a specific fan group (Hunt, 2003: 186).

Daz Jamieson's blog calls attention to these characteristics in that he also includes pictures of his children and says, "I popped into Toys R Us to buy my 2½ year old son a reissue of Optimus Prime for Christmas. I already have one, of course, otherwise I could never let him play with one in front of me." Such sharing of experience, and protectionism of perceived valued property from 2½ year old children, alludes to the "masculinity of cult" discussed in the previous chapter. Of course, there could be arguments put forward that Transformers were marketed as "boys' toys" and therefore would continue that pattern into adult collection, and Joanne Hollows (2003: 47) makes the case that "the collector is [not] an 'essentially' masculine figure", but it is interesting to see how Jamieson denotes playing with Transformers as a boyish pursuit (as long as there are duplicates) and therefore their collection as an adult male pastime.

Simon Plumbe and Sven Harvey, co-organizers of the annual "Auto Assembly" Transformers convention in the UK, have initiated a communal blog on their website where fans can leave and share their childhood memories of the series and toys. "Transformers Memories: 20 Years of Robots in Disguise" was conceived as "an extensive archive of fan memories of Transformers", including thoughts on episodes, characters, first memories and favourite toys. Plume's first entry likewise covers these main themes in that he says, "I was what you call a late starter to Transformers. Sven had been trying to convert me for years … since then, I've got a small corner of my room taken over with a toy display, comics and DVDs everywhere and I've even converted my fiancée into being a fan. Sven would be proud … " Not only does this show fans as adult collectors of child toys but it also challenges the common stereotype of them being socially maladjusted bachelors, Plumbe has friends, family and a fiancée – a situation counter to the stereotypes discussed in chapters one and three. The lifelong fascination for Transformer memories, to be retold and recounted in a communal weblog, can also be related to the notion of timeless film reception Annette Kuhn (1999) calls "enduring fandom" explored in chapter two. In the case of enduring Transformer fans, they remain loyal to the product long after Generation One stopped being made – collecting toys on eBay, at conventions, through fan clubs – but also continue to share in their memories of the brand by rewatching the cartoons and following similar patterns of induction into the collecting community.

Embodying the Memory: Adult Fans and Discourses of Play

Following the work of scholars who have concentrated their discussion of children's television and toy culture in the 1980s around notions of consumption, cultural hegemony and ideologies of conformity, those that study media fandom and the relationship between fans and cult television also relegate mass-produced and consumed texts such as *The Transformers* to the negative confines of the mainstream. In his seminal study of fan cultures Matt Hills (2002: 112) discusses fandom in terms of creating a space for "affective play", which "deals with the emotional attachment of the fan" and "suggests that play is not always caught up in a pre-established 'boundedness' or set of cultural boundaries, but may instead imaginatively create its own set of boundaries and its own auto-'context'". However, those texts that attract such engagement between fan and object of affection are defined by a sense of longevity and value, quality and exclusivity that consequently positions so-called mass "popular" media texts as insignificant, short-lived and culturally worthless. Hills specifically cites Dan Fleming's (1996) work on toy culture to posit that the reason why children's television such as the *Teenage Ninja Mutant Turtles* brand or *The Transformers* do not attract and retain a loyal and long-lived fan culture lies in the fact that the toys were so easily discarded and forgotten as commodities when the children grew up or even when they moved on to the next big toy craze at Christmas. Like the toys, the cartoons were fads, examples of "Fad TV" that focused on reaching the widest market audience and making the biggest return on sales rather than investing in quality. For Hills (2002: 110), shows like *The Transformers* cannot, and by implication should not, attract cult fan communities since cult texts "stand as the precise antithesis to the 'quickly abandoned' Turtles and Transformers". Specifically,

> Where the affective relationships of fan culture preserve an attachment which challenges the disposability, pre-programmed obsolescence and contained innovation of the commodity, the readily forgotten "Mutant Ninja/Hero Turtle" appears to be far more thoroughly integrated with the circuits of capital and consumerism.
>
> *(Hills, 2002: 110)*

However, as examples of *Transformers* fans already discussed in this chapter indicate, communities, personal identities and notions of cultural capital are very much in evidence in the fan practices of adults who not only perceive the texts of their youth as vitally important in adulthood but are also protective of the cult status they believe their favourite "fad" film or television series deserves. Transformer toy fans and collectors buy and watch the DVD box sets of *The Transformers* cartoons to reconnect with their childhood. Nostalgia for their youth and the media texts once consumed when they were young is an important part of being in a fan community. Shared stories between fans about their first Transformer toy or their favourite episode become ice-breakers in online blogs and at conventions, allowing for new networks of fans and friends to develop. Memory and nostalgia play a very important role in contemporary constructions of age and media, accessible through the remediation of old adverts, cartoons and the toys.

Nostalgia for childhood play and the media texts and physical consumer objects that symbolise personal memories of being a child is articulated through fandom – whether that be collecting toys fans once owned, and indeed never owned, or building an archive of old television episodes that then remain accessible and stand as physical reminders of when and where fans first watched them twenty or more years ago. Fandom thus becomes a connector to one's past, a reinvestment in what once made an individual feel comfortable and secure. However, this is not to say that the negative accusations targeted towards *The Transformers* and Hasbro about indoctrinating children into consumerism taint the fans' sense of the past. Nor does this mean nostalgia for an often criticised toy and cartoon prevents fans from growing out of this supposed indoctrination. Revisiting the past through watching old kids' TV or buying collectible merchandise becomes a way of reconnecting with youth and reasserting a sense of self based on an earlier version of selfhood. In defining melancholia, Mary Caputi draws upon the work of Walter Benjamin (2009) to assert that "the modern subject ... longs for an anterior richness missing from the present, a person driven by an internalized desire that, by definition, can never be filled". Taking this further she describes how for some "the present is filled with glimpses of a cohesion that has now been displaced" and that the contemporary is thus defined as movement forward in time albeit always containing "a longing to recapture or re-create something that went before" (Caputi, 2005: 27). Convergent media and the remediation of Transformer toys and cartoons allow for the continued presence of a childhood past in the adult fans' present. Therefore, they do not need to look back on the past with melancholic desire since new media keeps recycling images and artefacts of children's culture in the present.

Connecting with the Past: Nostalgia and Transformative Memories of Childhood

Popular publications that recollect childhood toys and games indicate a sense of nostalgia for the objects of yesteryear. The introduction to Steve Berry's *TV Cream Toys* states that the book,

> examines in detail the seven score or more toys we most yearned for as youngsters ... These are the peerless playthings of a nation's youth, the ones

that encapsulate a time and place to which we can never return ... TV Cream Toys is the Christmas morning you should have had when you were young enough to appreciate it.

(Berry, 2007: 18)

Applying the work of Susan Stewart one might assert that publications such as the above employ a narrative that is all about lack, gaining something from the past that we perhaps never had the opportunity to experience in the first place. She states:

> Nostalgia, like any form of narrative, is always ideological: the past it seeks has never existed except as narrative, and hence, always absent, that past continually threatens to produce itself as a felt lack.
>
> (Stewart, 1993: 23)

Yet Transformer fan memories demonstrate that while nostalgia for a past youth may be based on a current lack found in adulthood – a lack fans try to make up for by buying and rewatching toys and DVDs – it is also part of the process of entering a remediated world of Transformers fandom as an adult. This is a fully filled world where nostalgia encourages a sense of control over one's past and the media texts still consumed and valued. For example, as alluded to in Dan Jamieson's blog on TheTransformers.net, nostalgia clearly plays a key role in a fan's life. In one sense he looks back on his past, but in another he acknowledges that Transformers are still very much in his present – the path he started on leads from his childhood to adulthood where he now blogs about the toys on the website and plays an important part in the repackaging of the TV episodes. Jamieson is very much part of a current Transformer fan community where he contributes to and creates officially produced merchandise aimed at adult collectors, in the process counteracting Stewart's description of nostalgia being about living in the past to fill a "felt lack".

Fans like Jamieson are clearly asserting their cultural capital through the creation of new Transformer related texts. Another fan, J.E. Alvarez, writes in the introduction to his guide to Transformer toys and collectibles,

> Now my toys have become my escape from society's toxins, an alternative habit to poisons like alcohol and other such drugs. Now I have been given the opportunity to give something back to the manifestation that has brought me so much satisfaction.
>
> (Alvarez, 2001a: 5)

Here, Alvarez uses his collection of toys for a specific purpose, to catalogue and offer a guide to fellow collectors about what is out there and what it is potentially worth. Moreover, feeling a sense of responsibility and gratitude, he writes that he wants to give something back to the toys. But not solely because of what they gave him as a child but what they still give him as an adult: not least because they "have become [his] escape from society's toxins" and provide a source of income as an author and freelance journalist. Both Jamieson and Alvarez are writing about and for themselves but also clearly writing to fellow Transformer fans who will inevitably share similar feelings of nostalgia and gratitude. Thus, rather than seeing nostalgia in the case of Transformer fandom as being about lack and an individual sense of loss it is more about a collective feeling of remembrance for a toy and cartoon that served them well in the past and that they continue to embrace in the present. Both of these fans have risen to become respected experts in the Transformer fan community, they write books and lead forums – their jobs are based on their fandom. Transformers are very much part of their adult life and as a result that supposed "felt lack" characteristic of Stewart's definition of nostalgia cannot apply here. Alvarez speaks of escaping from society's toxins through his collection but he does not suggest he wants to escape society altogether and return to his childhood. He has brought his childhood forward with him so that it performs an important role in his adult life where he earns a living from it, acts as an expert, and is member of a Transformer community who thrive on engaging with the past in the present. Indeed, as Alvarez states in the introduction to his guide to the Japanese versions of the toys:

> [T]hese "robots in disguise" have been part of an incredible phenomenon which has no end in sight. Thanks to the Internet, VCRs, comic books, and the love of these toys and characters in the hearts of fans everywhere, Transformers will forever live on as part of our culture.
>
> *(Alvarez, 2001b: 6)*

Alvarez's view of *The Transformers* as an ever-present part of contemporary culture and reminiscent descriptions of his own toy collection in the guidebooks correspond to Paul Grainge's discussion of nostalgia in American culture. In contrast to Stewart's definition of nostalgia, he asserts that it "need not be seen as a troubled emotion but can, instead, respond strategically to the ambivalence surrounding sociocultural transformation and/or ideologies of progress" (2002: 26). Building on Grainge's work, Philip Drake summarises further that nostalgia as a mood "can be conceptualised as conveying a knowing and reflexive relationship with the past" as well as having the more familiar and negative connotations based on longing and loss and the fabrication of history: It "operates quite removed from this concept of loss, as evidenced by the popularity of retro objects that are less about articulating a connectedness to a lost 'authentic' past than with consuming objects whose signification has become loaded with connotative markers of taste in the present" (Drake, 2003: 190). This point is crucial in my discussion since the Transformer toys are physical objects, brought forward from childhood and regularly consumed and valued as authentic by adult fans and collectors. Using Svetlana Boym's definition, I would argue that nostalgia works here as a connector between past and present, the individual (Alvarez) and the community (the fans), channelled through an authentic object of signification (the toys). She writes, "nostalgia remains an intermediary between collective and individual memory. Collective memory can be seen as a playground, not a graveyard of multiple individual recollections" (Boym, 2001: 54).

Notions of communal and individual nostalgia for childhood are integral to the remediation of popular media texts like *The Transformers*. In the age of media convergence "old and new media collide" and once forgotten icons, symbols, images, sounds and series from music, comics, film and television are reborn and attract new fans with which to share and indulge. As Henry Jenkins asserts (2006a: 2), convergence allows for the archiving of and searching for new forms of entertainment where "the flow of content across multiple media platforms" links the web with older media forms such as film and television. *The Transformers* cartoon series becomes part of the Internet's vast archive of visual material. Fans are able to find their once favourite episode on either YouTube or another file-sharing site and buy the DVD box set from an online retailer, ultimately reliving the memory of watching it for the first time. *The Transformers* becomes real again for adult fans who desire a reconnection to their childhood. The physicality of the toy which had been lost as children grew up, returns as the Internet gives fans access to finding and buying what they had once possessed. Remediation "makes us aware that all media are at one level a 'play of signs'", but at the same time "this process insists on the real, effective presence of media in our culture" (Bolter and Grusin, 1999: 19). As such, *The Transformers* is a constant presence in the fans' lives as the remediation of the series and convergence of viewing technologies keep it alive and real in adulthood.

For Will Straw (2007: 3), "The relationship of the Internet to the past is typically talked about in terms of remediation," yet the old continues to have merit as new generations are introduced to images from the past and treat them as if they were seen for the first time. While the old becomes new in a remediated world he also reminds us that the Internet, the gateway to the digital world, "provides the terrain on which sentimental attachments, vernacular knowledges, and a multitude of other relationships to the material culture of the past are magnified and given coherence" (Straw, 2007: 3). So, for example, while fans are able to rewatch the cartoon and find recordings of the old Hasbro television adverts on YouTube they are also able to buy the toys from collectors and dealers who use websites like eBay to sell original and rereleased versions. Nostalgia and memory thus become the impetus for fans to search the web for their favourite toy and series and remediation and convergent technologies gives them the opportunity to reconnect with and purchase the physical artefacts from their youth. Straw contends:

> It is not simply that the Internet, as a new medium, refashions the past within the languages of the present, so that vestiges of the past may be kept alive. Like most new media, in fact, the Internet has strengthened the cultural weight of the past, increasing its intelligibility and accessibility.
>
> *(Straw, 2007: 4)*

Creating the New: Fan Videos as Convergent Media Texts

The Internet also allows for the affective play of fandom where fans can appropriate old media texts and combine them with new images, different sounds and produce new texts that attract their own fan following. In previous work on Transformer fan videos and fake trailers for the live action film from 2007 I discussed the emergence of a fan discourse "rooted in the personal value fans have attached to the Transformers toy and cartoon series" that was specifically targeted at defending the original over the Michael Bay adaptation (Geraghty, 2011a: 89). The videos made by fans used images taken from the original cartoon series and scenes lifted from the new film, mixing them together to create new Transformer texts. These videos were shared on YouTube and provide another example of how remediated children's texts are remodelled and recycled using convergent media technologies. Nostalgia for the old text was again an impetus to relive and reconstitute past memories and promote the original Transformers over the new. I argued that, for adult fans, valuing *The Transformers* from their childhood became "a process of textual negotiation and renegotiation," displaying "implicit and explicit value judgements, embedded within both critical and fan reception, that are based upon fidelity, authenticity, and nostalgia" (Geraghty, 2011a: 103). Videos of fans dressing up in homemade Transformers costumes and role-playing as their favourite characters follow in a similar vein as the fake trailers I mention above. However, the specific nature of these fans literally transforming their appearance to be like a Transformer toy they once played with as children needs further discussion and analysis beyond value and taste.

Transformer fan costumers display in their videos an attempt to physically embody their memories of childhood through a literal transformation into enlarged versions of the characters first brought to the television screen in the 1980s. One such video, entitled "Blue Steel Transformer Costume", depicts a fan's (he calls himself "Blue Steel") efforts in making a fully fitted costume made from metal with electronic sounds and lights for extra authenticity. The two-minute video is a record of the planning process, the key stages of manufacture, and the final artefact with the fan showing off how he can wear the costume, transform into a car, at the end. The video is set to *The Transformers* theme tune with sound effects for the transformation into a car and back again taken from the series and recent movies. The sheer amount of time, money and effort put into designing and making the costume must have been immense so it is no wonder that "Blue Steel" felt the need to upload his achievements on YouTube. For Heather Joseph-Witham, "costuming is an enjoyable pastime as well as a means to an end. When suitably attired, fans are transported to another world" (1996: 30). Furthermore, we can understand "Blue Steel's" efforts as a symbol of his fandom, his nostalgia for The Transformers as an icon of technological progress and homage to the physical toys themselves as they stand as models on which he based his own designs. Donning the homemade costume is an attempt to embody and make real a sense of identity "Blue Steel" gets from the toys, cartoons and films as well as a physical transformation that brings the memory and nostalgia for the franchise to life.

Henry Jenkins argues that fans must translate their "viewing into some kind of cultural activity, by sharing feelings and thoughts about the program content with friends, by joining a 'community' of other fans who share common interests. For fans, consumption naturally sparks production" (2006b: 41). Similarly, José van Dijck defines Internet users as "active Internet contributors, who put in a 'certain amount of creative effort'" (2009: 42). Therefore, in the "Blue Steel" video, we can see this production and creative effort in full as it documents the creation of a costume that allows the fan a closer connection to his favourite media text. The remediation of *The Transformers* through "Blue Steel's" costuming and video making brings nostalgia to life and underlines what both Grainge and Drake have argued about nostalgia being the signification of objects in the present. The mode of presentation is also important. Uploading to the web and using YouTube to display such fan creativity and its associated emotional connection with a popular media text works as a form of communal memory making – contributing to the remediation of nostalgia for *The Transformers*. For Juli Stone Pitzer, in her analysis of fan video making, "The visibility of fans as producers ... can help generate fan visibility" and "rekindle interest among former fans, or introduce new males and females of all ages and demographics" to a media text (2011: 123). In this sense, nostalgia is communicated through the convergent platform of YouTube and remediation provides the opportunity to reach other fans who may share similar feelings and memories as "Blue Steel".

YouTube, as online facilitator of media usage and self-expression, is perhaps an important example of where nostalgia in the media lies. The relationship between fan audiences and YouTube is an interesting yet contrary one which has only just started to receive critical attention. As Burgess and Green (2009: 78) contend, it operates as a corporate, commercialised concern that also enables "cultural citizenship" through its "communities of practice". They see it as an alternative public space that allows users, fan or otherwise, to participate democratically and interact globally through submissions of video content which is often deeply personal and reflective of the politics of the individual who posts it (78–9). YouTube can be seen as an archive of the social and the personal, a repository of visual material collated from film and television imagery throughout history. In a sense it represents a collective memory of us through the media. As more people view and upload to YouTube the web becomes a virtual space for multiple media memories and childhood memories form an important part of that. For Joanne Garde-Hansen "the Internet is distributing memories into personal, corporate and institutional archives" (2011: 71) therefore fans are presented with not only their own memories but also those of other fans which have been saved, archived and shared. A site of remediation like YouTube provides "a platform for the production of separate but connected containers of events, memories and identities and offers viewers an ongoing transformation of collective memory as a mosaic of media" (Garde-Hansen, 2011: 107).

Consequently, memories are a crucial component of media fandom, not least because new technologies allow for the remediation of old television series through websites, fan videos and online archives. Throughout this chapter I have argued that nostalgia for and the memorialisation of childhood texts like *The Transformers* should not be viewed as inhibiting or backward looking. Indeed, memories, as Alison Landsberg states, "are central to a person's identity – to one's sense of who one is and who one might become ... they become the building blocks from which to construct narratives of the present and visions of the future" (2004: 41). In other words, memories of childhood – brought to life in this case through the remediation of children's television – have a direct influence on the present and the creation of one's future.

Conclusion

As new toys are produced, old ones repackaged, and episodes remediated those fans that recollect them do so because nostalgia and intertextuality are key components of their postmodern identities and important tools in the continued understanding of contemporary society. Sharing thoughts and memories of an intertextual childhood phenomenon such as *The Transformers* is but one way of interacting with and within this modern age of uncertainty. Being part of a fan community, in an age of fractured society and social hierarchies, "can be viewed as a positive strategy" balancing alienation at work with camaraderie through group membership (Ross and Nightingale, 2003: 126). Sharing memories of a once mainstream children's TV show and popular toy range provides real satisfaction to individuals who have unwittingly challenged the notion of genre specificity.

The "Blue Steel" video is one of hundreds uploaded on YouTube, with most combining homemade footage, sampled music and clips from the cartoons and movies. Such additions and embellishments breathe life into the nostalgic memories that the fans are trying to enact through making and dressing up in their costumes. These visual displays of creativity and nostalgia for the franchise are clear examples of the "affective play" discussed earlier. The videos provide fans the space to experiment and play with new media technologies, identities, and their own memories. Paul Booth argues that a key characteristic of digital fandom "is how fans' use of technologies brings a sense of playfulness to the work of active reading" (2010: 12). The specific nature of the Transformer fan video, which involves costuming and the manipulation of a range of media images and sounds, brings certain corporality to this form of digital fandom. Nostalgia is again the inspiration for this and it is again more about living and creating in the present than it is a longing for a loss of the past. These videos offer "fans a space in which they can reproduce characters and situations from the extant media object, and then use those characters to reproduce fan cultures" (Booth, 2010: 167). "Blue Steel's" blue transformable robot costume is a new character, created by him and based on his passion for Transformers; not revelling in the past but more looking to the present and future as evidenced by his adaptations and improvements to the outfit.

Throughout this chapter I have tried to stress the importance of nostalgia in the practices and recollections of adult Transformer fans. Childhood, for them, has in many ways not ended as adult life begins and continues. But this is not because fans have regressed somehow or refused to grow up in that Peter Pan sense of rebelling against adulthood. For adult fans technology and the recycling of old media forms and franchises through remediation and collecting keeps childhood ever present. Remediation keeps old media forms, images and icons alive in the electronic ether and the physical objects that are kept, recollected and redistributed maintain a tangible link with elements of childhood that might have been thrown out, lost or just forgotten. Embedded within the practices of fans, whether they make costumes, write books, or post videos on the Internet, is a form of nostalgia for childhood that incorporates the past but does not mourn its passing as it remains very much alive in the present. I would argue that the examples of Transformer fan nostalgia discussed in this chapter are emblematic of a re-enchantment with symbols and objects from the past that are made available through new media technologies and rearticulated through the creative practices of contemporary fandom.

PART III

Places

5

FROM CONVENTION SPACE TO FAN HETEROTOPIA

Popular Fandom and the Cult Geographies of the San Diego Comic-Con

The convention has been the primary location for mass fan gatherings for over 70 years. From the first World Science Fiction Convention (WorldCon) held in New York in 1939 to the most recent San Diego Comic-Con in 2013, fans of all ages, nationalities and races, men and women, have enjoyed the unity of coming together and celebrating their favourite media or popular culture texts: whether literature, comics, films, TV, animation, sport, games, collectibles or memorabilia. The convention has provided a familiar and safe place for fans to meet, exchange, and communicate while perhaps not enjoying positive press or similarly appealing spaces during the daily routine of life outside the world of what they like most. In the epilogue to *Living with Star Trek* (2007) I posited that the convention space allowed for the sharing of an oral history that inspired fans to express their close connection with the fictional *Star Trek* text and the actors who appeared on stage to talk about their time on the show. At the same time "memory played an important part in the fans' sharing of oral history", with actress Nichelle Nichols' story about Martin Luther King Jr telling her to stick with *Star Trek* – so she could continue to be an inspiration for African Americans – acting as catalyst for fans to stand up and publicly recount moments in their own lives when *Star Trek*'s message of hope struck a chord (Geraghty, 2007: 171). While the convention allowed for emotional connections between fans and actors and between fans and fans, it also served as a space where commodities such as toys, props and autographs could be bought and sold. However, such objects did not symbolise mere consumption. Fans bought things because they meant something, it brought them closer to that very text they were remembering and celebrating in the main hall alongside fellow fans and collectors. Collectibles and souvenirs from a convention can be seen as mementos of the special moment when fans got close to the actors who inspired them and the television shows or films they cherish. Therefore, I would argue that memory and consumption, emotions and objects are joined together as part of the whole convention experience.

Journalists and critics might pour scorn on massive fan conventions like those organised for franchises such as *Star Trek* and *Star Wars*, or the biggest of them all in San Diego, but what they provide to fans is a location for the emotional connection with, and consumption of, their favourite texts. What is more, this connection with space and place needs to be understood as a transformative and unique experience rather than a commodified and generic one. Previous studies of conventions have compared them to religious sites, where fans gather to discuss their "sacred" text: "Although not sacred in the religious sense nor are they profane, and although non-ecclesiastical they may be perceived as holy by their visitors" (Shackley, 2001: 155). For Michael Jindra, fan communities like that of *Star Trek* represent "symbolic communities" (2005: 166) that take on "serious, religious functions" (171). Conventions therefore become sacred sites where fans can immerse themselves in the text through rituals of performance, consumption and worship; making the text all the more real and creating a mythology (169).

The notion of ritual is explored by media scholars who focus on the repeat fan viewing of series on TV and through DVD box sets. Roger Aden uses the term "symbolic pilgrimage" to characterise the process fans go through when they watch series repeatedly, getting closer to the text by shutting out the everyday distractions of life in their living rooms and other personal spaces. Will Brooker describes it as "a trip without drugs, a journey and return without leaving the easy chair" (2007b: 149). For Aden, the text itself becomes a sacred site, which fans travel to and return from when watching: "Symbolic pilgrimages feature individuals ritualistically revisiting powerful places that are symbolically envisioned through the interaction of story and individual imagination" (Aden, 1999: 10). There is a preparation ritual to ensure fans are not disturbed – getting snacks ready, locking the door, shutting off the lights, taking the phone off the hook – that "removes the participant from the everyday and brings him/her closer to the fiction" (Brooker, 2007b: 155).

Conversely, Jennifer E. Porter sees convention attendance as a form of physical pilgrimage in a secular context. Using the work of anthropologist Victor Turner she argues that the pilgrimage to a shared convention site is a liminal journey of transformation to find *communitas*, "communal fellowship", with other fans (Porter, 1999: 252). In so doing the site of the convention, whether it be specifically tied to the fictional text like film locations and theme park rides or neutral and generic sites like hotel ballrooms and community centres, provides "a time and space for fans to be free to explore their love of something deep and meaningful in their lives" (267). As a consequence, these atypical fan sites become important places for popular veneration. *Star Trek*: The Experience once located at the Hilton in Las Vegas (see Roberts, 2001; Karpovich, 2008) or the Adventure in Hyde Park (see Geraghty, 2003), Captain Kirk's future birthplace in Riverside, Iowa (see Figure 5.1), *Harry Potter* World at the Leavesden Warner Brothers Studios, the *Coronation Street* set in Manchester (see Couldry, 2000, 2003), a local cinema in Cloverdale, British Columbia (see Geraghty, 2011b), the Dracula museum in Whitby (see

FIGURE 5.1 Stone marking the future location of Captain Kirk's birthplace in Riverside, Iowa.

Reijnders, 2011), or a rain-lashed residential street in Forks, Washington (see Lundberg and Lexhagen, 2012) are examples of sites that through fan enshrinement and pilgrimage become venerated memorials to popular culture: "Traditional elite institutions build shrines to symbols of faith, patriotism, and knowledge. But popular shrines communicate the legitimacy of popular experience, even if it is lurid, frivolous, or downright kitsch" (Combs, 1989: 74).

Therefore, while this chapter seeks to understand the relationships fans have with their favourite texts and collectibles it also focuses on how notions of physical place and emotive space impact on the experiences fans have travelling through and within the "venerable" convention site, and also the geographical location that the site occupies in the city. If *communitas*, as mentioned above, is defined as "intense bonding and sharing of the pilgrimage and the connection with the sacred place" (Brooker, 2005: 18) then I want to show that while places like the convention site might control and limit the fan experience they also shape and define the physical surroundings which the convention temporarily inhabits. The interaction between people and objects within a real space enhances both the emotional and physical relationship fans have with popular media texts. Therefore, this chapter seeks to bring together ideas discussed so far about collecting, memory and merchandising to offer a reassessment of commodity consumption at fan conventions. How do fans create "deep and meaningful" connections with sites they have never been before? What role does memory have in making those unfamiliar sites seem more safe and familiar? Within the physical site of fan interaction, a panel or exhibition hall, how do the collectible and mass-produced objects that epitomise fan consumption bring fans closer to the fictional text and their geographical location? These questions inform the following analysis of the popular culture and merchandising phenomenon that is the San Diego Comic-Con.

San Diego Comic-Con and Fan Pilgrimage

Founded as the "Golden State Comic Book Convention" in 1970 at the Grant Hotel in downtown San Diego, the San Diego Comic-Con has become the premier site for fans and global companies to meet and share in all manner of popular media (including comics, film, TV and computer games). Moving to the convention centre in 1991, Comic-Con now attracts more than 130,000 people a year. So, from a hotel lobby hosting comic book dealers attracting roughly 300 die-hard collectors, the site for comics and the superhero stories contained within has changed dramatically to incorporate industry, artists, producers, celebrities, journalists, and fans. Drawing on field research and analyses of media texts and production histories, I argue that Comic-Con International (to give it its proper title) provides a space for the re-engagement of fan memory with past and long-dead popular texts and offers fans both a physical and emotional experience tied to textual- and object-centred pleasures. Booths that sell rare comic books or reissued toys from Mattel or Hasbro, autograph tables that offer fans the chance to meet their favourite actors, or giant rooms used by Hollywood executives to publicise the latest blockbuster to thousands of attendees all represent locations where fans, collectors, dealers and the industry can interact. While inside the convention centre space offers opportunities for the breakdown in fan hierarchies, the city space outside also becomes part of the Comic-Con experience. The streets are postered with adverts for new series, costumed volunteers hand out freebies on street corners, and local businesses welcome attendees by decking out their shops with cult merchandise. As a result, the San Diego Convention Center, the hotels and the city itself become familiar places returned to every year where fans and collectors can get spoilers, see special screenings, buy new products and old collectibles, and meet their favourite stars for the duration of the event. For one week in July, San Diego turns from Southern Californian family holiday destination to international focal point of popular culture fandom.

We can gauge the significance and popularity of Comic-Con in some of the references made to its popular media texts. In the episode "Hot Cocoa Bang Bang" (season 2, episode 22) from *The Cleveland Show* (2009–present) Cleveland takes his family to Comic-Con to set up a stall and sell copies of his new comic, *Waderman*. Whilst there his son revels in being a fan, dressing up as some of his favourite characters and engages in a fight dressed as a Nav'i from *Avatar* (2009) to save Comic-Con from the threat posed by network executives and their committee-designed sitcoms. Numerous episodes of *The Big Bang Theory* (2007–present) make reference of Comic-Con, with the four friends visiting the pop culture extravaganza on several occasions. In *Paul* (2011), Simon Pegg and Nick Frost start their road trip across America at Comic-Con. And, as a sign of the importance of Comic-Con in marketing DVDs with extras and special features several television series box sets include the panel discussions from recent Comic-Cons.

What this means for the actual products being launched in San Diego is that they are no longer aimed at a niche audience – they are mass-market commodities, with timeless comic book superheroes from DC and Marvel competing with new characters from the worlds of TV, film and anime. The fans that attend are old enough to remember the originals such as Superman and Batman and young enough to be interested in more modern incarnations of the iconic duo. Generations of fans collide in Comic-Con, offering producers and industry tycoons ample opportunity to market their brands and continue the shelf life of the comic book – whether in its paper, electronic, film or computer game form: "Indeed, the primary function of the megacon is, somewhat ironically, to encourage further capitalistic investment in comic book *culture*, not comic *books*" (Fawver, 2012: 8). An exhibition space, as described by Umberto Eco in *Faith in Fakes*, "assumes the form of an inventory" (1998: 292) and thus Comic-Con can be a seen as an inventory of popular culture and the associated memories and objects that keep it alive. Stan Lee, renowned comic book writer and legendary creator of Marvel Comics' most iconic characters, says of the San Diego Comic-Con: "The thousands of convention-goers are grown-ups, adults who are interested in movies, television, DVDs, and, of course, comic books … These fans are tremendously important to the comic book business, just as they are to any creative endeavour" (Lee cited in Spurlock, 2011: 5). These comments mirror Jenkins's opinion of the convention in that the "fans have become the leading edge of the studio's promotional campaigns" (2012: 25) and that trying to win over crowds in San Diego may lead to greater success for new television series set to launch in the autumn or blockbusters gearing up for battle the next summer.

If fans make the convention and prop up the media forms that flood the event year on year, then what of the space that contains this interaction? After moving from the Grant Hotel to the El Cortez Hotel in 1972 Comic-Con spent many years building a devoted and regular attendance. San Diego offered attendees good weather for the four days in July when the convention was held and enough space to offer a mix of attractions: from dealer rooms, to autograph booths, to the annual costume competition and Comic Book Expo (where retailers and publishers did business with each other). By 1979, however, the hotel space was no longer adequate so Comic-Con moved to the Convention and Performing Arts Center (CPAC) in downtown San Diego. During the 1980s more events were added to the programme; the Will Eisner Comic Industry Awards and international media markets such as Japanese anime became popular amongst fans and gained dedicated programme tracks. By 1990 the convention was attracting 13,000 attendees so another move in 1991 to the bigger and newly built San Diego Convention Center on the harbour allowed for more space and more opportunity to expand the daily programme (see Figure 5.2). The city council identified multiple income streams beyond comics and memorabilia, thus downtown streets and billboards were

FIGURE 5.2 An outdoor view of the San Diego Convention Center on West Harbor Drive.

plastered well in advance of the convention, using superheroes and popular animated TV show characters to advertise the location as well as the event (see Figure 5.3). By 1999, 48,000 people were attending Comic-Con and the city itself was becoming an attraction, not just the comics and people inside the convention centre.

At Comic-Con we see non-traditional fan spaces such as the more tourist-focused Gaslamp Quarter and Seaport Village utilised alongside more business orientated spaces such as hotel meetings rooms and exhibit halls. An empty and blank space, or "non-place" to use Marc Augé's (1995) term for generic places like airports, stations and hotels, that is used year round for national dental conventions through to local beer festivals, the San Diego Convention Center becomes an active and real fan space through nostalgia, collecting and personal interaction. Most sites of pilgrimage are "*multiply* coded" (Brooker, 2007a: 430), and thus fandom connected to place differs for each fan. Locations that inspire fan pilgrimage have real world uses, they are not just used or visited by fans, therefore they have to actively make these places special – through either physical transformation of the space (adding familiar objects) or performance in that space (costume and cosplay). According to Will Brooker, fan pilgrimage is about pretending, performance and making the new from "the familiar and quotidian" and so fans coming to San Diego and the convention centre are, borrowing Brooker's phrase, "approaching the location with their own agenda" and "are able to transform 'flatscape' into a place of wonder. They bring their own urban imaginary, their

FIGURE 5.3 Lamp post advertising on the corner of 4th Avenue and J Street in downtown San Diego.

own maps of fiction and their own angles on the everyday" (Brooker, 2007a: 443). For Gregson and Crewe (2003: 2), discussing flea markets and jumble sales held in car parks and church halls, "consumption occurs in sites and spaces that are ordinary and mundane in their location and in their situation in everyday life", thus the cavernous and versatile convention centre, along with the city streets and buildings that surround it, are also transformed into spaces that allow for multiple exchanges and mass consumption (see Figure 5.4 and Figure 5.5). Where multiple entertainment media forms converge on one city a new, albeit, temporary site for superhero creation and consumption grows there; in it, fans and the industry rub shoulder to shoulder and there exists a unique moment where both hold equal power. Joss Whedon, writer and director, reflects on Comic-Con:

> [It] has definitely gotten bigger and more mainstream. The industry has figured out where the true fans are. This has created a dichotomy between the comic fans and the movies – in some cases, a bitter rift. But I believe there could be harmony between the comic book folk and movie makers. Ultimately, they just need to sit down or possibly make out. This is the kind of place Comic-Con is: It's a place where people with the same passion – whether their obsessions are similar or very, very different – come together. To make out.

> *(Whedon cited in Spurlock, 2011: 11)*

FIGURE 5.4 Comic book stall inside the exhibition hall at Comic-Con.

FIGURE 5.5 An empty Sails Pavilion on the upper level of the San Diego Convention Center, used for registration and autograph signings.

While Whedon's view of the fan/industry relationship at Comic-Con seems a little utopic, Henry Jenkins proffers a more negative view: "Today, one of my big ambivalences about Comic-Con is how much it now emphasizes fans as consumers rather than fans as cultural producers ... [it] puts the professionals in the center and the subcultural activities the conference was based on at the fringes" (2012: 25). I disagree with Jenkins's assessment of where fandom is located in comparison with the industry at Comic-Con. For sure, consumption forms a large part of the activity that goes on in the rooms and main exhibition hall, and Hollywood studios have the biggest booths selling their latest wares. However, as I have already mentioned and will discuss further below, the convention spills out into the city streets and other public and private buildings. Fans occupy more places and create more spaces for their particular fandom than the industry can define and control. So, while the professionals are at the centre of the exhibition hall and panels (advertising their own creations) fans are inside the convention meeting new fans, arranging meetings and gathering new ideas (getting inspiration for future creative activities and projects). Outside fans revel in transforming San Diego into their space, daubing walls and windows with flyers and posters for fan clubs, groups, zombie walks and activist marches. Subcultural identity and the activities that go with it are at the heart of Comic-Con, therefore one has to reconsider what spaces constitute the convention and which geographic places act as sites for fan interaction and production.

San Diego, Comic-Con and Global Entertainment

Where Comic-Con was once entirely American in its focus (DC and Marvel, US comic artists, film and TV series dominated), the organisation has become a global nexus for all types of international popular media texts: British science fiction, Japanese anime and computer games, Spanish and Mexican horror, Canadian superheroes, Belgian adventurers, and Danish toy companies stand side by side with established American comic icons such as Superman and major Hollywood studios such as Warner Brothers. Comic-Con International, officially renamed in 1995, provides a space for the promotion of global popular media texts, where American and international comic fans can meet, and foreign media companies compete with US conglomerates. Its mission statement, also adopted in 1995, indicates a dual desire to both appreciate the comic book form that spawned the original convention in 1970 and expand its scope to include popular culture texts more widely:

> San Diego Comic-Con International is a nonprofit educational corporation dedicated to creating awareness of, and appreciation for, comics and related popular art forms, primarily through the presentation of conventions and events that celebrate the historic and ongoing contribution of comics to art and culture.
>
> *(Cited in Sassaman and Estrada, 2009: 9)*

In keeping with this mission other events have been initiated by Comic-Con International to support the comic arts, including the Alternative Press Expo and

WonderCon – both recently being held in San Francisco but now moving to Anaheim to accommodate larger crowds. Even the future for the San Diego Convention Center is uncertain as the space is becoming increasingly limited for the massive crowds and exhibitors that want to attend; Anaheim remains an alternative – yet unpopular – location. In promoting comics and the popular arts, Comic-Con International, and San Diego in particular, became an attractive destination for fans and Hollywood studio executives. The convention centre was expanded in 2001, adding two new halls, which could be used to gather thousands of fans for the Masquerade costume ball or seat the same for the latest blockbuster movie launch. Ballroom 20 can hold 4,250 people and hosted *Star Wars* film festivals and premieres of new comic book superhero storylines. However, with the opening of Hall H in 2004, which can seat over 6,500 people, Comic-Con became the perfect venue to host Hollywood movie-orientated programmes. Showcasing the stars and directors of some of the most popular film franchises, Hall H became a Mecca for fans eager to see sneak previews and hear hot gossip months before a film premiered in cinemas: "Comic-Con proved to be the launching pad for many popular films, especially those with their roots in comic books, such as the *X-Men* and *Spider-Man* films, *Iron Man, Superman Returns, Hellboy, Sin City, 300, The Spirit,* and *Watchmen,* to name just a few" (Sassaman and Estrada, 2009: 154). As popular genre programming on US television continued to attract global audiences, cult TV series also utilised Hall H to launch new series and preview current ones. Seen as a "testing ground" for ensemble cast series like *Lost* and *Heroes,* Comic-Con became the spiritual home for many writers and actors who would regularly attend the event seeking to boost awareness for an upcoming project.

Seeking higher esteem within the Comic-Con pecking order Hollywood studios compete to get their new film or television show into Hall H. Running from dawn to dusk, with queues often forming days in advance to get into the most popular panels, the mixed programme of film launches and television script read-throughs attracts not only thousands of fans during Comic-Con but also the world's press who flock to interview stars and get an angle on what new things will be out the following year. The big superhero franchises, like *Avengers* and *Spider-Man,* start off in Hollywood but make their way through San Diego to gather momentum and hopefully set up a lucrative box-office return. In 2010, Hall H hosted panels to launch Disney's *Tron: Legacy* and Marvel's *Captain America,* in 2011 *The Twilight Saga: Breaking Dawn Part 1* and *The Adventures of Tintin* (with a rare appearance by Steven Spielberg) were joined by television luminaries such as *Glee* and *Doctor Who,* and in 2012 television seemingly took over with panels for *The Big Bang Theory* and *The Walking Dead* proving very popular in addition to another appearance by *Doctor Who.* The expansion of Hall H's programme to include science fiction television as well as the usual superhero films further signals Comic-Con's shift to promote global popular arts beyond the comic book. The fact that the BBC's *Doctor Who,* broadcast on BBC America in the US, attracts thousands of fans dressed as Daleks and Doctors suggests a global audience for traditionally televisual texts which in turn not only solidifies their cult appeal but also transforms their central characters (in this case The Doctor) into international popular culture icons who sit side by side with their American cousins such as Superman and Captain America.

If Comic-Con has become a particular place for Hollywood promotion and superhero adoration then it is also a space for the recycling of old media and entertainment forms. Series like *Doctor Who* and comic books like *Superman* clearly have a pedigree that stretches further back into history than the convention. Old and new versions of both appear at the same time, with independent traders selling valuable original issues of *Action Comics* and toy action figures of William Hartnell's Doctor. In many ways Comic-Con represents the physical manifestation of Henry Jenkins's theory of "convergence culture" where the space allows for the archiving of, and searching for, new forms of entertainment and where "the flow of content across multiple media platforms" links the web and online gaming with older media forms such as comics, film and television (Jenkins, 2006a: 2). In convergence culture, old and new media collide and fans are able to remain loyal to favourite childhood series and characters at the same time that the very same media texts are recycled and reimagined for new audiences and new fans. John Fiske described the traditional fan convention, most famously illustrated by *Star Trek* and *Star Wars*, as a space where "cultural and economic capital come together" (Fiske, 1992: 43). A fan's love and valuing of the text is expressed alongside their financial investment in it, represented by them spending money on expensive tickets, souvenirs and memorabilia (something I will discuss in more detail in chapter six regarding *Star Wars* toy collecting).

Yet, the convention is also a site for communal nostalgia, collecting, sharing stories and the literal bringing of the past into the present as fans are seemingly "locked into an endless cycle of re-enchantment" (Gregson and Crewe, 2003: 112) with their favourite superheroes and animated television characters. Fans travelling to San Diego Comic-Con to have this experience go on a symbolic pilgrimage to an imagined space; a space for which most of the year is neutral but for one week in July is highly emotive. As Will Brooker (2007a: 429) describes of fan pilgrimages to filming locations, they become "sites of play and carnival, poetry and magic". Fans use stored memories of their favourite texts to interpret and find their way around both the fictional and real space – "viewing the present through an archive of the past" (433). Whilst not a filming location in fan-loved fictional text, I propose that the San Diego Convention Center, the city, associated buildings and tourist sites become a geography of nostalgic recollection where collectors, fans, producers, artists, writers, and stars all bring new meaning and history to the popular media franchises that Hollywood continues to market in those spaces. As Svetlana Boym (2001: 54) says of nostalgia, it "remains an intermediary between collective and individual memory. Collective memory can be seen as a playground of multiple individual recollections". As such, Comic-Con is a vast playground of memories and texts, superheroes and fans, signs and objects, ephemera and commodities. They all intermix in a neutral communal space, geographically San Diego but psychologically and emotionally unique to every individual that goes there.

"I'm 21 and I'm going to buy lots of toys!": Collecting and Liveness at the Con

As I have intimated up to this point, Comic-Con is a site of multiple activities and the consumption of popular culture in all its myriad forms plays a central part in most attendees' experience: from acquiring freebies and handouts to buying rare comics and queuing for autographs, texts are collected and kept as well as traded and discarded. The trading and collecting of toys, the latest product line release or second hand original, happens on a mass scale with dozens of booths offering fans the chance to recollect old toys from childhood. Every attendee receives a giant sponsored shoulder bag upon entry (with different pictures of Warner Brother productions on the side), big enough to carry daily purchases and freebies (see Figure 5.6). Independent dealers make a tidy profit over the four days of the

FIGURE 5.6 A Comic-Con attendee with freebie convention bag handed out at registration in 2010.

convention and fans often resort to Fedex-ing their purchases on site to avoid extra baggage charges on their return trip home. As the convention has expanded beyond the simple trading of comic books, some of the main global toy companies have taken the opportunity to use Comic-Con as a platform to launch new lines and bring back old favourites, rather like the main Hollywood studios use it to market forthcoming blockbusters. Where some fans wait hours in queues to see directors and stars talk through sneak previews of movies like *Pacific Rim* (2013) and *The Hobbit: An Unexpected Journey* (2012) others could not care less about Hollywood's latest and instead wait in line to meet their favourite toy designer who is there to talk about their newest action figure or play set. Thus, Hasbro and Mattel – America's biggest toy producers maintaining a presence on the same level as the likes of Warner Brothers and Twentieth Century Fox – actively engage in a dialogue with fan collectors to create brand loyalty but also get feedback on new products in an effort to respond to demand for what collectors want to see made. As the quote I overheard from a fan in a line to pick up entry passes suggests, some were there to "buy lots of toys" but Comic-Con is also an adult space where 21-year-old collectors can add to their collections without any stigma surrounding the fact that toys are negatively associated with childhood commodity consumption. The convention is a free space for multiple fan experiences and desires.

Physicality of place makes Comic-Con all the more special for toy collectors that make the effort (and are lucky enough to get tickets) to travel to San Diego. For while fans can share and trade online throughout the year, akin to keeping up with movie gossip and news on websites like Ain't It Cool, Hasbro and Mattel save their best to share with fans inside the convention. In 2011 Hasbro gave out free Kre-O (rather like Lego) Transformer figures of Optimus Prime to attendees, helping to launch the new line of toys on the back of the release of *Transformers: Dark of the Moon* (2011). As well as freebies, Hasbro release limited edition toys to sell at their pop-up Toy Shop in the main exhibit hall. In 2010 the range included *G.I. Joe* Sgt Slaughter figures (limited to two items per purchase), a 5-inch Strawberry Shortcake, a Generation One reissue of *Transformer*'s Blaster, Marvel Universe's Galactus (again limited to two items per purchase) and a 2010 My Little Pony. For the first few days of Comic-Con many fans are busy carrying boxes and bags away to their hotel rooms – once their collecting efforts are exhausted they can then enjoy the convention without hindrance and worrying whether limited edition items have sold out (see Figure 5.7).

Hasbro's selection of toys in 2012 included a *G.I. Joe* and *Transformers* comic crossover H.I.S.S. Tank and a fan inspired vintage *Star Wars* action figure set. Along with the six specially packaged figures inside the box came an extra toy: Jar Jar Binks frozen in carbonite, "MESSA FROZEN!" exclaimed the poster (see Figure 5.8). What was particularly attractive about this toy for collectors was the fact that it appeared to support the commonly held fan belief that Jar Jar Binks was a terrible addition to the *Star Wars* universe and should be killed off – suffering the ignoble fate of being frozen in carbonite (like Han Solo in *The Empire Strikes Back*) to be gawked at and ridiculed. Matt Hills discusses fan hatred of the Jar Jar

FIGURE 5.7 A Comic-Con attendee carrying assorted large toys back to his hotel room next door to the Convention Center.

character and argues that such vilification is emblematic of fans trying to claim ownership over the text: "'Hating' the 'childish', 'cartoonish', 'commercial' Jar Jar Binks, in this instance, is one tactic aimed at preserving the fans' 'good' object of *Star Wars* as 'serious' and 'culturally significant'. The discourse of hate is taken up, however excessively, within fan struggles over cultural value" (Hills, 2003: 89). With this said it was perhaps somewhat ironic that the "commercial" Hasbro produced a "childish" version of the very object of fan hatred it had originally produced in the millions for the release of *The Phantom Menace* in 1999 – consigning Jar Jar to a cruel and eternal demise in 2012.

Mattel, through their Matty Collector Club (see chapter three), also promote several lines of their popular toys including *He-Man*, *Ghostbusters* and the DC superhero range. At their booth, in the shape of Castle Grayskull from *Masters of the Universe*, you could not only grab free badges and paper hats to celebrate the 30th anniversary of *He-Man*, you could also meet live versions of He-Man, Teela and Man-at-Arms and get a picture for the convention scrapbook. As a tongue-in-cheek tribute to devoted fans who "brave" the sometimes humid and pungent conditions of the main exhibit hall crammed with thousands of people Mattel gave out free deodorant sticks in 2010. Branded as "Eternia ® Pine" (Eternia being the fictional homeworld in *Masters of the Universe*) with an image of Moss Man (Heroic Spy and Master of Camouflage) on the label, the strap line read "Fresh COMIC-CON

FIGURE 5.8 Poster at the Hasbro Toy Shop advertising the 2012 convention exclusive Jar Jar Binks frozen in carbonite figure.

Relief". The use of the Moss Man character provides fans with an intertextual joke since the original 1980s toy action figure was covered in a pine scented, moss-like material as a gimmick.

These small items, often throw-away and cheap, provide fans an extra connection to the text, event and the physical space where they acquired them. By tying together the convention (overcrowded and hot), the fans (who might need freshening up), and a character from Mattel's most popular line of toys they have connected franchise brand with Comic-Con brand through one small freebie – and thus part of the fans' enjoyment and association with the space and fictional text is founded in an object one could only get on site to be either used, kept as memento or even traded for something of equal cult value. The fact that attending fans of *Transformers* were at the Hasbro booth to get the first Kre-O figure of Optimus Prime or fans of *He-Man* were at the Mattel booth to get the badge, hat or deodorant meant their connection to the text and toys, their fandom, is proven to be that little bit more special than other fans who did not attend. Matt Hills describes a similar display of fan distinction in horror film festivals and conventions, whereby fans who attend can get to see things first or feel closer to the stars and directors. He argues that a "fan's convention/festival attendance becomes one 'authentic' marker of 'insider status'" and thus reflective of the importance of subcultural capital in the hierarchies of fandom (Hills, 2010a: 99). Further discussion of fan hierarchies and cultural capital can be found in the next chapter with regard to *Star Wars* toy collectors; however, I make this point here to highlight something else important to Hasbro and Mattel's use of space and collectible objects at Comic-Con, and discussed in connection with horror conventions by Hills: "liveness".

Liveness, for Philip Auslander, stands in contrast to the effects of a mediatised culture where musical performance can be reproduced and heard by millions of listeners who never saw the live performance on stage. The popularity of live events like music concerts, or comic conventions in this case, is founded on the immediacy of connection to the event (something different could happen every time) and also the fact they have some inherent cultural value that fans (whether they attended or not) consider important: "Another dimension to the question of why people continue to attend live events in our mediatized culture is that live events have cultural value: being able to say that you were physically present at a particular event constitutes valuable symbolic capital" (Auslander, 1999: 57). Thus, obtaining a limited edition toy or joke deodorant stick is physical proof of such attendance at a live and popular event like Comic-Con and helps to symbolise a fan or collector's devotion to, and endurance for, their favourite text or toy brand. In the case of Mattel's Matty Collector Club just being there might not be enough since a lot of preparation and planning has to go into obtaining the newest toy. Every year, around March or April, the club starts to sell vouchers to members online who must purchase them in advance of going to Comic-Con in July so that they are guaranteed the chance of getting their hands on that year's new toys. In 2013 the journey to Comic-Con (18–21 July) started on 29 April where new toys were revealed online, with voucher presale starting on 4 June. Inspiring fans to plan ahead the Matty Collector site posted on launch day, "There really is nothing that compares to SDCC ... except maybe the chance to be one of the first to get your hands on a great new figure or vehicle from your favorite brands ... Make sure you check back every day this week so you don't miss a single one!" Clearly, being a collector of Mattel toys does not simply involve mass consumption of objects, it means being selective of brand and meticulous in planning – most of all, it means being at the event with ticket in hand to pick up your limited edition toy as reward for being a fan all year long. San Diego Comic-Con is therefore both a live event and premeditated experience – it represents a destination for fans and a journey for collectors.

Toy collectors consume and produce. As well as journeying to San Diego and collecting toys through Mattycollector.com all year long they are also given the opportunity to design new toys to be made by Mattel. To celebrate 30 years of the *Masters of the Universe* cartoon and toy range Mattel held a competition for fans to enter designs for a series of new figures that would be unveiled at the 2012 Comic-Con. At a panel called "Mattypalooza 2012", held on the Friday, fans were treated to a special event hosted by Mattel designer Ruben Martinez and brand manager Scott "Toy Guru" Neitlich. The "Toy Guru" hosts a blog on Mattycollector.com and is well known to collectors. As one-off event held within the convention space Mattypalooza again confers special status on fan collectors able to be there and keen enough to stand in the long line for entry. However, the panel also acts as a confessional space for fans that have grown up over the last 30 years still collecting *Masters of the Universe* toys. A Q&A session allowed fans to ask what will come next in the product line but they also thanked the designers and managers for producing a well-loved toy that they have enjoyed for decades and still connects them with their childhood. This nostalgia for the toy object is important and also confirms status and distinction within the collecting community: those who can remember and talk about the original cartoon series and toys from the 1980s get credit from the creators who then in turn ask them what characters or vehicles they would like to see brought back and revamped for Matty Collector club members.

Mattel use fans and collectors to help guide their brand development and are clearly open to fan involvement. In recounting the history of how *Masters of the Universe* was brought back and relaunched at the 2008 Comic-Con, Neitlich writes in his blog about his rise from playing with He-Man at age 4 to being in charge of the entire line, designing the first King Grayskull figure for the new Classic range. In his case, fan consumer had transformed into fan producer and Mattypalooza at Comic-Con acts as a site for the revelation and expression of personal fan memories. For Robert V. Kozinets "consumers who have invested themselves in cultural texts are continually drawn into dialectical interplay with producers, subcultures, microcultures, and wider cultural meanings and practices in order to legitimate and express what matters to them" (2001: 84). Thus, the convention allows for this "dialectical interplay" between fans and producers and the objects and texts at the centre of this meeting point are shown to have important meanings; neither created or inscribed by toy companies like Mattel but nonetheless valued and celebrated by both those who collect and those who make. Over the course of the convention, at a booth or in a room where collectors and Mattel designers can share stories, the toy brand continues to have a life and give life to the year-round activities of fans.

BBC America, *Doctor Who* and Hall H

Because Comic-Con provides a space for toy brand promotion and nostalgic celebration, it is no surprise that media companies like BBC America also use Comic-Con to launch and build an audience for UK programmes in a crowded international TV market. The network was launched on 29 March 1998 and rebranded in 2007 as part of the BBC Worldwide brand. Distributed in association with the Discovery Network it is available on both satellite and cable through subscription. With a New York headquarters it has had a number of American executive officers with experience of working on US niche cable networks, including MTV and Comedy Central. Deriving most of its content from the BBC and other UK broadcasters means BBC America offers an interesting mix of drama, genre programming and documentaries, but it has also aired classic American series such as the *Battlestar Galactica* reboot and *Star Trek: The Next Generation*. Steadily growing an audience in the US, the latest sign of the network's international success came at the San Diego Comic-Con in 2011 where BBC America achieved first-time stellar status by holding a *Doctor Who* panel in Hall H. *Doctor Who, Torchwood, Being Human, Bedlam* (amongst others) have all had popular previews, panels and merchandise launches in San Diego but Matt Smith's 11th incarnation of The Doctor was the first UK TV series to be given such prime billing – something repeated in 2012. The presence of the cast and creators of BBC America's top-rated series is supported by a centrally located BBC America booth in the main exhibit hall which attracts hordes of fans and passers-by eager to purchase the latest *Doctor Who* merchandise and grab exclusive Comic-Con freebies. For 2012 fans could get foam Dalek hats to wear around San Diego, displaying their fandom with pride and attracting interest from those not lucky enough to get one but who wanted to trade.

Even in this environment of online branding and transmedia storytelling the presence of BBC America at Comic-Con, with *Doctor Who* as tent-pole series, proves the importance of place in the continued popularity of genre programming and popular culture icons. Fans gathering together en masse in San Diego to attend the panel in Hall H and see the stars create a media hype that helps promote the series to an international audience and offers a springboard for the latest episodes soon to air on television. It is a viral event where attendees can tell their friends through social media and word of mouth about previews and what's in store. The convention experience and "insider information" gained places the fan at the centre of production activity, albeit for a fleeting moment, but they then can share, post and tweet this enthusiasm for the series and pictures taken beyond the convention centre – thus making the experience more valuable, durable, and longer lasting. Organisers run both Twitter and Facebook accounts throughout the duration of the event and fans can post pictures of costumes, collectibles and celebrities on the Comic-con.org website. Apps available for the iPhone also keep fans updated with the latest schedule change and special appearances by authors, artists and stars. What attendees can see so too can fans unable to get to San Diego. Thus, the convention is just as much a viral event as it is a real one. Furthermore, national and local press host Comic-Con blogs and forums so that fans can share the latest gossip from the convention centre live online. For example, *USA Today* publishes daily front-page stories in their Life section about what is appearing on stage and then runs more focused reviews of TV, films and games on their Comics. usatoday.com website. Both spaces provide attendees opportunity to review what they saw the day before and plan what to see next as well as upload pictures and post their own experiences of the convention alongside news stories written by attending journalists. Comic-Con is "an economical way of producing buzz" (Coogan, 2006: 6) for the studios and newspapers that cover the event, and as such fans are active participants in the making and remaking of brands such as *Doctor Who* for international audience consumption through the web and press.

Moreover, being at Comic-Con in Hall H is a boon to organisers as well as BBC America. There appears to exist a reciprocal relationship whereby shows like *Doctor Who* gain more status, being compared to and billed with colossal Hollywood franchises that use the convention to premiere the next big release, and San Diego Comic-Con diversifies its market and cult audience to include international *Doctor Who* fans prepared to travel thousands of miles to get that live convention experience. In the history of Comic-Con, we can see an evolution of the convention space where in its generic nature it allows for multiple popular culture products to be sold and advertised as well as thousands of fans to interact and engage with their favourite media texts. The convention centre is both a business space and a fan place; a global entertainment industry, represented by the Hollywood studios and comic book publishers that gather there, mingles with fans in a localised environment. Costumed fans spill out onto the streets of San Diego, which are specially dressed themselves for the occasion. Within such an environment BBC America can capitalise on its back catalogue of shows, *Doctor Who* as headliner, attract new international audiences and build a fan community loyal to its brand and specific types of programming. Thus, in the process, *Doctor Who* becomes a recognisable international brand, moving away from the traditional UK series and adopting American format and production methods more familiar to millions of viewers across the globe.

While San Diego Comic-Con offers BBC America and *Doctor Who* the status of appearing in Hall H and a merchandising booth in the main exhibit hall to sell toys and pass out goodies, what it also offers by way of cult esteem and the opportunity to connect with fans is priceless in an increasingly saturated popular media culture market. Just by being there, in the city and in the convention space, it has become part of the fabric of Comic-Con. Gathering in Hall H with thousands of other fans gives the individual *Doctor Who* fan an experience that creates an indelible memory and becomes part of how they share and present themselves as fans within the community. Comic-Con has in effect changed *Doctor Who* as international cult text and *Doctor Who* has helped to change Comic-Con by broadening its cult audience. The two together demonstrate how physical place and fan space contribute to the experience of being at the convention and successfully extend the life of a global media franchise.

Comic-Con as Fan Heterotopia

As I have argued thus far, Comic-Con offers multiple experiences and locations for all its attendees. Whether they are part of a toy collectors' club like Matty Collector or gathered in one giant space like Hall H clamouring to get a sneak peek at the latest blockbuster or TV series, all fans gain a connection to the physical surroundings of the convention and the city of San Diego. What is more, often the objects of fan affection that brought them to Comic-Con in the first place (e.g. *He-Man* or *Doctor Who*) recede into the background as other elements of the city and convention attract and vie for their attention. Indeed, for those fans that regularly travel to Comic-Con every year it is not just the convention or the events contained within that serve to characterise their time there; it is what goes on in the fringes and outside the main building that makes it a truly different yet familiar experience year after year. For Kurt Fawver, Comic-Con provides an escape for fans wanting to flee themselves for a few days (2012: 13) yet the city offers more than a simple getaway. San Diego becomes a destination that confirms what fans like and, more importantly, who they are. Texts and contexts combine to make Comic-Con a safe place in which fans revel, or, as Yi-Fu Tuan argues in his book *Space and Place*, "When space feels thoroughly familiar to us, it has become place" (1977: 73).

For the week when Comic-Con is in town San Diego takes on a new identity; temporary posters, signs, marquis, buildings and stalls are put up by the city local authorities and private store owners and shops splash colour and decoration through the streets to make the city as welcoming and engaging for visitors and locals alike. When over 130,000 extra people come into a city with a population of just over a million, filling hotels and public amenities to bursting, there clearly has to be some thorough planning and preparation beforehand. Yet, while streets and public transportation routes are blocked off and expanded, the city manages to create a feeling of ease and familiarity which makes the fan experience all the more engaging. The cooperation of, and blending in with, other city businesses and buildings means the Comic-Con experience is entirely holistic within the city space. Fans might queue up to see celebrities in Hall H at the convention centre but they can also walk two blocks and line up to get into a special exhibition on comic art at a local gallery in the Gaslamp Quarter. Thus Comic-Con is the city and the city is Comic-Con, it is an "experiential accomplishment binding people and environments" (Moores, 2012: 27) which evolves and adapts to the changing tastes and interests of the fans that travel there.

In 2010 the San Diego Metropolitan Transit System (MTS) decorated the trolley stop for the Gaslamp Quarter (the closest stop for the convention centre) as if it had been invaded by a group of *Star Trek* fans (see Figure 5.9). The direction signs and information posters at the stop had all been translated into Klingon and a temporary notice for passengers explained that "Klingons have taken over this station for the duration of Comic-Con and have demanded transit signs be posted in the Klingon Language. MTS appreciates your cooperation during this friendly takeover". For 2011 MTS decided to be a little more esoteric and decorated the same stop as if it were taken from the pages of a comic book (see Figure 5.10). The graphics and lettering familiar to comic readers adorned notices, with "THWOOM!" and "THWAK!" adding colour to the Gaslamp Quarter sign, and fans could stand behind comic book speech bubbles, containing phrases like "WH–WH … WHAT'S HAPPENING TO MY HAND?!?", allowing them to literally become part of the textual and physical environment. In conjunction with each other, fans and public bodies (such as MTS) contribute to the physical transformation of the city with even the smallest of street furniture becoming part of this textual interplay. On the crosswalk buttons surrounding the convention centre fans stuck painted transfers over the walking man, transforming him from generic street

FIGURE 5.9 Sign at the Gaslamp Quarter trolley stop indicating a Klingon invasion at the 2010 Comic-Con.

sign to *Doctor Who*'s Fifth Doctor (a Peter Davison impression replete with hat, cricket whites and the famous stick of celery) (see Figure 5.11).

Zombie fever has hit Comic-Con in the past two years, with both a hotel chain and local baseball team joining in the fun to help energise the fan experience. Next door to the convention centre on Harbor Drive the San Diego Marriott Marquis and Marina offers both industry and fans convenient (and highly expensive) accommodation. Since many of the events and activities at Comic-Con cannot fit in the convention building, both the Marriott and Hilton Bayfront (on the south side of the convention centre) host panels and events – staging some of the costume competition, gaming booths and film screenings. Both hotels also provide excellent frontage to display giant posters for upcoming film and television releases, dominating the skyline and providing Hollywood a canvas to paint the city in a cult hue (see Figure 5.12). To help the Marriott blend in with its cult surroundings and appeal to the costumed fans who use its facilities, in 2011 the lift doors were adorned with posters for season two of *The Walking Dead* (see Figure 5.13 and Figure 5.14). Yet they are not just advertising billboards. In a recreation of a scene

FIGURE 5.10 The same trolley stop decked out like a page from a comic book at the 2011 Comic-Con.

FIGURE 5.11 A crosswalk button outside the Convention Center transformed into *Doctor Who* themed street art in 2011.

FIGURE 5.12 The south tower of the San Diego Marriott Marquis and Marina in 2010, decked out in advertising for the forthcoming movie *Skyline*; with Optimus Prime standing guard.

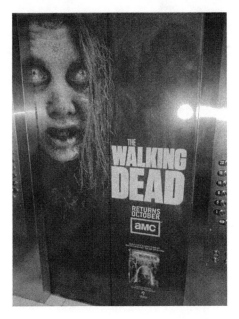

FIGURE 5.13 *The Walking Dead* posters decorating the lifts in the Marriott's north tower in 2010.

FIGURE 5.14 Zombies (or long dead Comic-Con attendees) trying to escape into the Marriott hotel lobby.

from the pilot episode, where Rick Grimes wakes up in an abandoned hospital confronted by a locked morgue, some lifts displayed scrabbling hands giving the appearance that trapped zombies were reaching through the gap with the doors daubed with the painted message "DONT OPEN, DEAD INSIDE". Zombies also appeared to infest Petco Park (home of the San Diego Padres baseball team) in 2012. "Dawn of the Con", sponsored by VH1 Classic and hosted by director Rob Zombie, gave Comic-Con badge holders the opportunity to get into Petco Park for a free music concert with a horror theme. This was preceded by a zombie run competition where volunteers performing as zombies (in full make-up and dress) tried to touch (or "infect") runners who had to traverse obstacles dotted throughout the ballpark, as well as avoid being caught, to reach their escape. The physical environment of the Padres' Petco Park was turned, temporarily, into a post-apocalyptic wasteland that encouraged fans to interact with live performers and a fictional horror space. For those who did not enter the run videos posted on YouTube of people's "death defying" endeavours in the ballpark gave other fans vicarious insight into the themed competition and again highlighted the transformative nature of Comic-Con activities taking place in different parts of the city.

In reconciling the contradictory nature of the fan experience at the San Diego Comic-Con – in their relationship with the objects collected, travelling in and around the physical place of the city, running through Petco Park, entering a themed lift in the Marriott hotel, blogging and tweeting about the panels on a virtual space – we might use the work of Michel Foucault and his conception of the heterotopia. In opposition to the non-physical spaces of utopias, which Foucault feels are "unreal spaces", heterotopias are

> real places – places that do exist and that are formed in the very founding of society – which are something like counter-sites, a kind of effectively enacted utopia in which real sites, all the other real sites that can be found within the culture, are simultaneously represented, contested, and inverted. Places of this kind are outside of all places, even though it may be possible to indicate their location in reality.
>
> *(Foucault, 1986: 24)*

Following Foucault, Ken Gelder sees the heterotopia as imagined "but it also has some kind of realisation, somewhere" (Gelder, 2007: 81). For fans then, the heterotopia is realised in the objects collected during the convention as they combine and simultaneously represent, contest and invert, the physical real place of where there were bought and acquired and the virtual spaces of the web where fans share their experience of the convention, the city and pictures taken. Comic-Con is therefore both things at the same time: a real event and ephemeral experience. Ultimately, all spaces that fan collectors inhabit in San Diego are lived spaces, spaces of possibilities that are at the same non-places (as defined by Augé) and real places. They offer a dialectic space important to communal life and community: absolute, relative and relational (Harvey, 2007: 45). For fan collectors of bought merchandise and give-away souvenirs plucked from industry booths, place and space are in constant flux as individuals within the entire Comic-Con fan community move between the object, convention centre, city and the multiple spaces of their online presence. Fans, in their online activity and conversations between each other in the convention centre, report their experiences and confirm their efforts yet concepts of the fixed space are no longer relevant, particularly in an age of convergence where all things and all people can play with and interpret objects in different ways through different media. The San Diego Comic-Con represents a heterotopia, containing real objects from real places, in which and through which fans can access new worlds, meet new people and travel through different physical spaces – celebrating their passion for popular culture and displaying their investment through the things they wear and collect.

Comic-Con is not just a convention held in one building and one building does not define what Comic-Con is to every person that attends. One must recognise the different spaces that constitute the official convention (panels, booths, Hall H, online chat rooms and other social media) and the geographical places within San Diego (the streets, hotels, bars, restaurants, shops, ball park, trolley stops) since they all act as sites for fan veneration, interaction and production. They have helped make Comic-Con a global and ever-growing heterotopia which attracts industry and fans and yet because there is a multiplicity of space and place no fan experiences the convention in the same way. It is both an individual and communal encounter with the cultural outpourings of the creative industries and yet it manages to offer every fan the opportunity to engage with physical and ephemeral products of popular media culture on a very personal level.

Conclusion

As I have argued throughout this book, and will continue to explore in remaining chapters, the collected objects of popular culture symbolise important aspects of fan identity whose inherent meanings are changed depending on how they are used to construct and maintain said identity. Likewise, in this chapter, I have argued that the spaces in which these objects are collected, venerated, displayed and traded also change depending on how fans use them and interact within them. Concepts of place are always in flux considering the transformative nature of fandom and the thousands of objects and texts consumed, produced and exchanged. Comic-Con changes year on year and San Diego as host city also changes, a new experience for fans every time they go. That so many long-time attendees bemoan the fact that Comic-Con has "grown too big for its own good" and that it has become "too commercialized" suggests on one level that Hollywood has completely taken over (Bowles, 2010: 3D). However, on a deeper level I would argue such complaints indicate that it remains what all fan conventions have historically been for fans: sites for contestation, exploration, and experimentation. Repeated calls for Comic-Con to scale back and reduce the presence of Hollywood intimates that fans still consider it an important place where they, for a few days in July, can be who they dream themselves to be. Physically immerse themselves in media texts they can only imagine for the other 360 days of the year.

Comic-Con clearly means big business for fans and industry executives alike. While consumption is a central activity within the confines of the convention centre, looking outside confirms that fans engage in other activities that are just as important in the creation of an enjoyable and immersive convention experience as purchasing collectibles or sitting in celebrity panels. Fans travelling around the city and attending events attached to Comic-Con, but not actually in Comic-Con, means San Diego also becomes a site of fan pilgrimage and veneration. Fan tourism in this sense is not just about buying lots of stuff and accumulating goods – it is about experiencing a geography of the popular which become a safe and familiar space for fans to celebrate who they are and interact with their favourite media texts. Cities are usually considered traditional sites of consumption (with businesses, malls, shops, restaurants, bars, etc.), emphasising the dominance of a consumer society. However, San Diego as site of consumption does not just offer outlets for commerce and profit and Comic-Con is not about selling Hollywood merchandise. As Steven Miles argues about the city, "they provide spaces within which we negotiate our own symbolic relationship with consumer society"; and as such we are free to create our own identities defined by the things we collect, buy, trade and sell: "Spaces for consumption are effectively the arenas within which the emotions, dreams and wounds of a consumer society are played out" (Miles, 2010: 184). What Comic-Con shows us is that memories of and nostalgia for media texts from yesteryear contribute to the negotiation between fans as creators and consumers, individuals and members of a community. San Diego as a city takes on new meanings for every fan that goes there because it is not defined by mere consumption; it is defined by what the fans and industry do creatively within that space.

6

PLAYING WITH THE FORCE

Fan Identity, Cultural Capital and *Star Wars* Toy Collecting

This chapter examines the cultural and social importance of one particular aspect of the *Star Wars* franchise: the toys. Specifically, I suggest that the action figures bought, sold, and collected around the world are an intrinsic part of the *Star Wars* franchise universe and its meaning making. The commercial success of the 3¾-inch action figures is well known. In previous work I contended that the production and collecting of *Star Wars* toys from the first trilogy of films represented a return to the tradition of war "play" in American youth culture (see Geraghty, 2006). This was in response to America's own lack of self-security after defeat in Vietnam and the effects of the "end of victory culture" as described by Tom Engelhardt (1995). Those children who watched the films and then played with the action figures were participating in a "fictional world" created by adults (the toy company, the government, and the parents who bought the toys) that represented a redressed and revised form of reality in which the psychic wounds of Vietnam could be healed.

As the original films passed into Hollywood legend and the prequels moved to the forefront of Lucas's mind, *Star Wars* fandom continued to thrive and toy collection became an integral part of belonging to and participating in adult fan groups just as it still remained part of traditional child "play". As the children who once played with Luke and Leia were growing up and learning the fiscal advantages of having kept some of them sealed in their original packaging, notions of "war play" were changing due to the reactionary nature of contemporary American foreign policy. Adults who used to play with the original action figures did not necessarily understand them to be representative of the American national consciousness, or part of a specific reaction to American military action overseas. As the franchise grew and new toys were released to coincide with the three new prequels, issues over fan collecting became far more significant than the experience of playing at war. Therefore, I argued that the production and collection of toys in the late 1990s and early 2000s represented a new form of cultural capital where fans collected the actions figures as part of their, as Anthony Giddens (1991) would say, "self-identity" and at the same time claimed some form of personal ownership over the *Star Wars* movies and texts (Geraghty, 2006: 210). *Star Wars* toy collecting is about constructing an identity as a fan and creating new meanings from a pre-established universe. The acts of preserving objects from childhood, accumulating new additions and creating new toys from old are all part of expressing one's own *Star Wars* fandom and claiming some form of individual ownership over a franchise that is adored by millions and controlled, until recently, by one person: George Lucas.

It is my intention in this chapter to develop some of the ideas introduced in my previous work on *Star Wars* toy collecting and understand more fully the importance of the physical object to the collector and how each toy takes on new meanings brought to bear by the individual. Where I had acknowledged the influence of war play on previous interpretations of meaning with the original toy action figures I would want to posit in this chapter that the act of collecting and recollecting these objects from youth overrides any and all possible culturally embedded meanings. For Fiona Candlin and Raiford Guins "objects have symbolic functions, embodying and representing our gods and spirits, averting demons and encapsulating memory" but they also "have social meanings". These meanings can be used to "assert status or power, circulate value, demarcate our habitats and habits ... as well as to connect us to and disconnect us from friends, colleagues or strangers" (2009: 1). Therefore, with these qualities in mind, I want to re-examine *Star Wars* toys and the collecting of them within the contexts of material culture and the processes of meaning making that collectors undergo with every object in their collection.

Toys as Important Objects

Within scholarship on material culture and the study of objects there is debate on the extent to which objects should be understood as pieces of social history or things devoid of meaning and outside the contexts of social life. Arjun Appadurai contends that "human actors encode things with significance" and "it is the things-in-motion that illuminate their human and social context" (1986: 5). Therefore, the collecting of *Star Wars* action figures and other merchandise, bought and sold online, at conventions or in stores, is about object being in motion and accumulating human and social significance as each object comes to be in the possession of an individual with their own story to tell and their own reasons for buying and collecting. Objects from history "accumulate meanings as time passes" but are also "active and passive" in meaning making as the viewer/owner learns more about them and observes them in a continued state of preservation and display (Pearce, 1994: 19). Christopher Pinney sees the socialisation of objects as an inevitable outcome of prioritising the subject and the social. Objects "can only ricochet between the essentialized autonomous object and the dematerialized space of things whose only graspable qualities are their 'biographies' and 'social lives'" (Pinney, 2005: 259). Yet, what appears to be missing from his interpretation of objects and their meaning is the impact the collected object has on the collector, how the object works to change the individual and their own personal story – who they are and where they have come from.

Susan Pearce's work on objects as meaning contends that they help to narrate the past, the past of the physical object and also the owner's. They fill in the blanks of an individual's personal history but also the act of collecting and preserving the object helps to fill in the blanks of its own story that remain unfilled until confronted by the collector or viewer. Thus, while objects might be reduced to having qualities bound by the owner's biography and social life, the historical nature of such object (whether it be passed down through generations of the same family, changing hands in the same generation, or moving from maker to collector as in the case of *Star Wars* toys) assures that meaning is always changing and the blanks can never be fully filled. Objects are dynamic and their stories never fully told as history, and collectors construct new narratives of ownership and meaning:

> As the viewer stands in front of the showcase, he makes use of the various perspectives which the object offers him, some of which have already been suggested: his creative urges are set in motion, his imagination is engaged, and the dynamic process of interpretation and reinterpretation begins, which extends far beyond the mere perception of what the object is. The object activates our own faculties, and the product of this creativity is the virtual dimension of the object, which endows it with present reality. The message or meaning which the object offers is always incomplete and each viewer fills in the gaps in his own way, thereby excluding other possibilities: as he looks he makes his own decisions about how the story is to be told.
>
> *(Pearce, 1994: 26)*

It is through the lens of the object as meaning that I want to analyse those examples of *Star Wars* toy collecting I discussed in previous work and extend my focus on the collector/object relationship to include a case study of self-confessed *Star Wars* historian and the biggest collector of franchise related ephemera, Stephen J. Sansweet. Before I do so I will discuss some of the contemporary media scholarship on toys and merchandising that has been published since my first work and consider the processes of meaning making recent scholars suggest are integral to the interpretation of media objects.

Toys as Paratexts

The first steps toward a wider consideration of consumer products like *Star Wars* toys and the relationship between the fans and their object of fandom is to acknowledge the prominent position of what Jonathan Gray calls media *paratexts* as opposed to the centrality of specific *texts*. Indeed, we are now accustomed in fan studies to state that the productivity of fans and their related fan practices represents an appropriate and worthy text to study just as much as the original media text to which they are related or inspired. So, rather than studying *Star Wars* as cult text, we might study fan produced videos on YouTube as important texts of fan activity that carry inherent meaning and significance in and of themselves. However, the peripheral texts – those associated with the commercialisation of the franchise or brand such as the lunchboxes, toys, video games, and websites – are so much part of the meaning making process that they become texts to study in their own right. Gray argues that "the paratexts may in time *become* the text, as the audience's members take their cues regarding what a text means from the paratext's images, signs, symbols, and words" rather than from the original (Gray, 2010: 46). Therefore, in relation to the *Star Wars* toys and the collector community, what the fans buy, make, transform and display online are crucial and interconnected parts of the entire *Star Wars* phenomenon and need to be analysed to fully understand the toys' appeal and fan nostalgia for them.

In *Show Sold Separately* Gray discusses the importance of branded merchandise such as toy action figures in that they can assume and carry new meanings beyond those intended by the media industries. Extending the narrative, taking it away from the cinema screen and bringing it into the home, means *Star Wars* as a closed text becomes open and replete with multiple meanings. He acknowledges the first stage of meaning making in childhood, using the work of Dan Fleming (1996), to argue that the "action figures underscore the plural in [*Star Wars*], declaring the central frame and theme to be that of a never-ending series of grand and cosmic battles of mythic proportions" (Gray, 2010: 180). So, again using Fleming, the popular effect of the *Star Wars* figures can be in part due to what he calls "narrativisation"; whereby toy versions of TV and movie characters, such as the Lone Ranger and Tonto, represented both the specific series and familiar stories and relationships informed playing with the toy: "Throughout the 1960s the toy industry became increasingly dependent on cinema and, especially, on television for play-worthy objects that could borrow the popularity of a screen character or story. Such objects then came with a narrative attached" (Fleming, 1996: 102). Narrativisation helps children interact with fictional reality, or make-believe, during play. This creates what Fleming terms "a semiotic space" (201) where toys can act as transitional tools allowing children to experiment with their own developing identities and understand the adult world (202).

Returning to Gray, where the toys remain in circulation – collected by the parents that still buy their children a lightsabre for Christmas – it means that as texts themselves they have become just as important to the continued proliferation of *Star Wars* merchandise and the ever-reaching influence it has on contemporary popular culture. They assume primary status as paratexts in the world of the fan and thus acquire important and unique meaning in the life story of that fan, as suggested by Susan Pearce in her work on objects and narrative histories. Gray argues that in passing on the toy, from parent to child, what adults were handing over as a gift was "their own nostalgically remembered relationship with the text that came at least in part from the toys" (2010: 185). An assertion similar to Gary Cross's where he argues that in giving toys as gifts parents were attempting to pass on part of their childhood to their offspring, as a sign of generational transference and moral guidance (1997: 44). Still, when the toy remains part of the adult world, treasured as part of one's fan identity and valuable collection, they take on new significance. Their mass-market nature does not detract from or destabilise the meanings inscribed by the fan onto their collection. Preserving the toy that is meant to be played with in pristine condition (in plastic, on a shelf, locked behind glass) is a sign of the value fans put on paratextual artefacts, it tells us that "the uses of objects cannot always be culturally predicted or assumed, even (or perhaps especially) mass-producted [sic], mass-marketed objects" (Hills, 2009b).

In her study of the Hello Kitty phenomenon in Japan, where cuteness (*kawaii*) is marketed to both young children and adults through consumer goods, cartoons, and fan clubs, Christine Yano explains that the toy brand "becomes a form of selfhood" where experiences of it in childhood are "retrieved from the past through goods, connecting friend to friend" (2004: 64). Adults that continue to buy Kitty products embody the *kawaii* and enact it every day through their engagement with fellow fans, wearing of Kitty T-shirts and display of Kitty toys at work (see also McVeigh, 1996, 1997, 2000). Likewise, in the continued collecting and playing with *Star Wars*, adult fans are constructing and reconstructing a form of selfhood, or identity, that connects them with periods of their own lives and initiates them into a community of fans who are doing exactly the same. This might at first appear problematic in that someone would want to build an identity around an ephemeral consumer product, but the reconnection with a valued toy is not simply about recycling consumption. It is about sharing stories with other fans in the *Star Wars* community; it is about a shared childhood experience. No different, in many ways, to fans of a sports team or television show who connect with other fans through the shared experiences of social media, going to a game or watching TV.

For Jason Bainbridge, the possibility for children's entertainment to become part of adult culture has always been present but the fact that these toys are an integral part of the textual/paratextual world of the franchise brand means they are points of "intersection for adult pleasures and childish fantasies, structured narratives and free-ranging play, material culture and digital culture – and through this breaking down of barriers, arguably become one of the most potent (if overlooked) symbols of media convergence" (2012: 41). While I agree with Bainbridge's sentiments, and will continue to explore in relation to *Star Wars* fans in the remainder of this chapter, I would want to stress that he is not the first to make this observation. Scholars mentioned in this chapter already – Jonathan Gray, Matt Hills, Dan Fleming, Ellen Seiter (1995), Gary Cross and myself – have discussed the importance of toys as symbols of media diffusion and adult meaning making. Likewise, Bob Rehak, in a recent article on monster movie merchandise, toys and model kits, argues that such physical ephemera help map the history of fantastic media franchises and that ignoring the material incarnations of film and television texts means we lose an understanding of their cultural persistence and commercial viability. "Object practices", such as modelling, collecting, making and modifying, bring to the fore "the physical artefacts and processes by which popular culture both remembers and recreates itself" (Rehak, 2013: 43). Therefore, it is to such *Star Wars* related object practices that I now wish to turn my attention.

Creating an Industry

The impact that the *Star Wars* figures had on the toy industry was phenomenal, "in 1978 Kenner sold over 26 million figures; by 1985, 250 million". Profits from the toys, figures, lunchboxes, and video games eventually totalled $2.5 billion by the end of the first three films (Engelhardt, 1995: 269). This was in addition to the huge takings at the box office where *Star Wars: Episode IV – A New Hope* (1977) would follow Steven Spielberg's lead with *Jaws* (1975) and *Close Encounters of the Third Kind* (1977) and achieve blockbuster status. *A New Hope*, which only cost $11 million to make, "began as a summer movie, ran continuously into 1978, and was re-released in 1979". It earned "over $190 million in U.S. rentals and about $250 million worldwide, on total ticket sales of over $500 million" (Thompson and Bordwell, 2003: 522). It is no secret that Lucas kept the rights to the merchandise in order to get the film made, and no doubt has been smiling ever since, yet what is important about the first movie is that it helped to cement the summer blockbuster as part of American film culture and make merchandising an integral part of the Hollywood production plan. Jeremy Beckett (2005: 5–17) and Stephen Sansweet (2009: 22–7, 2012: 6–9) offer detailed histories of *Star Wars* merchandising, licensing agreements and the growth of the collectible market; interestingly, they both identify dips in popularity during the 1980s when few new products were being made – which at the same time drives up the value and rarity of those items that fans consider highly desirable.

Justin Wyatt sees *Star Wars* as a high concept franchise, the first to really approach toy merchandising with vigour, and, as a result, increase its market appeal. Although, quite rightly, Eric Greene has pointed out that *Planet of the Apes* (1968) created a similar buzz around its toy and comic merchandise (1998: 164–9) and S. Mark Young (2012: 159–60) sees the legacy of toys produced for *Buck Rogers* and 1950s TV series such as *Captain Video and His Video Rangers* (1949–55), *Rocky Jones, Space Ranger* (1954), *Space Patrol* (1950–5), *Tom Corbett, Space Cadet* (1950–5) and *Captain Z-Ro* (1954–60) still attracting adult collectors today. For Wyatt, the "high concept" movie was an important part of the New Hollywood film industry. High concept films are those that are conceived as highly marketable, and therefore highly profitable, as well as being visually striking and stylistically innovative. Such films, for example *A New Hope*, are different through their "emphasis on style in production and through the integration of the film with its marketing" (1994: 20). In terms of the *Star Wars* features, we can describe them as "high concept" since they are comprised of what Wyatt labels "the look, the hook, and the book": "The look of the images, the marketing hooks, and the reduced narratives" (22). The fictional world of Star Wars that had kept children engrossed for two hours also had underlying marketing advantages: "The film's novel environment and characters have been so striking that Kenner Toys has been able to go beyond the figures in the film by adding new characters to the Star Wars line in keeping with the film's mythological world" (153). The infinite potential for expansion kept the figures popular throughout the 1980s as children continued to watch and re-watch the movies and play with their own make-believe worlds. A contemporary franchise example of this would be the 2D animated series Star Wars: Clone Wars (2003–5) and its CGI follow up, Star Wars: The Clone Wars (2008–present), which have produced their own brand images and tie-in products (Clone Wars action figures, DVDs, and books) as diversification within diversification – a fictional universe within a fictional universe.

Evidence for the Kenner toys' impact on the toy industry can be seen in the proliferation of toys and cartoons created in the early 1980s modelled on the Star Wars theme of rebel heroes versus evil empire: Kenner's own M.A.S.K. (1985–6), Hasbro's The Transformers (1984–7) and Mattel's He-Man (1983–5) to name a few. These new futuristic and fantastic worlds showed war without human loss, machines doing the fighting, and technology saving the day. Star Wars-size figures "were transported into millions of homes where new-style war scenarios could be played out" without acknowledging America's delicate position after Vietnam (Engelhardt, 1995: 269). In 1982 even G.I. Joe had a makeover with Hasbro making the figures 3¾ inches and deciding to create a new, faceless enemy (COBRA) for America's heroic fighting force to be screened in an animated TV series, G.I. Joe: A Real American Hero (1983–7). Each Joe would be an individual team member with their own identity and personality; as with the Star Wars toys, children could collect and play with a range of figures that represented variations of good, evil, skill, and visual appeal. "War play on 'Earth'", as opposed to the "alien" play of Star Wars, "would be in the reconstructionist mode" supported by collector's cards, TV cartoons, movies, video games, and comics. Children were now totally ensconced within a manufactured world, with war as the background and America still victorious (Engelhardt, 1995: 284). Extending the war play metaphor to a post-9/11 context David Machin and Theo van Leeuwen (2009: 62) contend that contemporary military toys emphasise "individualism, the small flexible team able to operate swiftly" in reaction to unforeseen threats as seen in the attacks on New York and Washington DC and America's war on terror.

Toying with Identity

For Kendall Walton, as children grow up, their props (transitional objects) within their fictional world of make-believe, dolls, hobbyhorses, toy trucks, and teddy bears, are transformed as part of adult life: "The forms make-believe activities take do change significantly as we mature. They become more subtle, more sophisticated, less overt" (Walton, 1990: 12). Therefore, for children growing up imagining themselves part of the *Star Wars* universe, the toys are integral props in the make-believe relationship they have with that fictional world. Playing and collecting the toys affirms and brings the *Star Wars* story to life. Consequently, those adults that used to play with the robots begin to have a more complex relationship with the toys they collected as children. They are no longer seen as objects of play but as markers of their personal memories of childhood, as well as symbols of subcultural capital, that can be bought and traded within a fan community. There are multiple readings to be made about the playing with, and collecting of, *Star Wars* related merchandise, the most significant now being that adult fans are collecting them as part of their own search for personal memory. Art historian Michael Camille views collecting as "a socially creative and recuperative act", where the identity of the collector is self-fashioned through the accumulation of collectibles (cited in Monaghan, 2002: A18). The following extracts from a range of fan websites, blogs and fan produced merchandise highlight the ways in which *Star Wars* has for some fans become an integral part of personal memory, and how a child's television show and toy has remained a valuable asset in modern day life. After all, as Roland Barthes observed in *S/Z* (1975) about the nature of the text:

> Rereading is no longer consumption, but play (that play which is the return of the different). If then, a deliberate contradiction in terms, we *immediately* reread the text, it is in order to obtain, as though under the effect of a drug (that of recommencement, of difference), not the *real* text, but a plural text: the same and the new.
>
> *(16)*

In other words, there are multiple readings to be made about the playing with, and collecting of, *Star Wars* action figures, the most significant now being that adult fans of all nationalities are collecting them as part of their own search for personal identity. Collecting is less a pathology centred on economic consumption and more of a process, where the identity of the collector is self-fashioned through the accumulation of collectibles. For Jeremy Beckett, life-long *Star Wars* fan and toy enthusiast, adults collect the action figures because of one of three reasons: the renewed interest in the franchise created by the prequels, suffering the "Peter Pan Syndrome" (i.e. trying to recapture one's youth), or getting involved in a phenomenon that "has encompassed hundreds of millions of people around the world" (2005: 4). Whereas the second reason sees collectors returning to a nostalgic personal past where they played with toys and re-enacted scenes from the movies, the first and third reasons hinge on the collector never having experienced the thrill of the original toys or movies because they neither could afford nor have permission to buy them in the first place. In other words, the *Star Wars* collector chooses to collect the toys – they might not necessarily be connected to any past history as a child – and thus the act can be inferred as something which is more about the community or environment in which the collecting takes place rather than about the objects themselves. Beckett points to this external influence in his comment about the collecting community: "Luckily for me *Star Wars* has not only led me to have a room full of colorful plastic toys, but it has also provided me with a multitude of highly educated, knowledgeable, and articulate friends and colleagues" (2005: ix).

In terms of sales figures, before the May 2005 release of *Revenge of the Sith* the franchise had accumulated $9 billion for the merchandising (Abraham, 2005) and $3.4 billion in worldwide box-office receipts (Crawford, 2005). During the March run up to *Revenge of the Sith*, Krysten Crawford pointed out in "The Jedi Jackpot" for CNN/Money.com that Darth Vader was unsurprisingly the focal point to the merchandising tie-ins. For the prequels, the action figures and play sets were specifically targeted at two markets: the children's toy market and the adult collector. The latter was undeniably the one that the toy industry saw as the "cash cow". According to Jim Silver, an industry expert, "in terms of action figures, *Star Wars* has the biggest collector base of any brand" and license holders have been able to bank on that base, no matter the age, buying the latest new release (quoted in Crawford, 2005). However, for Jonathan David Tankel and Keith Murphy collecting "collectible" artefacts has become more than just trying to make money from the nostalgic yearnings of some die-hard fans: "For the fan, the potential for profit at some future date, while always present as in any economic transaction, is often overshadowed by the value created by the ownership of the artefact in the present" (1998: 56). John Fiske sees "the accumulation of both popular and official cultural capital", signalled through the fan collection (records, toys, books, etc.), as the "point where cultural and economic capital come together" (1992: 43). In other words, fans of popular culture such as *Star Wars* or The Beatles and avid buffs of official culture such as opera or fine art share the same desire to both know as much as they can about their subject and to collect as much physical material as they can (42–3). A simple search on eBay notched up hundreds of potential purchases of rare, yet more often common, *Star Wars* action figures: I searched for stormtroopers and found 218 hits ranging from an original priced at $2.75 to a "The Power of the Force" version priced at $5.00 and a vintage re-issue priced at $9.95 to a selection of original stormtroopers, biker scouts (*Return of the Jedi*, 1983) and snowtroopers (*The Empire Strikes Back*, 1980) somewhat overpriced at $69. There is obviously a fan market where profit is important, nevertheless, it seemed more significant that there was also a community where fans got together to not only trade but also discuss the implications of their passion for collecting toys that they used to play with as children. Annette Kuhn's term "enduring fandom" (as discussed in relation to Hollywood memorabilia and collectibles in chapter two) would seem applicable here, although she defines it as "loyalty to a star" throughout a fan's life "beyond the star's death" (135), it is quite clear that *Star Wars* fans are still loyal to their childhood plastic play-mates even after they have reached adulthood. It is to this type of fandom and fan community which I will now turn; specifically, identifying and examining the collecting practices of *Star Wars* toy collectors and the meanings those toys assume when made part of a collection.

Collecting and Creating

For Susan Pearce there are three predominant modes of collecting – souvenir, fetishistic and systematic (1995). In souvenir collecting, "the individual creates a romantic life-history by selecting and arranging personal memorial material to create … an object autobiography". These objects remain in service to the collector, they don't define them. With fetishistic collectors "the objects are dominant and the collector responds to his obsessive need by gathering as many items as possible". For Pearce, these objects than create a sense of self. The third type of collector, the systematic, follows a rationale for collecting – perhaps to complete a set which demonstrates "understanding achieved" (32). All three types of collecting might appear at the same time, elements contributing to the comprehension of what, why, when and how somebody put together a group of objects they see as a collection. Thus, in the examples discussed below, we might observe that while *Star Wars* fans collect as part of a need to complete a set or obtain every item released by Kenner they might also buy items that represent something more personal. A rare item acquired during a trip to a convention, specially made for the occasion and of a limited production run, or an item that fits particularly into the individual fan's collection, the one toy they never managed to get when younger but now made available through intense research, hours spent on eBay and access to increased funds.

Indeed, for Beckett we can see in his reasons for collecting *Star Wars* memorabilia (remaining loyal to the franchise from childhood, acquiring an intense knowledge of the merchandise over the years, and having special access to items as an author of the "official" price guide) a mixture of all three types of collector outlined by Pearce. *Star Wars* toys both define and are defined by him: his memories of playing with the originals as a kid define them as objects of his past but his hints and tips at how to be a good collector and suggestion that one needs to decide what type of merchandise to collect before you start out (Beckett, 2005: 34) indicates a systematic approach to the hobby and that the collection defines him as a person in some small part – he is, after all, setting himself up as an expert by producing a price guide for fellow fans. Beckett is not alone in his passion for collecting *Star Wars* toys and is not unique in displaying all three characteristics of the collector. Without fellow enthusiasts access to and availability of memorabilia would no doubt reduce, so collector fairs and conventions (as discussed in the previous chapter) become important sites for trade and information exchange. What happens when rival collectors and sellers convene to increase the size of their collection and make a living reveals interesting parallels between the organised nature of an established fan community and the structures put in place that drive the fan collector to continue their efforts.

In 2003 the official *Star Wars* fan club in Mexico put together a convention to celebrate 25 years of *Star Wars* toy collecting. Fans and collectors from all over the world gathered in Mexico City to see, trade, and talk about the latest toys as well as the classics; what *Star Wars* fan Dustin calls in his conference diary, "*Star Wars*

Collectors Convention in Mexico City" (2003), as "pure heaven". This convention attracted "celebrity" collectors, described as "Super Collectors" by Dustin, who even signed autographs for fans eager to hear about their collecting and toy anecdotes. This particular revelation was interesting since it is well documented that fans have great admiration for the stars of their favourite films and programs, yet it slightly alters the fan/star relationship when the "star" is a collector like themselves. Quite clearly, toy collecting fans have created their own hierarchy of esteem that includes the actors and producers of *Star Wars* but also members of their own community. In this case, making your own bootleg versions "brings the collector heightened status (within his or her collecting sphere) and feelings of pride and accomplishment" (Belk, 1995: 68).

Those, like Joseph Iglesias, who have collected toys since childhood astounded Dustin because he was fascinated to hear about bootleg copies of his favourite figures: "From Brazilian figures made out of lead to the infamous Uzay 'Head Man' Joe [Joseph] seems to be on top of it all." *Star Wars* toy collecting has become a real universe within the fictional universe created by the franchise: collector Joe can make his own Brazilian versions of famous figures, the Turkish company Uzay can make affordable bootleg figures to sell all over the world, and Kenner can produce an exclusive members-only "*Star Wars* Convention Exclusive Silver Boba Fett with Star Case" that was distributed in Mexico City, yet all are in great demand. Exclusivity is clearly paramount when it comes to bootleg and special issue figures and this clearly corresponds with Russell Belk's description of competition within collecting circles. In a consumer society where success is often measured by material gain, the collection itself can often emphasise collector competition where monetary value and the number of objects act as "a way to 'keep score' or monitor growth and progress, even though [collectors] may well have no intention or even a possibility of selling the collection" (Belk, 1995: 80).

This example implies that *Star Wars* toy collectors follow similar patterns of fandom and belonging to a community, where entry and status can depend on expressions of fan expertise and/or creativity. Fan communities are often deeply hierarchical and involve a systematised structure of subcultural taste and political discourse which Mark Jancovich terms "cult distinction" in his 2002 article on cult movie fans (306–7). These discourses of taste and distinction are rooted in the personal value fans attach to the central media text and its associated paratexts. Fans either produce a sense of distinction between themselves and the mainstream (non-fans), defining the fan community in opposition to how they are constructed by other groups and the media, or they distinguish levels of fandom amongst the group, testing status and knowledge through quizzes and accumulation of rare goods. Likewise, both Matt Hills and Lynn Zubernis and Katherine Larsen recognise the importance of established hierarchies in fandom. For Hills, fan culture can be seen "not simply as a community but *also as a social hierarchy* where fans share a common interest while also competing over fan knowledge, access to the object of fandom, and status" (2002: 46). Fans are competitive. Zubernis and Larsen posit that where "academics were reluctant to recognize hierarchies in fandom", seeing it as being supportive of difference, aggressive behaviour within fan groups online and at conventions indicates a high level of policing in the community known as "wank" (2012: 13).

Personal attacks between fans could relate to the outward emotion one fan displays towards their favourite star or show but in the case of collectors I would argue it rests on the comparisons between collections or how one person obtained a hard to find object. Beckett devotes a lot of space in his guide for *Star Wars* collectors warning people about scalpers, those who drive up the price of memorabilia by buying cheap at retail price and doubling their margin at conventions, and against buying fakes or reproductions, since they could be misrepresented at resale by someone wanting to earn a dishonest profit. Descriptions of the "Collect to Collect" credo show that collectors do try to police the hobby so that people are not cheated from acquiring special items or forced to pay too much. Beckett suggests that while scalping is not illegal, "in the long run it can only hurt the community and the hobby" and it "promotes decay" (2005: 46).

Similarly, he argues that while reproductions might help collectors fill a gap in their collection current owners might deceive future buyers by selling on an item they know not to be authentic, this being "dangerous to the hobby" (77). While being first and foremost a price guide these examples of policing the *Star Wars* collecting community suggest that Beckett's book acts also as a moral guide to the continued success and communal spirit of *Star Wars* toy collecting. That there are certain rules and codes to the hobby make it more of a systematic endeavour than individual collectors might acknowledge in their own personal choices for collecting. Whether they collect to achieve completion, remember past times or obtain rare items, conflicting stories of competition and camaraderie within the community seem to define the nature of *Star Wars* toy collecting. Rules that might appear the antithesis of what collectors do, "Buy only what you need and make sure others get one before you get many" and "Help others achieve their collecting goals for the sake of the hobby, not profit" for example (46), give meaning to the very act of collecting these mass-produced commodities. The objects themselves are enhanced by the fact that they encourage collectors to think beyond their own collection and look to how it represents the *Star Wars* community as a whole; the collection itself is a paratextual element within the textual world of *Star Wars* fandom.

According to Beckett the "Turkish line of Uzay bootleg figures is without a doubt the most well-known line of *Star Wars* bootlegs in the world". The specific figure mentioned by Dustin, "Head Man", is an ultra rare figure based on the official Emperor's Royal Guard figure from *Return of the Jedi* but with a chromed head and shield (Beckett, 2005: 209). The "*Star Wars* Convention Exclusive Silver Boba Fett with Star Case" is also available online with Amazon.com if you live in the United States or Canada. These specialist items give status to the maker and the collector and the fact mass-produced toys are made unique through modifying suggests, as does Paul Martin with regard to the act of collecting, that it "can be seen as a means of individualizing the uniformity of the mass produced. In a consumer society, we all look for ways to alleviate the routine of the functional. In collecting, a certain depth or another dimension is found" (1999: 146–7). Modding, bootlegging and MOC action figures, My Own Creations, are often central to a fan's collection because of the very fact that it makes theirs different to others. Indeed, the making of the modified toy adds even more personal value to the object as it stands as an intermediate between the mass produced and the uniquely created; helping "to close the symbolic gap between 'ordinary' cultural life and 'extra-ordinary' media fiction … [T]he materiality of toys makes them especially useful in this respect they quite literally materialise the immaterial and the intangible" (Hills, 2009b).

Furthermore, Joe's and Uzay's appropriation and modification of what Tom Engelhardt (1995) has described as a very American product, is similar to the relationship scrutinised by some scholars between international women and the American Barbie doll. Barbie was first released in 1959 and quickly became a homogenised American idol. But what is interesting for Pamela Thoma (1999) and J. Paige MacDougall (2003) in their studies of Barbie collecting around the world is that Barbie's meaning was changed and adapted to suit personal and international tastes. Thoma's study of beauty pageants argues that Asian American girls used Barbie's glamorous image as a template for their own "transnational feminism"; in other words, gaining acceptance in a stereotypically white female environment. Ann DuCille has also looked at the Barbie doll in terms of African American female identity and commented that black Barbie dolls have problematised race and racial issues in America: "The particulars of black Barbie illustrate the difficulties and dangers of treating race and gender differences as biological stigmata that can be fixed in plastic and mass-reproduced" (1996: 57).

MacDougall goes further and argues that appropriation of the Barbie doll in Mexico offered young girls a "local identity rather than emulating the meanings and values she was attributed by Mattel" (2003: 257). Through a process of "creolization" consumers in the Yucatan region of Mexico gave their Barbies new Mayan identities, complete with self-woven traditional dresses: "Overall, the creolization of Barbie dolls in this context demonstrates the power of consumer agency to contain global images within local systems of meaning" (273). Both of these studies, and the example of Joe turning *Star Wars* figures in Brazil into per-sonalised bootlegged collectibles, follow David Hesmondhalgh's analysis of the cultural industries where he asserts that local markets can compete with the hegemonic forces of American cultural imperialism, for example Latin American *Telenovelas* (2002: 182–3). Local and personal identities act in opposite ways to the American meanings inscribed at the point of production. Similarly, for artists who make designer toys, resistance to the dominant design and production of the mass-pro-duced toys means "material objects or things may function as nodes through which to transform the proliferating networks of images, things and the agents that bind them within late capitalist consumption" (Steinberg, 2010: 211). The fans at the Mexico City convention were working out a new identity in relation to their favourite collectibles, not one based on a particular political viewpoint, but one based on postmodern concepts of self-identity and society. This in turn situates those fans outside the dominant capitalist model of consumption where making your own figures and modifying commodities inverts the structure of production and consumption with the fan on top over the toy industry. It is ironic that collectors have chosen to use a licensed corporate product to define their identity, yet one might call it a form of surrender to the influences of American cultural hegemony.

However, the fact that collectors also go beyond the boundaries set by Lucas and Kenner, creating their own versions of figures, buying and selling bootleg copies that are just as rare as official figures and revered in equal measure, signals that the hegemonic framework does not necessarily hold true when examined on a global scale. Collectors all over the world dip in and out of the imagined fantasy world of *Star Wars*; adding to and expanding the universe created by Lucas. We might even see fan craftwork and creativity, in making new figures from parts of old or redesigning established characters to fit within the fans' vision of how their favourite figure should look, as emblematic of David Gauntlett's concept of "making is connecting". Even in an age of increased digital domination and creativity, with the Internet and social media allowing people to edit, cut, make, colour, and create any manner of visual media product, he argues the "resurgence of interest in craft activities, clubs, and fairs" intimates a continued attraction to the non-virtual world where an emphasis on recycling and the reuse of material propels people to be more imaginative and resourceful (Gauntlett, 2011:13). Additionally, the effort that goes into making and doing, building and crafting suggests that pleasure is found in the process, not the product of one's labours (70). While an appreciation of the cultural contexts in which *Star Wars* fans remake and modify toy figures can give us insight into their hobby as a craft (being an offline rather than online activity), examples discussed in this chapter would also indicate that makers of bootleg figures do get pleasure from the product as well as the process since it brings them both income and hierarchical status in the fan collector community. Indeed, their craftwork gives them a different sense of identity distinct from other fans that collect but do not sell, display but do not make.

In his explorations of the dilemmas of modern selfhood, Anthony Giddens sees "What to do?", "How to act?", "Who to be?" as the "focal questions for everyone living in circumstances of late modernity [the here and now]". As well as asking these questions people try to answer them "either discursively or through day-to-day social behaviour" (1991: 70). In what Giddens calls "the trajectory of the self" people are constantly trying to define themselves and their self-identity through reflexive examination of their "life-cycle" (14). In the *Star Wars* fantasy world, the collector-fan's self-identity is in a constant state of reflexive examination as new films are released, toys are produced, and conventions are organised. Beckett, Dustin, Joe, and all the "star collectors" adapt and change their lives as they write about and interact with the new toys they collect as well as meet and trade with fellow collectors. Joe makes new bootleg copies to sell and display at conventions, people like Todd Chamberlain give lectures on the art of making vintage display cases (quoted in Dustin), and Dustin himself feels he "can hold [his] own now after hearing these guys talk about" collecting "Lili-Ledy" collectibles. *Star Wars* toys, and all their related packaging and display paraphernalia, carry intensely individualised personal meanings that define who these fan collectors are and help guide their own "trajectory of the self". For Janet Hoskins, "an object can thus become more than simply a 'metaphor for the self.' It becomes a pivot for reflexivity and introspection, a tool of autobiographic self-discovery, a way of knowing oneself through things" (1998, 198). Similarly, Cornell Sanvoss' study of fandom suggests "the more that approaches to fandom emphasize the element of the reader's self in the construction of meaning", or in terms of this study, their determination to collect all the figures and toys available, "the greater the degree of polysemy [multiple readings] they imply". Self-reflection in fandom has often been taken to mean that texts become a blank screen on which fans reflect their own self-image; they "are *poly*semic to a degree that they become *neutro*semic – in other words, carry no inherent meaning". Sandvoss asserts that "neutosemy" is the "semiotic condition in which a text allows for so many divergent readings that, inter-subjectively, it does not have any meaning at all" (2005: 126). *Star Wars* toys then do not carry inherent meanings, collecting and modifying them in pursuit of self-identity creates the meaning.

From Collector to Curator: The Case of Stephen J. Sansweet

As I argued above, within the *Star Wars* fan collector community there are often hierarchies of fandom that suggest status is achieved through the amount of objects collected and the levels of creativity employed to make new and modified collectibles out of old. Without a doubt the most successful and renowned *Star Wars* fan collector is Stephen J. Sansweet, whose collection of franchise related objects has given him special access to the George Lucas inner circle, afforded him the opportunity to write 16 books on *Star Wars*, and, ultimately, allowed him to turn his hobby into his day job. Admitting he does not know the exact figure of how many items are in his collection (in 2009 an inventory to that date had counted 55,352 items in the database [Sansweet, 2009: 18]) the sheer size of his collection is enhanced by his knowledge of the history of every toy, branded object and marketing curio ever produced. As an authority on the franchise he has achieved a status almost on the same level as Lucas himself. In 2011 he retired as the Director of Content Management and Head of Fan Relations at Lucasfilm, having performed the role for 15 years, and opened up Rancho Obi-Wan, a 9,000 square foot former chicken farm turned museum in Sonoma County California, so that he could share his immense collection with other fans.

Sansweet's privileged position as Head of Fan Relations at Lucasfilm meant he was heavily involved in the marketing of the re-released Special Editions of the original trilogy in the late 1990s. He also helped set up the annual worldwide and popular Celebration conventions that gave fans greater access to the stars, creators and artists of the *Star Wars* world. Going from fan (situated outside the creative centre of the *Star Wars* franchise) to Head of Fan Relations (part of the corporate structure of Lucasfilm and advisor to Lucas on numerous fan-related enterprises) meant Sansweet's status as fan also changed. He no longer could be seen as a "poacher" but a "gamekeeper" within the fan community. "Textual Poaching" is Henry Jenkins's term, derived from Michel de Certeau (1984), to describe the process by which fans embrace and transform the original text which, in the case of *Star Wars*, then becomes a catalyst for a network of new elaborate interpretations and meanings (Jenkins, 1992: 24–7). "Textual Gamekeeping" is explained by Matt Hills as the process through which "poacher" fans become legitimate producers and owners of cult texts, storywriters for example, within the "cultural parameters of niche marketing" and an "interpretive community" of fans (2002: 40).

There are several examples in contemporary media where long-time fans have managed to shift from the periphery to the centre of their favourite texts. *Doctor Who*'s reboot was the result of the BBC giving screenwriter (and long-time fan) Russell T. Davies overall charge in bringing the franchise back to TV screens in 2005 – moving from fan to creator thanks to his writing talents and the status he achieved through other critically acclaimed and award-winning television series. Sansweet's transition in fan status mirrors Davies' in that his was born out of the accumulation of *Star Wars* knowledge and ephemera, the talent and acclaim not resting in screenwriting and credits but in his ability as a collector and researcher knowing where to find the best collectibles and juggle his work commitments with an expensive and time-consuming hobby. Still Sansweet can clearly be seen as a fan turned producer, poacher turned gamekeeper, and thus his status as ultimate *Star Wars* collector is assured.

Returning to Sansweet's collection, we can see all three of Susan Pearce's types of collector (souvenir, fetishistic, systematic) in his approach to accumulating stuff. Rancho Obi-Wan is full of items that help him recall specific moments of his life, objects with attached memories that define who he is and how his life has unfolded. Souvenir objects include his very first collectible – the one that started it all – which was the 1976 *Star Wars* promotional book sent to his place of work at the Los Angeles bureau of the *The Wall Street Journal*. In taking the opportunity to "rescue" the pack from an office bin, Sansweet describes how he "looked on covetously" as his colleague "skimmed the pages … and then tossed" it in the trash (2009: 8). The significance he places on this first item suggests the importance of memories about the start of his collector journey but also shines light on his concerned attitude toward preserving and remembering each item. However, a more fetishistic approach to collecting is reflected in his comment about the release of *The Empire Strikes Back*: "I wanted everything – the books, comics, kids' pajamas, posters, fast-food premiums (and the containers and placemats), eating utensils, furniture, lunch boxes – you get the idea" (Sansweet, 2009: 12). Thus the objects started to take over his life and dictate what he should consume and prioritise. As a systematic collector Sansweet also sees his endeavours as a type of mission, having a plan and goal; in an online interview advertising the opening of Ranco Obi-Wan he says: "I'm being more selective these days, but I still call myself a completest [sic]" (quoted in Berkowitz, 2013). The system of collecting is also suggested in how he organises his collection in the museum and the books he writes about it. In *Star Wars, 1,000 Collectibles* (Sansweet, 2009) he divides his survey of items into categories/chapters ranging from play, wear, eat and look to use, fan-made, one-off and props.

While Sansweet's collection can be judged and analysed by fans and critics alike, the fact that he has created a museum to house it makes him a curator as well as a collector. Paralleling his rise from fan to Head of Fan Relations, poacher to gamekeeper, moving from collector to curator means Sansweet is an example of the contemporary trend in popularising the museum. Paul Martin argues that museums have been changing rapidly as they have had to compete with other entertainment and educational institutions that offer service and access to the heritage industry. He sees the work of independent collectors and collector groups as "eclipsing the work of museums" as they no longer can afford to keep acquiring objects (Martin, 1999: 4). Individuals like Sansweet, who have the personal income, space and time to focus on acquisition, can become curators and help to redefine what is considered worthy of keeping and made available to visitors. Rancho Obi-Wan is a space where traditional notions of the museum are copied and also transformed. For Tomislav Sola "there are three basic functions of a museum: collecting, research and communication" (2004: 260) and in each case Rancho Obi-Wan performs its role as collectible museum. Sansweet is curator with knowledge but there is also a board of directors who operate as researchers, communicators and organisers of the membership club. They do so because they want to give fans the opportunity to visit and enjoy the collection. It moves from private to public, shifting from "old-style" museum to "new museum" (see Message, 2006), and destabilises established hierarchies of historical and modern, high and low culture, artefact and commodity, worthy to keep and throw-away. This last point is confirmed by the fact Sansweet has been approached by the Smithsonian National Air and Space Museum who want to inherit the collection (Sansweet, 2009: 520).

Conclusion

In this chapter I have examined the various meanings *Star Wars* toys have assumed in the past 35 years, from the idea of the action figure being part of America's tradition of war play to it representing the self-styled personalisation of fans from all over the world that collect the toys as part of their self-edification. Through an analysis of *Star Wars* merchandise and the ideological implications of a pop-culture phenomenon, I have attempted to understand the connection between fandom, identity and collecting. Whereas scholars have previously placed *Star Wars* within its national contexts, myth (Galipeau, 2001), American society (Engelhardt, 1995), and the changing political landscape (Krämer, 2000), or studied the community of its more active fans (Brooker, 2002) within the confines of either textual poaching (Jenkins, 1992) or textual gamekeeping (Hills, 2002), this chapter has charted the developing significance of the *Star Wars* toy and collectible from child play to adult collecting. Meanings are given to objects and each object means something different and unique to every collector.

Star Wars collectors clearly see the toys and physical ephemera as meaningful and thus they "are not so much objects as they are congealed actions, passionate acts of seeking, selecting, and situating" (Brown, 2003: 146) the fan in an age of mass-consumption and global media markets. The acts of collecting, modifying and curating as seen in the three examples drawn from Beckett, Dustin and Sansweet show that the acquisition of commodities is not about consumption but "presents a metaphor of 'production'" (Stewart, 1993: 164). Indeed, collecting *Star Wars* toys because they represent a connection to a childhood past might fit Jean Baudrillard's contention that "what you really collect is always yourself" (2005: 97) but it also represents a creativity and imagination that extends from the past and into a present and a future where joy comes from the new things that are created from old (as in the remodelled and bootleg action figures) and in the opportunities to preserve artefacts for the community (as with Sansweet's Rancho Obi-Wan museum).

Star Wars has clearly affected the lives of millions who not only believed as children in the make-believe world of a "galaxy far, far away" but also see the products of a multi-billion dollar merchandising campaign as integral components of their adult lives. *Star Wars* can no longer be analysed solely on the basis of the changing American political landscape, and the ideological contexts surrounding the production and release of the first three movies cannot fully explain the continued popularity of the toys for contemporary adult/child collectors. Those who collect the merchandise today like Beckett, Dustin and Sansweet do so because the act of collecting, playing and recapturing one's youth is bound up in the modern desire to define oneself through symbolic possessions rather than through shared national beliefs. It also affords them opportunity to acquire status within a fan collecting community that sees value in the accumulated knowledge of and devotion to a popular culture text. From a fixed and undeniable meaning established by Engelhardt, that hinged on the national psychology of America's "end of victory culture", to a multilayered and interchangeable framework that allowed for personal empowerment, *Star Wars* toys have not only been "played with" but have also been "played up" in the day-to-day lives of fans growing older.

PART IV
Spaces

7

TRADING ON THE POPULAR

Shops, Megastores, Online Spaces and the Culture of Fan Consumption

Perhaps a sign of the impact that the San Diego Comic-Con has had on the circulation of popular culture is that so many similar conventions and events have grown up in its shadow. As I have already pointed out in chapter five, the history of the convention is a long one. However, the importance of Comic-Con in terms of scale and opportunity should not be overlooked. The super convention, which combines industry, fans and retailers is now an established means for textual consumption and commodity exchange. Fans are an important part of this exchange process, and the spaces in which this takes place are modified and controlled in such ways so as to make that process all the more attractive and entertaining for those who enter it. The convention centre, the hotel ballroom, even the sports hall have become integral to the creation and longevity of popular fan cultures. So, alongside the fictional spaces of the media text (as seen on screen) and the geographic locations for filming those spaces made accessible through fan pilgrimage, the convention space as site for fan consumption and exchange is all about making the text more real for those who enter it. In terms of aesthetic quality and original use value conventions may not fulfil every fan's desire to feel connected to their favourite film franchise or television series, but in the objects and ephemera on sale and display within these generic spaces fans are able to reignite their passion for popular culture texts in physical ways that are not typically afforded to them at home.

Nonetheless, while the convention space is more important than ever in the formation of a fan culture the content and design of said space has changed significantly since the 1970s. As discussed in chapter five, San Diego combines all elements of a typical fan convention including autograph booths, comic stalls, ballroom costume competitions, celebrity panels, films screenings and marketing stands (to name just a few). Largeness of scale, in order to accommodate the 130,000 people, and the heterotopic nature of the surrounding geography characterises Comic-Con in ways most other conventions could not imagine. However, what other conventions do imitate and augment is the focus on commodity exchange and object practices of fandom that Comic-Con simply does not have the capacity to include other than through professional dealers and licensed merchants. So, for those few comic book sellers, merchandise dealers, and toy experts that attend Comic-Con (paying over $1,000 to hire the smallest pitch within the exhibition hall) it may seem worthwhile to do business. However, on a much smaller scale, there are thousands of independent dealers, collectors, hobbyists and fans who utilise stalls and booths at conventions – not necessarily to make a living – but do so as part of their enduring fandom and passion for collecting. Indeed, such conventions are advertised purely for the nostalgic fact that there will be fan merchandise and collectibles on sale, alongside some of the stars and actors from yesteryear signing autographs and posing for photos. Two such conventions, the UK's Memorabilia and Collectormania, are important examples of the coming together of fandom and commerce under the auspices of celebrating popular culture and memorialising those texts and commodities that have long since disappeared from mainstream entertainment markets.

This chapter will focus on the various spaces of cult consumption that exist in the more mundane and functional environments of the high street and Internet. As places that accommodate all types of consumer, from casual shopper to fan collector, these sites for the exchange of cult commodities highlight the continued importance of physical interaction and the centrality of the physical object in the construction of fan subcultural capital. However, through my analysis of events such as Collectormania and Memorabilia (more collector fairs than typical fan conventions), independent cult stores on the high street and the defined spaces of Forbidden Planet's London Megastore and website, I argue that notions of space (and the potentials different spaces generate) evolve depending on physical surroundings, assumed and actual audience, and the use of new media technologies.

In terms of the fan collector, the variety and sheer amount of collectible media merchandise is often curtailed by the lack of access to desired and long-lost items; however, with the development of stores and websites that act as real and virtual archives for recycled and remediated toys and cultural ephemera, collectors are now able to acquire images and knowledge, if not the real thing. These digital images become part of that same commodity exchange process that characterises fan conventions, shops and online retail sites but it is arguably more democratic in that the images themselves cost nothing to view, bookmark, download or post comments about. Thus buying the object is one way of owning it, if that is not possible then a sense of ownership is achieved through the searching, collecting, and displaying of images online – creating an archive of collectibles bigger than most fans could gather themselves. Online space is used to present merchandise and collectibles in a way that supports the values and distinction inherent within cult fan communities and acknowledges the continued importance of collecting media texts in the creation of subcultural capital.

Second-Hand Fandom: Memorabilia and Collectormania

Memorabilia is described as the UK's ultimate collector's show, with two locations in Birmingham and London used at seasonal points throughout the year to attract thousands of fans and collectors. The National Exhibition Centre (NEC) in Birmingham often hosts the spring and winter shows, while the ExCel Centre in London's Docklands provides the location for the summer and autumn events. Both locations have large exhibit spaces in which to display props, hold screenings and set up merchandise stalls. Combined with the existing offer of refreshment stands and cafes, pop-up booths cater for attendees in all manner of costumes and outfits. Space, while generic, is demarcated in various ways so as to allow fans and collectors maximum pleasure and optimum buying potential. Attendees are given programmes at the entrance, which contain maps of the floor, highlighting key merchandise booths and stages. Rather like the exhibit hall plan of the San Diego Comic-Con, with colour-coded key and list of stalls to aid exchange, Memorabilia's map highlights from the outset the type of enterprise on which fans and collectors are embarking: a trip down memory lane. Both the map for NEC and ExCel have the hall set up so that tables and dealer booths are arranged along a number of straight rows, with the wide central aisle from the entrance marked out as "Memory Lane" so that people can easily get their bearings (see Figure 7.1). Clearly, nostalgia plays a big part in the marketing and construction of fan experience even before fans set foot in the hall.

FIGURE 7.1 Memory Lane at the November 2010 Memorabilia Convention at Birmingham's NEC.

The hall, either at NEC or ExCel, contains certain zones that cater for different fan tastes and collecting practices. The signing zone is structured in such a way that celebrities are on show but also separate from the main stalls. Lines form at the tables of the most popular actors, usually from franchise films like *Star Wars* or cult TV series like *Doctor Who*. Those whose fame is obscured by the fact they were heavily made-up during their performance use posters listing their major acting roles to jog fans' memories as they walk by. Zones containing replica vehicles, props and on-screen items attract fans rather like a museum – they can interact with the artists and builders who have brought their creations and get their photos taken whilst imagining they are really in the movie. For the briefest moment, sitting on the hood of the General Lee or opening the door of the TARDIS affords fans the pleasure of what Will Brooker describes as "viewing the present through an archive of the past" (2007a: 433), and being able to touch these "different objects become[s] a means for people to enact fantasy, to panoptically display themselves" (Lancaster, 1996: 32) within the public arena of the convention space. Other zones, including a wrestling ring and Robot Wars arena, illustrate that Memorabilia is an eclectic mix of sports and media fandom, building hobbyists and creative professionals arranged side by side in a heterotopic space for memory and nostalgia.

Collectormania displays a similar blend of commerce and nostalgia, despite the fact that Memorabilia is organised by the MCM Expo Group (www.mcmexpo.net) and Collectormania is run by Showmasters (www.showmastersonline.com). Both companies manage a host of popular culture conventions and events, using some of the largest commercial spaces available in the UK. The sister event to Memorabilia is the London Comic-Con (very much in the vein of San Diego) also held at the ExCel. As well as Collectormania, conventions in London's Kensington Olympia, Milton Keynes, Manchester, Glasgow and Coventry, Showmasters promotes and organises a range of events at local hotels for specific series such as *Torchwood* and *True Blood*. More in the mould of older conventions, where rooms are booked out for the weekend and fans can mingle with stars in the panels and bars of a chain hotels, these events continue to combine collecting and commodification with more traditional displays of fan adoration and personal interaction. Collectormania's mass marketing and merchandising conventions in the style of Comic-Con remain far more generic and utilise space much like Memorabilia. The London Film & Comic Con held at Earls Court 2 in July every year reminds us that Showmasters is trying hard to bridge the gap between text and object, fictional narrative and commercial reality. By placing well-known actors from popular series alongside dealers, cosplay, costumed record breaking attempts, and volunteers giving out freebies, it attracts a diverse array of fans – maximising footfall and justifying location.

For Göran Bolin (2004: 126), "consumption is a prominent feature of everyday social life" and as such the spaces in which this consumption occur must be conducive to the nature and type of product being bought and sold. To make the process of purchasing faster, thus increasing profits and demand, there has to be a rationalisation of both production and distribution (getting the goods made and to shops quickly) as well as in exhibition (putting items on display for the customer). In the form of a shopping mall, we can see this final stage of the consumer process most obviously in that it makes "places of consumption, the sites where consumers meet with commodities, make their choices, buy and then leave, as functional as possible" (Bolin, 2004: 127). Functionality is built into malls as they house every type of shop and commodity that consumers might want, alongside services and facilities that aid in the process of purchasing such as cafes, cash machines, toilets, and parking. Likewise, the large exhibition halls that serve as temporary homes for Collectormania and Memorabilia perform a functional role that emphasises consumption within the contexts of the media texts contained under the one roof. Posters, costumed fans, and the usual display of merchandise on sale remind fans and collectors that they are at a media inspired event, but the presence of Costa Coffee cafes, Upper Crust stands and ATMs also confirms that this event is taking place in mundane and functional surroundings. How these surroundings are laid out follows again, like the shopping mall, a design "for the purpose of keeping the flow of customers steady" (Bolin, 2004: 127). So, while "Memory Lane" provides fans a visual aide memoire of objects and images from their past it also funnels them into and through the massive exhibition space, setting the limits of where they can go and what they can see at any one time.

However, while consumer-orientated spaces such as the shopping mall have been much maligned – seeing them as homogenous profit-orientated sites for mere consumption – some critics have asked why then do they remain so popular if they are offering everyone the same experience, with little sense of individuality or personalisation. If the experience in large shopping spaces is apparently so passive, why is it sought so repeatedly? Similarly, why do fans repeatedly go to conventions and sites of textual consumption if the experience is so generic and impersonal? The answer to this question has been addressed in relation to Comic-Con in chapter five but it is worth repeating here in the contexts of Collectormania and Memorabilia since those fan spaces are often so generic and focused on the buying and selling of goods. Indeed, while the purchased object is so central to the bringing together of fans and collectors at venues like NEC and ExCel, other fan activities (such as the costume competition, screenings and discussion panels) are pushed to the fringes; adding colour but not distracting fans from the central premise for the event – buying stuff.

Yet, critics still see value in the mall experience of shopping that would also apply to Collectormania and Memorabilia. For Nancy Backes, malls may be functionally designed for the purposes of profit but they "are re-appropriated by visitors into resistant and generative practices far different from the intention and purpose of the space. Visitors, in short, reappropriate the space to satisfy their own purposes in contemporary life" (1997: 5). We can see this working for generic spaces like those offered by NEC and ExCel in that their demarcation as fan spaces allows a temporary break from the norm for fans who want to shop for the things they cannot find on the high street or in shopping malls. A blank space becomes a site that "offers an escape from boredom and a search for meaning" (Miles, 2010: 111).

Furthermore, using the work of Sharon Zukin (2005) who argues that shopping forms a public space in which people create new ideas and assign new values onto consumer products, I would argue that while Collectormania and Memorabilia are all about consumption they also constitute similar sites for re-evaluation of mass-produced goods – particularly second-hand items as I will discuss below. Generic fan convention spaces offer alternative sites of consumption, often in opposition to the usual brands and stores fans buy and visit for most of the year, which act as liminal spaces between the self and the community. Zukin argues,

> Neither free nor completely democratic, the public sphere of shopping is a space of discussion and debate. It is a space of manipulation and control, but also of discretion and fulfilment. It is, in fact, an ambiguous or heterotopic space, where we struggle to combine principles of equality and hierarchy, and pleasure and rationality, to create an experience we value. Shopping could in turn be suggested to actively hide the means of exploitation that underpin a market economy, thus shopping offers us a world of commodities that restore, rather than steal, our souls.
>
> *(2005: 265)*

The most striking and similar aspect of both the Collectormania and Memorabilia events is that they use space in the same ways. Zoned areas for themed activities and screenings (Collectormania's zones include the Anime Zone, Artists Alley and the Video Game Zone), aisles full of dealers' tables groaning under the weight of old toys and collectibles, and autograph booths that pitch legends of sport alongside cult media stars from home and abroad. The October 2011 Memorabilia fair in London boasted the first appearance of *Doctor Who*'s Freema Agyeman signing autographs sitting side by side with boxer Nigel Benn and footballers Frank McLintock and Billy Bonds. The crossover potential between fans was not entirely obvious, small children queued to see Agyeman as middle-aged men swapped sporting memories whilst waiting for a chance to speak to a former West Ham United player, in Bonds, who has long since retired. Similarly, at the Entertainment Media Show in March 2011 (combining Collectormania London and Sportsmania) fans could witness the rare sight in Photo Area A of Kenny Baker (*Star Wars*), Lester Piggot (horse racing), Michael Biehn (*The Terminator*), Ahmed Best (*Star Wars*), Cary Elwes (*The Princess Bride*), Carl Weathers (*Rocky*), Sir Stirling Moss (motor racing), Mercedes McNab (*Angel*) and Philip Glenister (*Life on Mars*) all signing pictures and posters for a small fee (ranging between £15 and £20). The sheer eclecticism becomes part of the attraction for fans as they walk past witnessing such intermedial spectacles, whether they recognise any of the personalities on display or not.

The jumbled and miscellaneous nature of the celebrities and texts on show is underscored by the range of dealer tables and stalls containing all manner of merchandise. From Lego to Transformers, trading cards to lunchboxes, merchandise is both brand new and second-hand. As the following image taken at Collectormania

FIGURE 7.2 A jumble sale style presentation of mixed cult merchandise at Memorabilia.

at NEC in November 2012 suggests (see Figure 7.2), many of the dealers at these types of event do not specialise in what they sell, and what they sell often comes incomplete and out of box. Still, the presence of such material indicates that part of the attraction for dealers and collectors is to display all their wares and to see what other people have in their collections (whether they are for sale or decoration). In this respect, the conventions that prioritise the selling of objects and collectibles through independent traders are more akin to the jumble sale or car boot sale than they are of the mass market or chain stores that often set up shop at events like the San Diego Comic-Con. For Nicky Gregson and Lousie Crewe part of the appeal for shoppers that frequent second-hand consumption spaces like jumble sales, car boot fairs, charity shops and retro/vintage stores is the potential for "capturing 'the bargain'" (2003: 94). Objects bought in these space are seen as "treats", in that "the pleasure lies as much in the practice as in the purchase" (95) and the search means just as much to the collector as does the final outcome. This is something I elaborated on in chapter six when discussing *Star Wars* toy collecting.

Gregson and Crewe (2003: 100) also acknowledge the importance of "discursive communities" in second-hand shopping, or fan collectors as is the case in this chapter, in that "practices of shopping" rely on the skills of the individual and their identity as experts (or fans) within their particular community. Again, like those individuals who engage in toy collecting as part of a social hierarchy of *Star Wars* fandom, sharing an interest in the same objects but competing over knowledge and items acquired, fans attending Collectormania and Memorabilia scan the piles of assorted unboxed figures, vehicles and mismatched weapons in an attempt to find that one valuable item. Value in this case, however, is not based on quality, condition or rarity but is found in the fact that such items can help to complete their collection back home. Second-hand collectors clearly display their fandom through the skills they have as shoppers and the knowledge they use to find the best deal:

> Practices of shopping are ones that rest on the existence of specific discursive communities. These, however, are not just important to identity formation. Rather, standing and kudos even within these discursive communities is related to the skills of shopping itself. So, the more outlandish and obscure the site of purchase, the more symbolic value comes to be invested in particular purchases and the greater its "boast" value within friendship networks. Seen to encode knowingness and skill, these subcultural shopping practices are ones that clearly elevate cultural over economic capital.
>
> *(Gregson and Crewe, 2003: 100)*

The display and purchasing of popular culture, both old and new, at stalls and autograph booths characterises what I would call second-hand fandom. With such a range of texts for sale, and multiple film, television and sporting celebrities on show and accessible, every fan is potentially catered for – whether they are the youngest Jar Jar Binks enthusiast or oldest aficionado of British motorsport. If one is unknown to the other then both become familiar in the contexts of the geographic location. Texts, objects, collectibles and autographs are traded and recycled as memories are shared between fans, dealers and celebrities. Indeed, the memories being talked about and nostalgia on display on dealer tables and through posters are as much part of the collecting experience as are the physical acts of purchasing goods and grabbing a signed photo. These convention spaces act as a place where second-hand objects and second-hand stories circulate – all with their own subcultural capital value attached depending on exclusivity, price and popularity. Second-hand toys, autographs, collectibles, ornaments, and games that make up the majority of the stalls at these conventions remind us of the value of the memories that keep them popular enough to be sold and resold every year. There is clearly a market for second-hand fan commodities and that market undoubtedly relies on the memory and nostalgia of fans who return to see which celebrities are signing this time around and what sought after object might lurk at the bottom of a dealer's bargain bin. Second-hand fandom relies on the exchange of objects and memories at events like Collectormania and Memorabilia (whose names inherently suggest the primary function and thing for which fans attend), and is propagated by the generic and adaptable nature of the locations used to contain the stalls, booths and pop-up stands within.

The Local Markets of Cult Collecting: All the Cool Stuff

If cyclical and temporary conventions specifically aimed at selling collectible items, second-hand goods, and mass market products offer fan collectors the chance to add to their collections, find a bargain, and enter typically non-fan spaces then the independent retailer store provides fans a constant and familiar place to which they can return throughout the year. In conjunction with their online store spaces, retailers that specialise in the toy and collectible market have a ready-made community to target and a host of product lines they can advertise and sell. We can track the birth of the toy and collectible store alongside the history of the comic book shop, which many argue became popular in the 1970s. When faced with declining sales on newsstands publishers started direct marketing of comics to specialty retailers that had a loyal and local clientele. Weekly publication meant regular customers and regular mass orders that could be shipped out to shops that acted as distribution centres (Woo, 2011: 127). Similarly, independent record stores provided a sound model for toy and collectible dealers as, again starting in the 1970s, they specialised in particular genres and attracted regular customers (Shuker, 2010: 117). Both types of retail space inform an understanding of how the toy and collectible shop has developed over time and why it is so important in the creation and development of a fan experience.

Independent toy and collectible shops have inhabited the high street and shopping malls for some time, taking advantage of the popularity of re-released toys and games from yesteryear and the general mood of nostalgia that permeates popular culture. Large toy companies such as Hasbro and Mattel view such retail spaces as suitable but different outlets for new products and old favourites compared to established mega chain stores like Toys R Us, as they come with a loyal fan clientele. The marketing and selling of nostalgia in these shop spaces is characterised by the very same things that drive adult fans to return to the toys of their youth, attempting to complete collections and acquire that one item which had eluded them since childhood. Indeed, for some of the fan collectors I discussed in chapter four, the experience of entering a shop space that contains items from their past is often the catalyst for renewing their passion for the original toy and restarting the collecting process. Stores that cater for fans by using childhood memories and nostalgia are by no means just for adult fans, they would go out of business very quickly if they were; instead, they act as sites for multiple generations of fans, for kids, collectors and enthusiasts. As such, they provide a secure and familiar space for the continued presence of the fictional franchise texts and the objects of fan desire that typify fan consumption such as the toys.

One such independent store, All the Cool Stuff, provides an interesting case study of the fan collector retail space (see Figure 7.3). Situated on the high street in the small Hampshire village of Fordingbridge, on the River Avon not far from Salisbury in Wiltshire and a short drive from one of England's most famous landmarks, Stonehenge, All the Cool Stuff might seem a little out of place considering its rural surroundings. Yet its presence there suggests that location is not the most important factor in establishing a clientele since social media and online marketing provide access and communication with fans and collectors from all over the country. Indeed, the shop's online and physical high street presence combine to create a cult brand that stands out in the village and attracts customers driving

FIGURE 7.3 All the Cool Stuff on the high street in Fordingbridge, Hampshire.

through and surfing online – taking advantage of lower property rental costs in Fordingbridge but being just close enough for people across the south region to be able to visit, browse the latest merchandise, and get the latest news on what products will be released next. Like the comic book shop then, All the Cool Stuff acts like a hub where fan collectors can talk to the knowledgeable staff, get gossip, view the toys and buy what they need: It "is a meeting place, like the clubhouse at a country club or small-town barbershop. It is a place for commerce, but, more importantly, it is a place for culture" (Pustz, 1999: 9).

Similarly, for Brian Swafford, comic book shops "become safe havens for fans to gather and participate in comic fan culture. Patrons of the comic shop are free to interact with other fans and be open in their fandom while in the shop" (2012: 295). Therefore, All the Cool Stuff as toy and collectible retail space offers collectors familiarity and safety; familiarity with the items on display and the people who work there and safety from non-fans and the homogeneity seen on the typical high street found in every village, town and city in the UK. Stores such as All the Cool Stuff and other specialist bookstores might attract what Larry Leslie calls, somewhat derogatorily, the "True Bookstore Rat" (2012: 119), or someone who regularly comes in, peruses the shelves, reads magazines and books on display but does not buy anything – preferring the experience of the books *in situ* rather than taking them out of the shop. Benjamin Woo's analysis of comic book shops and the fans that regularly visit them posits that there is a process attached to the relationship between consumption and space. As social settings, comic stores act in three ways: as "locales providing spaces for interaction among participants" (rather like the conventions I discussed earlier); as "nodes, interlocks, and regions relating contingent communities of practice"; and as "'sanctuaries' from mainstream hierarchies of taste and status, and arenas of competition for social and subcultural capital" (Woo, 2011: 125). This latter point again can be related to my analysis of both the fan communities that buy and collect toys and merchandise (as in chapters four and six) and my study of the San Diego Comic-Con (in chapter five). However, Woo's description of the comic book "locale" is instructive for an understanding of what goes on in toy and collectible stores like All the Cool Stuff: "Locales are constituted by the interactions taking place within them. Moreover, they locate practices in a structured/structuring context. Comic-bookstores are locales in this sense, and reception practices are transmitted through interaction among members of the communities that inhabit them" (Woo, 2011: 128).

The range of products on sale at All the Cool Stuff is typical of such establishments. Mainstream items from the Lego, Transformers and *Star Wars* toy lines are mixed with vintage and reissued items, with posters, T-shirts, games and other bits of cult ephemera making up the decorative display on shelves and in the shop window. As with comic book shops, All the Cool Stuff sells an array of products so as to diversify its range and increase its profit margin – therefore, perennial favourites are sold side by side with the latest new cult item or relaunched toy line from the 1980s. Online and in store the gendering of cult collecting (see chapter three) becomes apparent, with My Little Pony and other female coded brands having a presence but not in such large quantities as the boys' toys. Diversification is a key component of survival, and attracting loyal fan collectors as well as selling the more mainstream and popular brands ensures longevity. Woo's work on the social practices of comic book readers and the retail space of the comic book shop suggests that these specialist and niche spaces are always under threat – that is why so many independent retailers maintain an online shop and have a presence on Facebook and Twitter to attract and contact costumers (2011: 134). Nevertheless, both online and in the store the positioning of the same products highlights a balance between keeping up to date and selling the most profitable toys and also stocking older (often pre-owned) toys so as to keep keen collectors coming back. Woo argues that the ways in which owners set up their stores (categorising popular items, brands, toy lines) reflects how they "designate a set of genres and forms that are valued within the subcultural scene while excluding others that are equally or more popular among 'mainstream' audiences" (2011: 129).

So, while trying to stock toys that will attract serious collectors and fans, and at the same time selling more mainstream items that will appeal to new customers and widen their profit base, All the Cool Stuff sponsors collecting and fan events locally and across the UK which advertises its brand to existing and new collecting communities. Thus, the store acts like similar subcultural retail establishments in that they "are nodes in a wider network defined by relationships of sponsorship and promotion" (Woo, 2011: 129). In March 2011, All the Cool Stuff sponsored and organised a Transformers/G.I. Joe convention, held across the street at the Village Hall (see Figure 7.4). "Roll Out/Roll Call 2" was the third event to be held at the hall, and second focusing on the popular 1980s toy brands. Popularity increased so

FIGURE 7.4 Fordingbridge Village Hall, venue for "Roll Out/Roll Call 2" in 2011.

much that the event moved to a hotel venue in Southampton for the 2012 and 2013 dates. Using the show as a platform to increase regular customers but also act as a physical space to bring artists, celebrity fans, and other independent retailers together, All the Cool Stuff constructed (albeit temporarily) "a fixed space that multiple, contingently related groups and communities [could] access" (Woo, 2011: 130). However, as the following image highlights (see Figure 7.5), the use of

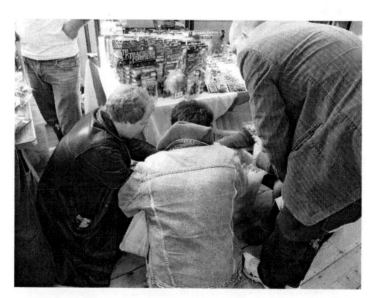

FIGURE 7.5 Convention attendees in the hall rummage through discounted items in the hope of finding a bargain.

the Village Hall combined with the jumble sale aesthetic of wooden tables and bargain bins is more demonstrative of second-hand fandom as described in relation to Collectormania and Memorabilia earlier in this chapter. In fact, I would argue that despite the attempts to keep the store branded as being "for both kids and those kids that never grew up" (www.allthecoolstuff.co.uk), All the Cool Stuff still serves as a space for nostalgia that is recycled and returned to every time fans gather at a themed show like "Roll Out/Roll Call". It acts as a commercial venture but, crucially, it serves as a physical space for fan interaction, competition and subcultural capital accumulation.

This notion is further underscored by the fact that the store paid for and sold specially designed toys at "Roll Out/Roll Call", available for pre-order and pick up in the hall. Items such as Kraken Bio Armour Pilot with Treadshot (underwater monster with robot inside), Break-Neck (a mini transforming car) and White Shadow (a Lego mini figure repainted and adapted to look like a military soldier) represent a form of subcultural capital in that they are fan designed and made toys based on the Action Force (UK version of G.I. Joe before it moved across the Atlantic) and Transformer brands. In the vein of the fan modifications of Boba Fett, so highly prized by *Star Wars* fans discussed in chapter six, these limited edition modifications emphasise All the Cool Stuff's credentials as a centre for rare and unique collectible merchandise. They promote amateur fan makers and fund their creative work, thus making them an underground and alternative business. But they also follow the more mainstream marketing strategies employed by the largest toy companies at Comic-Con when they give out freebies and sell limited edition items in that they act as physical objects that connect fans to the store, the convention, the Village Hall and the physical location of Fordingbridge. The memory of obtaining the modified toys (complete with specially commissioned artwork, packaging with All the Cool Stuff logo and website details) forever situates the store and its contexts in a subcultural fan experience that cannot be replicated. It puts All the Cool Stuff inside and outside the mainstream of mass-market consumption. In the same way as Steven Miles (2010: 174) describes the liminal space of the mall, I would argue the collectible store "operates as an enabling space, exuding theatrical excitement and the promise of a consumer-life fulfilled". However, "consumer-life" in the case of a store like All the Cool Stuff is more "subcultural life", where fan desire and collecting practices are fully expressed and satisfied.

Marketing Mainstream Cult: Forbidden Planet

Following in the history of the rise of the independent comic book and record stores mentioned above, Forbidden Planet has grown to become one of the most recognisable brands for selling comics, graphic novels, books, film and television collectibles, and other cult merchandise. Beginning life as a small shop on London's Denmark Street the company has expanded to encompass megastores, international shops and an online store. Building on the style and characteristics of the local retail shop, Forbidden Planet caters for both mainstream and niche tastes. It promotes both an image of the alternative and cult as well as keeping up with the latest fads and stocking the most popular toy and merchandise brands. Over the years, like independent retailers of toys, comics and music, it has had to diversify as the market for cult and fan merchandise has become crowded and responsive to the shifting tastes of mainstream media culture. The following analysis of the London Megastore continues this chapter's focus on venues of fan consumption and posits that while cult fandom has entered the mainstream (as argued in chapter one), Forbidden Planet treads a thin line between both camps: as a physical location it remains a safe destination for fans to enter and connect with their favourite media texts but also it performs a role akin to the department store in that it sells something for every type of fan, whether you are a novice or die-hard collector. In this way, its locality as safe haven and connective space (including its online shop) serves to underline the potentially liberating and fulfilling aspects of fandom and cult collecting. As such, Forbidden Planet can be described as a place of "popular veneration" (Combs, 1989: 71) within which all forms of popular culture are celebrated and fans come to buy merchandise in a ritualistic practice that affirms their passion and commitment to their favourite cult texts.

As well as the London Megastore (which moved from Denmark Street to New Oxford Street and then to its current location on Shaftesbury Avenue in 2003) there are two megastores in Bristol and Southampton, along with smaller shops in Birmingham, Cambridge, Coventry, Croydon, Liverpool and Newcastle. These are all owned by parent company Forbidden Planet Ltd. Forbidden Planet International, a second company owned by some of the original Forbidden Planet partners, has opened shops in other UK cities such as Edinburgh, Cardiff, Nottingham and Manchester, with a shop in Dublin and flagship store on Broadway in New York City. The success and continued popularity of the brand is in part due to the locations it picks, not far from existing shopping thoroughfares and main roads with easy access to public transport. The London Megastore is in the heart of the world famous theatre district, minutes from Oxford and Regent Streets, Tottenham Court Road, Covent Garden market and its boutique shops popular with fashion conscious youth, a thriving music scene and the more affluent middle classes. However, being so close to some of London's most popular tourist and shopping attractions, Forbidden Planet benefits from a regular stream of foreign travellers who are attracted into the store by the colourful and ever-changing window displays of popular comic book superheroes and the latest fantasy blockbusters.

The only other major work on the culture of the Forbidden Planet consumption experience is Kurt Lancaster's article on the simulated environments of science fiction tourism. In this work he argues that the New York store serves as "a 'clearinghouse' for science fiction commodities that allow people to enter worlds of fantasy ... The objects purchased in this store become a means for branching out into other worlds (by reading and fantasising)" (Lancaster, 1996: 34–5). As customers walk amongst the aisles of books, comics, toys and DVDs they are transported to the fantasy worlds those products depict, bringing the reality of their environment closer to the fiction of their imaginations. The range of science fiction ephemera on display makes the store a destination in itself, where fans can go to immerse themselves further into their favourite texts. So, watching Darth Vader on screen is enhanced by purchasing a novelisation, ceramic cookie jar, poster or picture book and is made more real in that a cardboard cut out of the character welcomes you upon entry: "Forbidden Planet, by its very nature, not only offers the means to enter fantasy worlds, but it is in itself a fantasy world" (Lancaster, 1996: 33). While I agree with Lancaster's assertions about the fantasy aspects of the store in relation to the London location I discuss here, I would contend that the contemporary diverse media landscape necessarily challenges some of the qualities of fantasy and escape Lancaster saw in the store when it was marked out as a science fiction genre space.

The London Megastore is not just for science fiction. The floor plan lists dozens of genres, global media products and blockbuster franchises, organised by popularity, audience and type. So, for example, as you enter the double door entrance the usual glass cabinet containing miniature figures, props, models, busts and collectibles is on your left, with the rest of the ground floor devoted to the most popular brands and merchandise from the latest blockbuster films and television series: *Star Wars, Doctor Who, Harry Potter* and *Lord of the Rings* have permanent shelf space, but then other shelves devoted to film and TV alternate between retro products from 1980s movies like *Gremlins* and cult series like *Battlestar Galactica*; shelf space is also devoted to Japanese anime, wrestling toys from the WWE, gaming merchandise from the *Halo* and *Resident Evil* franchises, superhero action figures from Marvel and DC, vinyl and art toys, seasonal gift products, calendars, magazines, posters and T-shirts. The lower ground floor appears more niche as it contains bookshelves for thousands of comic books and graphic novels, horror, fantasy and science fiction books and DVDs. This underground space is coded as cult through the eclectic mix of posters and adverts for forthcoming personal appearances by authors and screenwriters. Indeed, book signings are a regular occurrence at all Forbidden Planets stores, making them "nodes" in the wider fan community that frequent them (Woo, 2011: 129). However, the sheer variety and amount of product lines and media texts on sale and display makes the Megastore more like a department store of cult merchandise than a local comic book shop or independent retailer. Attempting to have something for everyone, therefore, promotes a sense of plenty with which other venues cannot compete. Like a department store it appears "to offer the consumer everything they wanted under one roof ... putting the consumer into the debt of those who make that provision. The daunting size of the department store is, from this point of view, intended to intimidate" (Miles, 2010: 102).

Forbidden Planet might offer a potential fantasy space for fans but it also inundates them with products and images that characterise it as a space for industrial marketing practices. Taking advantage of what is popular and currently in cinemas and on television, Forbidden Planet achieves a level of immediacy that other fan spaces like All the Cool Stuff, Collectormania and Memorabilia cannot maintain. However, following a policy that prioritises the new and latest release means that vintage and second-hand goods – often the target of fan collectors – do not appear on Forbidden Planet shelves, or even in their online store. Although, the store often carries stock first made available at the San Diego Comic-Con, complete with iconic logo to emphasise exclusivity. Ironically, then, smaller and less obvious merchandise stores can still compete in the cult marketplace because they are able to specialise and sell vintage toys and collectibles alongside newer products. If the London Megastore works to mainstream cult media texts and their associated merchandise, it still offers customers a shopping experience that emphasises possibility over the act of simply purchasing. In this way the Megastore resembles in the contemporary department store in that it offers "a world of apparently endless possibility, where the experience becomes more important than the purchase. In effect, the process of consumption starts before the actual purchase of the product" (Miles, 2010: 103–4). Indeed, for the fan approaching the Megastore from the street, the experience starts with the spectacle of the window displays that hint at the abundance and range of cult merchandise that waits within.

The Megastore has two large windows (see Figure 7.6) that are filled with posters, cardboard cut outs, busts, props and samples of books, DVDs and toys. These are changed regularly and correspond with what is in vogue and currently on our screens. Working towards cross-marketing and cross-genre appeal, items from different media franchises are often bunched together highlighting a broader and more mainstream audience that might feel compelled to enter. So, for example,

FIGURE 7.6 The Forbidden Planet Megastore on Shaftesbury Lane in London.

posters advertising *The Walking Dead* comic book series and DVD release sit side by side with other zombie texts such as *Resident Evil* statues and products related to George A. Romero's *Living Dead* films. Likewise, multiproduct versions of the same media franchise are grouped together; Wolverine figurines alongside *X-Men* graphic novels and Magneto children's costumes advertise Marvel's transmedia and cross-generational appeal. These arrangements emphasise the spectacle of cult media entertainment and are symbols of the subcultural capital that fans value within their own communities. Indeed, for Peter Gibian, looking at shop window displays is part of the appeal of shopping – emphasising a sort of cinematic spectacle that entices customers to enter stores and turns the process of buying into entertainment:

> When the "buying act" becomes so deeply associated with this kind of illusionistic visual spectacle, a very special mode of shopping is involved: it enters an arena of entertainment in which experience of looking is as important as the object found, in which customers are willing to pay for the atmosphere, for just looking, and their surplus money goes for emotional rather than physical necessities.
>
> *(Gibian, 1997: 270)*

Benjamin Woo argues that comic book stores are sectioned off into regions that bring to light the hierarchies of subcultural communities. Starting with the window displays, he argues that "products simultaneously advertise the store's product range to outsiders *and* block windows, closing its interior off from view" (Woo, 2011: 130). When inside, more mainstream and commercial products are pushed to the front, near the door, and the exclusive items are located at the back – implying that regular fans work harder to attain those products and are deemed more worthy of them as they progress further into the shop. In many ways Forbidden Planet follows this pattern of using regions, or zones, to demarcate cult products along more mainstream and subcultural lines. However, Woo's analysis does not account for the plethora of merchandise on display and the sheer breadth of media texts contained on the shelves. Forbidden Planet's zones of merchandising repeat media franchise texts in cycles based on format, platform and product. All the toys are together, separated by brand, so too the DVDs, comics, trading card games and books downstairs. Only the major perennials, *Star Wars*, *Doctor Who*, *Star Trek*, etc., have sections to themselves. So, whether you are a zombie novice or frequent cult collector, you have to pass through the store and go to every zone (merchandise, comic, book, film and TV) to see what is in stock related to your favourite text. Hierarchies are therefore flattened out by multiple zones and the mixed product displays in the windows and on shelves, indicating the increased mainstreaming of cult media.

Forbidden Planet is following in the footsteps of contemporary quality and cult television series in that it represents the breaking down of boundaries between mainstream and cult discussed in recent scholarship. Matt Hills, in his work on mainstream cult, describes how the popularity of cult series on network and cable television is indicative of more complicated forms of storytelling that are "engaged in deconstructing the cult versus mainstream binary, presenting commercially driven TV drama which self-consciously draws on discourses of authorship, sophistication, and quirkiness which have been more traditionally linked to cult TV in its telefantasy mode" (2010b: 73). In this way, we might read Forbidden Planet's window displays, zoned arrangement, and mix of franchise products as symptomatic of audiences'/customers' changing tastes in more sophisticated cult programming. This in turn highlights the need to increase the range of products on sale and make those links between genre texts and different media products more obvious to both regular fans and tourists that pass by. Similarly, while Henry Jenkins argues that "as fandom diversifies it moves from cult status towards the cultural mainstream" (2002: 161), I would argue that Forbidden Planet follows this trend by providing the latest merchandise to a fan community who is in constant need to have the most up to date item, collectible toy or special issue of a comic book. In this sense, then, the Megastore must stock the most popular lines as fan communities are constantly evolving, growing and changing in line with the expanded networks on the Internet and social media which publicise what is cool and what is soon to be released. As a location that offers a shopping experience enhanced by visual spectacle and a connection to imagined fantasy worlds, Forbidden Planet is but one place that ensures fans are welcomed and appreciated. In this sense, while physically different from them, it resembles the various spaces of fandom epitomised by Comic-Con, Collectormania, and the independent retail shop discussed throughout this book.

Online Stores, Digital Collecting and the Archive

As I have argued above, in spite of its more mainstream credentials Forbidden Planet still markets itself as an alternate space for cult merchandise. The physical layout of the store aids in the presentation of diverse media texts, ranging from genre television to erotic fiction, and as such all types of fans find it a potentially liberating and familiar space. This notion is itself played up by the store in its marketing. A black and white poster depicting a group of aliens, monsters, goths, and mutants leering at the audience with the tagline, "People like us shop at … ", asserts that Forbidden Planet is part of an underground economy of misfits and outsiders. The cartoon image is used on plastic bags, flyers and is now a big seller on Forbidden Planets T-shirts available in store and online. Perhaps in recognition, even false denial, that the store has become more middle-of-the-road in its stocking of popular items such as "Keep Calm and Carry On" tourist merchandise, the poster has had an update: the tagline now reads, "People like us *still* shop at … " While this may be wishful thinking for the most part, Forbidden Planet's online store provides a more private space for cult fans and collectors.

ForbiddenPlanet.com, like any online shop, can provide the store unlimited space to sell goods. The website is designed to highlight the bestsellers but also devotes pages to more niche products like manga and vinyl dolls. Within sections goods are organised by type and media, textual relationships between items are maintained via pages devoted only to the big franchises as identified in store: *Star Wars*, *Doctor Who*, DC and Marvel. So, searching through the "Collectable" pages you can find posters, prints, props, busts and statues for blockbusters such as *The Hobbit* and cult 1980s television animation such as *Thundercats*. On the "Vinyl" pages, the main doll producers Mighty Muggs, Ugly Dolls and Pop Vinyl are all together with items listed alphabetically by character – that way you can compare how a Mighty Muggs version of Jason Voorhees looks against one made by Pop Vinyl and make your purchase accordingly. This in many ways contradicts the attraction and unique qualities inherent in the vinyl or designer toy discussed by Marc Steinberg. He argues that "The designer toy generates an expanded field of creative and critical practice that simultaneously invokes and works against the grain of character merchandising" (2010: 227). However, the fact that the alternative design aesthetic which makes these dolls stand out in comparison to mass-produced characters makes them big sellers for Forbidden Planet is a sign of the store's increasing tendency to market itself as both mainstream and cult, as I have argued throughout this chapter.

The store's online layout promotes loyalty to film texts and characters, fans looking to add to their collection of *Friday the 13th* (1980) memorabilia, for example, but it also encourages a form of loyalty to particular toy and collectible brands that real shops could not support due to lack of space. Through range of stock and the continued trend to appeal to both cult and mainstream audience, the online store acts as both an introduction to the cult-collecting world and a site for more complex levels of cult fan distinction. Forbidden Planet can stock all the vinyl toy brands online and offer a range to suit most fans' tastes. Indeed, as Michele White argues about brand communities, "members ... are inclined to celebrate and buy the brand's products and to identify with the associated corporation" (2012: 4–5). Thus, online users of this site are fans of the Mighty Muggs or Pop Vinyl brand, in whatever shape or design the object comes, and look to add to their collection in a "systematic" process that aims to complete the set to achieve some form of closure and/or understanding (Pearce, 1995: 32).

Earlier, I argued that the London Megastore differs from collector conventions and independent shops in that it does not supply items that support my concept of second-hand fandom: the used and rare items either recycled and bought from childhood collections or found in lofts and storage cupboards. Apart from exclusives that it gets from Comic-Con to sell in store at a higher price it does not promote objects considered collectible in the sense of vintage, antique or used. However, the website offers the opportunity to do just that, as space is not a premium and online retailers are keenly aware of the fact that collectors carry out many of their searches for rare and highly desired items from the comfort of their armchairs. Signed originals and limited editions of comics and other bits of memorabilia are promoted heavily online, with descriptions that emphasise authenticity and value used to catch the collector's eye.

The June 2013 preview of the *Superior Spider-Man* (UK Edition – Signed Forbidden Planet Exclusive) exclaims: "Signed by Dan Slott with a wonderful Ed McGuiness bookplate! It is the story that turned Spider-Man's world upside-down as a dying Dr Octopus hatches his master plan for vengeance against Spider-Man: He will become him!" In many ways such marketing of collectibles mirrors how auction site eBay targets collectors and antique enthusiasts in that it tries to create hype to increase demand and sales. For Ken Hillis, "the experiential claims of authenticity, memory, and truth that sellers fabricate through the images and textual narratives they upload to the site together produce narrative effects crucial to profitable sales outcomes" (2006: 168). That is not to say Forbidden Planet operates like an auction site, it obviously does not, but the hyping of rarity and exclusivity tied to specific cult merchandise is similar to the ways in which online commerce in all its forms has adapted to use memory and the lure of the authentic to attract new media users by recycling and remediating older media texts and objects. This is something I will explore further in the next chapter. Perhaps what the website offers most to its customers – and copies from other sites like eBay – is a visual archive of images. These images of merchandise, branded products and fan favourites constitute a digital repository of fan ephemera that underlines the stores' original claim to cater for cult collectors and the "people like us" seen in the marketing poster. Indeed, if its primary function as selling website is obvious to the more mainstream buyer then its use as an image archive for exclusive items and collectibles suggests that it remains a destination for fan collectors who crave the organised spectacle of an amassed collection not offered in store.

For Zoe Todd, Internet-based archives like eBay, and I would also argue amateur fan sites and Forbidden Planet's online store, constitute the digital versions of Allan Sekula's term for the archive as "a territory of images" (cited in Todd, 2006: 80). Retrieving images from online databases, intended as fan repositories or originally designed for commodity consumption, is important for the "fabrication of history", preserving "past collections" and "making meaning today" (Hillis, Petit and Epley, 2006: 10). Thus, while collectors might struggle to complete their collection, afford that rare item or retrieve a physical sample of a long-lost product the visual archive online allows for ephemeral ownership of the image. Forbidden Plant, as database for all cult merchandise, is then more ably placed to offer collectors and fans a view of their favourite texts as an imagined archive – an archive of photos that bring to life the objects to which they have attached meaning and value. This concept follows Roland Barthes's description of the "image-repertoire" as outlined by James Leo Cahill. Repertoire, in this sense, "is a reservoir of shared knowledge, committed to memory, and easily recollected … A temporary recollection of images, a site of transient storage, accumulation, circulation, and investment" (Cahill, 2006: 194). Likewise, Forbidden Planet's website lists, categorises, repeats, and recycles images of cult objects in such a way that it allows fan collectors to take possession of, rather than be possessed by, the artefacts on display. The online image archive, whether it is part of a corporate or fan site, offers both visual spectacle and a sense of ownership that parallels the textual practices of cult media fandom.

Conclusion

Recent reports in the UK press about the decline of the British high street suggest that more and more people are turning to the Internet to buy their shopping, books, DVDs, gifts, and other luxury items. The Centre for Retail Research warns "that High Streets could see 20% of their shops close down within five years as more people" go online to buy the basics and find a good deal ("One in five shops could close by 2018"). For some media chains like HMV (music, games and DVDs) this threat is imminent and is a direct result of websites like Amazon, which undercuts prices and provides convenience to shoppers. However, as we have seen in this chapter, local shops like All the Cool Stuff and big chains like Forbidden Planet that sell cult media merchandise are still popular despite their high street locations – they do not cancel each other out of the market either. Indeed, the repeated appearance of Collectormania and Memorabilia at urban venues like ExCel, NEC and Earls Court suggests that being able to go somewhere and buy what you want and witness the physical spectacle of toys, props, books, games and other collectible items is an important part of being a fan that the Internet cannot fully replace.

Nevertheless, new digital spaces such as eBay, shop websites and fan-made pages offer the fan collector the potential for unlimited archives of images, knowledge and other digital ephemera that are important aspects of being a fan and displaying a sense of identity as a collector. For Kelley C. Smith Feranec, "Audiences, then, have not only created communities of culture around such sites, but have also generated nostalgia and a desire to collect the digital information itself" (2008: 9). The next chapter will focus on the remediation of the classic toy brand, Lego, and discuss examples of Lego collectors who use web spaces to display and archive their collections. Thus, it is important acknowledge here that the consumption practices examined in this chapter inform an understanding of how notions of space are being changed and adapted by collectors eager to build their reputation and display their skills in acquiring cult objects. Displaying a successful collection to others online "brings the collector heightened status (within his or her collecting sphere) and feelings of pride and accomplishment" (Belk, 1995: 68) and so we might understand the importance and continued popularity of physical sites such as the convention, cult shop and Megastore in relation to this very real need to show off in the digital domain.

8

(RE)CONSTRUCTING CHILDHOOD MEMORIES

Nostalgia, Narrative and the Expanded Worlds of Lego Fandom

The remediation of classic and long-lost children's film, television, games and toys as discussed in the previous chapter and chapter four highlights the increasing importance of nostalgia within contemporary popular culture. The proliferation of official and unofficial, corporate and fan produced websites and online databases allow access to media from a pre-Internet era. Tied to this digital rebirth of children's media is a growing adult fan culture centred on the remembering and recollecting of childhood where memory forms the basis for active online communities that engage in the trading and (re)purchasing of new and old toys and games from their youth. These activities can be seen as part of what epitomises the "rejuvenile", a new breed of adult described by Christopher Noxon (2006: 4) as someone "who cultivates tastes and mind-sets traditionally associated with those younger than themselves". Similarly, Gary Cross's work *Men to Boys* (2008) argues that we are in an age personified by "boy-men" where traditional notions of maturity and masculinity are being transformed alongside an increasingly attractive return to the pleasures of youth. Both authors choose broad-ranging examples from popular culture to illustrate their points and media is central to their analyses of when and where these cultural changes have occurred. Hollywood and the entertainment industry have not only responded to this shift in adult identification but they have actively encouraged people to want to reconnect with their youth and not feel juvenile when enjoying the latest superhero blockbuster or buying a toy action figure (Noxon, 2006: 12–13).

Toy companies are keen to cash in on the rejuvenilisation of a media fan culture. For example, as discussed in chapters three and four, American corporations Hasbro and Mattel have rebranded and relaunched classic toy lines from the past 30 years like Transformers, G.I. Joe and He-Man specifically to target older fans as well as entice younger markets – supporting this with a string of blockbuster live-action movies. Danish toy company Lego, on the other hand, has been a perennial favourite with children since its mass-marketing rebirth in the 1950s and 1960s.

The attraction of being able to build almost anything a child can imagine from a pile of colourful interlocking bricks proved a valuable selling point for parents concerned that their children should be learning something as they played (Cross, 1997). However, following developments in the American toy industry in the 1970s and 1980s, where fantasy and action toys became central components of movie merchandise and licensing agreements, Lego turned to creating its own ranges of themed building sets and minifigure characters where before children built what they wanted (limited only by their own imagination) they now followed plans and built within prescribed "systems": city, space, medieval, pirates, etc. (Kline, 1993). In 1999 Lego decided to buy into the merchandising market starting with its range of very popular *Star Wars* themed sets tied into the release of the first prequel film, *The Phantom Menace* (Lipkowitz, 2009: 29).

Lego's shift to producing product tie-ins has been supported by the creation of online fan clubs aimed at both children and adults. One of them, the VIP Program, boasts a members' only website, special offers and a point reward system, specifically targeting grown-ups and encouraging them to collect Lego rather than play with it, display it rather than pack it away. This convergence of popular fandom, new media, nostalgia and contemporary toy culture suggests that the lines between past and present, technology and culture, childhood and adulthood are increasingly porous. Memory is an important component of being a fan and the remediation of childhood toys like Lego through online communities helps to reconstruct memories of youth that are subsequently used to negotiate digital collaborative spaces shared by other fans. In these web spaces personal memories and histories of children's culture are constantly negotiated and reshaped, taking on new meanings (van Dijck, 2007). These negotiations affect the construction of a fan identity.

As outlined in the introduction, nostalgia has had much critical attention paid to it as a theoretical concept and as a way of understanding how we relate to time and place. Often being seen as an inhibiting and emotional phenomenon that reacts against change and modernity, nostalgia not only represents a longing for the past, it is also manifested as dissatisfaction for the present. Moreover, according to Susan Stewart (1993), nostalgia reconstructs the past through an ideological narrative: "the past it seeks has never existed except as narrative" (23). Henry Jenkins (2007) extends this by arguing that in order "for nostalgia to operate, we must in fact forget aspects of the actual past and substitute a sentimental myth about how things might have been" (157) or "objects we never possessed" (Jenkins, 1998a: 4). As contemporary culture recycles images and media texts from the past, nostalgia felt for them "intensifies a 'superficial' sense of history" (Grainge, 2002: 28) and thus "the present is denied and the past takes on an authenticity of being, an authenticity which, ironically, it can achieve only through narrative" (Stewart, 1993: 23). Debates on nostalgia have taken on renewed significance since Svetlana Boym reappraised its problematic and conservative readings in her work on former communist countries in Eastern Europe. Boym differentiates between "restorative" nostalgia and "reflective" nostalgia, where the former reconstructs "emblems and rituals of home and homeland in an attempt to conquer and spatialize them", the latter "cherishes shattered fragments of memory and temporalizes space" (Boym, 2001: 49). Thus nostalgia can be a more active agent, reflective and exerting a shaping influence on the past and present; bringing the two periods in an individual's memory together, making a new and more fulfilling experience of history and the possibilities it holds for the future. In many ways, then, nostalgia is not about looking for something previously denied or non-existent from the past as argued by Stewart and Jenkins. I would argue that it is about the ways we remember and use memories to actively engage in the present.

Lego, a children's toy originally based on the physicality of construction, has similarly taken on a historical significance in contemporary media culture as it allows adult collectors/fans to reconnect with their past and define a fan identity through more ephemeral and digital interaction. Now that the Lego "system" incorporates global franchises like *Star Wars* it means collectors/fans of one brand cross over to become collectors/fans of the other. The Lego *Star Wars* universe develops a fandom of its own with the minifigure versions of Han Solo and Darth Vader becoming just as iconic and desirable amongst collectors as the "real" toy originals. Therefore, I argue in this chapter that Lego's shift from educational children's toy to transmedia adult collectible may not just be part of the wider trend of "rejuvenilisation" described by Noxon or about nostalgically repossessing objects never previously owned but is, more importantly, characteristic of contemporary convergence culture. It highlights the importance of nostalgia in the transformation of childhood media and toys and how they are remembered. Rather than staying stuck in the past or remaining unchanged, nostalgia acts to enhance the original potentials of those remediated texts and commodities (such as Lego) and transforms their very nature as childhood objects for future use.

Therefore, building on Boym's idea of "reflective nostalgia", I want to offer another perspective on how nostalgia is utilised by, and thus transforms, those who actively connect with items from their past in the present. The examples of adult fans talking about Lego as their favourite childhood toy or adult fans that make their own Lego characters and movies, which I discuss in this chapter, are examples of what I will call "transformative nostalgia". Where Boym's reflective nostalgia leaves room for irony, humour and play, the types of nostalgia at work in Lego fandom in this chapter display a characteristic more discernible as transformative: transforming the original use for Lego, from childhood to adulthood, and transforming the experience of the toy as it passes from one generation to the next. The memories of Lego that serve as models for future play allow for a transformation of object and transformation of identity. The things that we continue to hold dear from childhood, remediated and recycled by the new technologies of modern culture, are evocative and thus serve to bring together ideas of thought and feeling. For Sherry Turkle (2007a), "evocative objects" act as "companions to our emotional lives" and "provocations to thought" (5). They mean something, as a link to the past and an object in the present, so "the meaning of such objects shifts with time, place, and differences among individuals" (2007b: 307). Playing with these objects (touching, holding, filming, remaking, displaying and collecting) "engages the heart as well as the mind; it is a source of inner vitality" (2007b: 309). There is an inherent conflict between how childhood texts are rebranded by producers and how fans choose to remember and negotiate those texts online. As a consequence, this chapter will also consider the reconstruction of personal and public memories of childhood in the digital sphere and assess how adult fans use Lego in the transformation and construction of a new media identity – as "a source of inner vitality" – within the wider online community and through video gaming.

AFOLs, Fan Clubs and Online Memories

In 1966, ten years after Lego founded its first international sales company in Germany, the official Canadian Lego Club was established. Lego was sold in 42 countries around the world and a year later Sweden became home to the second Lego Club. By 1968 the company had expanded considerably, from bricks, to "systems", to the first Legoland opening in its hometown Billund, Denmark (Lipkowitz, 2009: 20–1). The UK saw its own club start up in 1978, whose monthly magazine, *Bricks 'n Pieces*, offered enthusiasts (kids and adults) deals, ideas and blueprints to build new and exciting toys (22). In 1987, a similar magazine, *Brick Kicks*, became the official publication of the American Lego Club (24). Club publications offered collectors of the various systems the chance to expand their collections (buy special offers) and also gave Lego builders instructions to make their own scale models out of generic Lego bricks. In a relatively short space of time Lego had become a global toy brand and with a diverse array of products it had expanded its opportunities to not only attract young children to the fold but also teenagers and adults who enjoyed the thrill of planning, designing and building practically anything they could imagine – similar, in many ways, to model railway enthusiasts who could build their own sets and town plans out of the various products and accessories sold by companies such as Hornby. The longevity of both these brands allows for their multigenerational appeal; older generations pass on their affection for the toy to their children and their children's children, all the while still holding on to that original connection made with it (see Cross, 2004). If Lego is made timeless through cross-generational appeal then Lipkowitz argues that the global reach of Lego increased when the first website was launched in 1996 (2009: 29).

In a highly competitive market, where movie and franchise themed toys were saturating the market the creation of Lego.com, intended as both an ideas platform and a shop, can be seen as a strategic move to reassert a traditional toy brand that may have been waning in popularity. The use of the web, along with high street stores, meant as soon as new sets and themes were launched they could be bought and shipped immediately. Tied in with Lego's decision to make themed sets based on popular film franchises in 1999 and the growing popularity for Lego theme parks in the UK and USA the website provided a virtual and omnipresent platform for the company: advertising the "system" and the brand. As old media turned to new the website negated reasons for having local fan clubs: Lego.com could be the club for the whole world. Individual clubs merged under the banner of Lego Club, with regional editions of the magazine being available in print, then only online. By 2009 Lego Club had three million members signed up through the website (Lipkowitz, 2009: 182). Acting as the hub for members Lego.com became the primary means to advertise and launch new products to kids and their parents and a new conduit for lifelong adult fans of Lego to communicate. Recognising the communal aspect of the website Lego made it possible for fans to create their own homepages as part of the Lego Network. By 2009 one million fans had created their My Lego Network homepage. These fan designed pages acted as a "one-stop starting place" for "information, games, and activities for Lego fans" featuring "links to customer service, a company history and timeline, official press releases and sections for parents and educators" (184). Interaction was now an important part of the Lego experience; originating as simple one-on-one interaction between child and toy in the 1950s and 1960s, the "play" experience had become all about interaction with other kids and collectors online and across the globe. The Network was a community of fans who could use the site for chat, trade and making new friends.

Adult fans of Lego (AFOLs), who have grown up with the toy and taken it from childhood play to pleasurable hobby and pastime, actively engage in community activities – both online and at meetings. Those who build scale models, entire outdoor cities and imaginative pieces of art are called "Master Builders" who are specially selected by Lego to work in model shops and theme parks around the world (Lipkowitz, 2009: 188). These enthusiasts are the inspiration for the fan builders I will go on to discuss in the second half of this chapter. They are an interesting mix of professional and hobbyist, taking their love of the toy and literally building it into their lives as part-time employees of the company. The website, which services both adults and children, is a constant gallery for the Master Builders' work and designs. "Brick Artists", who use the multicoloured bricks in increasingly surreal and imaginative ways, transform the toy from a childhood plaything to a form of adult expression. In turn, these artefacts become cult signifiers of the toy's lifelong and cross-generational appeal; encouraging more people to join in, have fun and create. The toy thus becomes less "just for kids" and increasingly about ageless personal expression and communal activity. Subsequently, products like the toys, clubs, fan-made models, website, blogs and the personal homepages are important component texts of the whole Lego brand that require study in and of themselves. They are "paratexts" (Gray, 2010: 46) that signify meaning and meaning making that will be analysed throughout this chapter.

As I have argued, Lego.com encourages interactions amongst a community of Lego fans: kids can talk to other kids and parents can share stories with other parents. For both Joli Jenson and Paul Booth, fan communities (particularly those online) offer a number of potentials that extend the experience of being a fan. They are "supportive and protective" because "they are believed to offer identity and connection" (Jenson, 1992: 14). The blogs, chats and posts that fans exchange encourage "collectivity and unification" (Booth, 2010: 60) that stem from a shared passion for Lego and a desire to be further immersed within the Lego community.

The Network homepages that people can create thus represent attractive posters that display and advertise to other online members an individual's enthusiasm, knowledge, cultural capital and, most importantly, personal identity. Whether this virtual identity is entirely accurate or a facsimile, an exaggeration, or even false, it is a personal reflection of how club members want to be seen by others and thus stands as a marker of personal meaning: "[T]o represent their own conceptual sense of self – their "me" identity – as it applies in the 'real world'" (Booth, 2010: 163).

Fan activity on Lego.com is varied and displays characteristics of fandom in terms of competition, hierarchy and status. For example, on the message boards, fans have lively debates about how inauthentic some new Lego minifigures are compared to original ones. One member, "Jesusfreak1757" with the title of "Initiate", posted "LEGO has replaced the LEGO yellow heads with the ugly pink-ish skin color heads/hands. I DON'T LIKE IT!!!!!!!!!" Fellow member "Ze-NerdOnline" who is a "Craftsman" responded by asserting their own personal opinion over the skin change, "I always make switching my LEGO guys's head and outfits a hobby. This completely curbs this hobby of mine. GO BACK TO YELLOW SKIN!!!!" Notions of authenticity and fan investment will be explored in more detail later in connection with fan-made Lego videos. However, it is important to point out here that whether or not Lego fans enjoy interacting online because it offers a protective community or a sense of identity, what underlines AFOL dedication to the toy is a sense of nostalgia for the history of the brand itself (e.g. harking back to the original yellow skin Lego figures). Memories of having Lego as a child, and what that represented on a personal level, merge with the corporate history of the toy to become a nostalgic framework for conversation and new products, new creations, new images and new fans.

Joanne Garde-Hansen describes how retro-acts, vintage gatherings, and events like collector fairs and fan memorabilia conventions "all speak to a voracious culture of nostalgia". An important media driver for this shift is the Internet which is "distributing memories into personal, corporate and institutional archives" that can be accessed and shared by people that want to experience those familiar things again or wish to view and hear them for the first time (Garde-Hansen, 2011: 71). Lego.com performs a similar role in that AFOLs can access pictures of, and fan stories about, favourite Lego themed sets and minifigures from yesteryear and younger collectors can find those same things, incorporating them into their own conception of the Lego universe. That AFOLs and children can actively create individual homepages and post comments about how old Lego is better than new Lego reflects an engagement with memory, past and present, and suggests that those memories are changeable and interchangeable while at the same time have the same, if not more, currency over newer versions of Lego. This is not surprising if we accept Garde-Hansen's definition of the Internet as providing a platform for "(re)mediated history" and "the production of separate but connected containers of events, memories and identities and offers ... an ongoing transformation of collective memory as a mosaic of media" (Garde-Hansen, 2011: 106–7).

While technologies of media production rely on the remediation of history, both personal and collective, I would argue that memory and nostalgia are also inherent qualities of the Lego experience. This is perhaps not unique to Lego, however, as similar arguments could be made for model railway enthusiasts, teddy bear and doll collectors or board game players. As stated earlier, longevity is the key to the nostalgic appeal of these childhood playthings. The simple fact that the toy has been around for so long has meant that parents who have grown up playing with it pass it on to their children through a nostalgic process of remembering their own childhood. But this nostalgia is also market driven and is part of contemporary consumer culture. Dan Fleming sees this as important for the sustainability of the toy market where familiar brands like Corgi and Lego can "evoke memories of one's childhood that seem more trustworthy than the brasher demands for our attention" from more modern companies (1996: 118). Similarly, David Buckingham argues that in a risky and flooded toy marketplace "Integrated marketing, strong branding and the incessant recycling of past successes (particularly those that capitalize on parents' nostalgia for the toys of their own childhood) have become crucial in the attempt to manage the market" (2011: 95).

MOC Figures and Constructing a Fan Identity

My Own Creation (MOC) is the official term for a figure, set, model or vehicle that has been designed and built by fans. These MOCs can be constructed from pre-existing Lego sets (borrowing heads, wheels, accessories, etc. to make new things from old), assembled from large quantities of plain bricks (often recreating original models in a larger scale) or they can be Lego bricks and figures which have been literally remoulded and repainted to become something never seen before. In many ways, MOCs can be seen as replicating the unique appeal of Lego right from its inception: that almost anything can be built from Lego through the ingenuity and creativity of the builder. As with other fan communities, it is not typical that Lego fans partake and enjoy making and collecting both types of MOCs, the two activities are often mutually exclusive. However, both types of MOCs are the very definition of fan productivity; taking the original object of affection, fans recreate something entirely new to reflect and express their own identity. Fan scholars have for many years analysed the multiple ways in which fans of popular culture engage with, poach and transform their favourite texts. Lego fans are no different since MOCs are the physical manifestation of such transformations. As Henry Jenkins writes, when fans embrace popular texts they "claim those works as their own, remaking them in their own image, forcing them to respond to their needs and gratify their desires" (Jenkins, 2006b: 59). Moreover, the very nature of Lego as a toy that encourages creativity, design, skills and imagination (building brick by brick) lends itself to what Jenkins sees as integral to the process of being a fan. The fact that this is how adult Lego fans actually experienced playing with the toy when they were young makes this connection even more palpable: "Fandom is not about Bourdieu's notion of holding art at a distance, it's not that high art discourse at all; it's about having control and mastery over art by pulling it close and integrating it into your sense of self." (Jenkins, 2006b: 23). Fans "actively assert their mastery over the mass-produced texts" which provide the building blocks "for their own cultural productions and the basis for their social interactions" (Jenkins, 1992: 23). Indeed, as the following analysis of Lego *Star Wars* MOCs, fan collectors, and gamers will demonstrate, adult Lego fans that create and build their own figures and sets use the toy in a process of identity construction that is built upon established modes of fandom and personal narratives of self.

Lego are keen to capitalise on the rejuvenating effects of MOCs for fans. Clubs formed for the sole purpose of designing and building new sets from pre-existing bricks number in their thousands across the globe. National and international Lego conventions serve as perfect sites to display their efforts, and with *Star Wars* MOCs often these creations sit side by side with official props and costumes from the films at *Star Wars* events like the 2007 European Celebration. The community of builders and fans are recognised by Lego in several publications, with pictures of their creations taking centre stage in a bid to promote the never-ending versatility and attraction of the toy. Simon Beecroft (2009: 94) describes how "The LEGO fan community spans generations, reaches across continents and bridges languages". His section on the fan community at the back of the *The Visual Dictionary* is an interesting counterpoint to the rest of the book, which serves as a simple guide to all the *Star Wars* Lego sets created and sold since 1999. On one level *The Visual Dictionary* is a marketing device to get kids and adults to buy more Lego – you've bought this, now see this and add it to your collection. On another level, however, for fans and collectors that buy the book and who are unaware of what else can be done with *Star Wars* Lego sets, the community section introduces them to a world that they might perhaps want to enter. Buying the toy is not enough, now you can join the community and build on your passion for Lego by building MOCs with other fans. Lego becomes a socialising activity rather than just a commercial product. Daniel Lipkowitz, in *The Lego Book*, not only references fan builders and the community of Lego fans but also stresses how important AFOLs and MOCs are to the longevity of the toy:

> All over the world, grown-ups are rediscovering their childhood love of LEGO building – except for the ones who never lost it to begin with! With incredible talent and imagination, these AFOLs, or Adult Fans of LEGO, are pioneering new building techniques and detailing, attending fan groups and conventions, and showing off their passion for the LEGO brick every day.
>
> *(Lipkowitz, 2009: 192)*

Lego are clearly keen to point out that adult fans are builders and that they use their talents to create new Lego products, they are not simply playing with their toys of old but they are using Lego as it originally intended to be used: as part of an educational process. The ways in which Lego fan communities are described and mediated by the company emphasise worthiness. Whether fans use the bricks to recreate the Mos Eisley spaceport from *Star Wars* (saving up thousands of tan coloured bricks to get the scene just right), build scale models of the Empire State

Building (recreating details with the eye of a professional architect), or create new designs for *Star Wars* characters and ships (fulfilling their desire to visualise what has not so far been depicted on screen) they are actively engaged with a pursuit that is not childish but commendable, innovative not unoriginal.

Rather than simply being consumers, trapped in an endless cycle of buying just to have, fans "engage in symbolic sojourns that transcend a consumerist culture" (Aden, 1999: 80). Lego collectors, like all fans of popular media texts, are engaged in a process of "textual production" (Fiske, 1992: 30) that separates them from the mass market and defines them as active producers of new things that represent more than just the financial investment. MOCs are physical markers of fans' personal investment in the Lego toy and their *Star Wars* universe creations, like all fan objects of attachment, are "intrinsically interwoven with [a] sense of self, with who [they] are, would like to be, and think [they] are" (Sandvoss, 2005: 96). The following Lego *Star Wars* MOCs and online videos are evidence of a particular combination of self and fantasy that illustrate the limitless creativity of fans and collectors.

The minifigures offer fans the perfect object to customise. They can either remould or repaint to make the figure look like them or they can mix torsos, legs, heads and hats to make new figures based on established characters or completely original minifigures that attract multiple bids on sites like eBay. Nevin Martell, in a book celebrating the 30th anniversary of the minifigure, describes their appeal:

> As soon as minifigures made their debut in 1978, fans started customizing them. They created completely new characters using official LEGO parts and then adding their own stickers, paint jobs, and handmade accessories. Suddenly a banker's torso with a formal black jacket might be used to make an Abraham Lincoln minifigure ... over the years MOCs (My Own Creations) have become a vital part of the LEGO fan experience.
>
> *(Martell, 2009: 92)*

Lego minifigures have become popular articles of collecting, trade and fan work because they can be so easily manipulated and by the fact they represent Lego's universal playability and versatility: either as part of a set or standalone the minifigure literally embodies the player's presence in the Lego world. Described as "fascinating and highly collectible" by the authors of the *Character Encyclopedia* "minifigures bring the LEGO *Star Wars* galaxy to life" (Dolan, 2011: 2). They are small enough to fit into the built environment that the builder has created and thus become the physical avatar of the master who controls their domain. With the added dimension of creating new characters for the *Star Wars* universe the Lego minifigure becomes a transformative extension of the self that can be inserted into the fictional narrative of the saga, thus allowing fans to become part of, and own, the very text they adore. On Lego.com fans can upload pictures of their recent creations to show off to fellow enthusiasts. Over 49,000 pictures as of May 2012 suggest that this is not a small community or even a shy one. Fans of all ages, both male and female, post images and comments about their creations and of those of others.

One fan, prinscessleia667, shows off her new "Lego me" with pride saying, "This is a Lego me for Brayden's competition. He asked for Lego me, so here I am ... Aren't I adorable?" Clearly recreating herself as a Lego Jedi Knight prinscessleia667 uses lightsabres and Jedi accessories to dress up a female minifigure. The head has a smiley face and a long brown hair headpiece and the torso is adorned with a cape. Interestingly, not only does prinscessleia667 have a physical Lego form (now immortalised in the picture) but she has also created a virtual icon with the same painted torso that identifies her as prinscessleia667 on the Lego message board. Both images represent her to fellow fans and both images serve as visual extensions of the *Star Wars* universe in which she is now a Jedi character. Another fan, bgirlabby, posts that she will put up a new figure each month to show people her creativity and start competitions for best speeders, figures and guns. Like prinscessleia667, this fan has created a minifigure of herself with lightsabre and torso borrowed from elsewhere but is clearly keen to customise other Lego sets, including vehicles. Typical of fans and fan communities, bgirlabby wants to compete, to challenge other fans to be the best minifigure customiser. She says "I will be having several contests ... I will happily accept any contest ideas!" This suggests, as in all fan communities, that there is a hierarchy of *Star Wars* Lego minifigure builders that is defined and distinguished by knowledge, creativity and imagination. Matt Hills explains that seeing distinction as an important part of fandom "allows us to consider any given fan culture not simply as a community but *also as a social hierarchy* where fans share a common interest while also competing over fan knowledge, access to the object of fandom, and status" (Hills, 2002: 46).

The personalised *Star Wars* minifigures in these instances can be described as the physical manifestations of what John Fiske sees as the contradictory relationship between fan and producer (in this case Lego and George Lucas): "The reverence, even adoration, fans feel for their object of fandom sits surprisingly easily with the contradictory feeling that they also 'possess' that object, it is *their* popular cultural capital" (Fiske, 1992: 40). Building on this, I would argue that their physicality and nature as objects of fan affection make them more than just possessions – they *are* the fans that make them. Both objects of fan cultural capital and markers of fan identity MOC Lego *Star Wars* minifigures are the internal made external: evidence of the link between "the 'external' world of objects and the environment, and the 'internal' world of our experience, feelings and identity" (Gauntlett, 2007: 139). Furthermore, displaying these material "selves" online appears to make the experience of building a unique minifigure more real. They become part of the extended *Star Wars* fan community online, characters that act as virtual avatars of individual people who interact and communicate with others through the web.

Rather like Goffman's "presentation of the self" (1959) fan MOCs online are constructions that are meant to give a particular impression to the external audience but are, importantly, more autobiographical than imaginary. They are attempts to transform and build a coherent and real identity using the *Star Wars* universe from childhood as a framework. Merging memories of *Star Wars*, nostalgia, and the desire to own the text with the need to establish and present an identity within the fan community, Lego MOCs are mnemonic devices of fandom. As Tony Whincup describes of memory and materiality:

> As a group, mnemonic objects generally encapsulate the best of people's reflections about themselves. It is in these object attachments that a personal and "advantageous" sense of self can be sustained. Objects as mnemonics are a complex business intertwined with edited past experiences, current constructions and orientations towards future aspirations.
>
> *(Whincup, 2004: 81)*

Within the Lego *Star Wars* fan community MOCs are not just displayed they are also played with and used to make ancillary texts that further the *Star Wars* narrative. From videos on YouTube that flaunt the huge collections of bought and built sets and figures at other fans (in a competition to see who has the biggest collection) to fan-made sketches that use MOCs and official *Star Wars* minifigures to subvert and reinvent the fictional text, Lego is central to personal and public world building. The Internet is the perfect platform on which to display fan creative work since it can be updated, augmented and viewed by millions across the globe. Therefore, personal collections can become very public and popular through file sharing and social media. One particular Lego fan practice is to film a video of your collection on display in your house and talk through it for the benefit of the audience, picking out favourites, rare items and original MOCs. Dozens of these collector videos on YouTube speak to each other as fans routinely try to outdo each other by adding more figures or vehicles to their display and inventing exciting new ways of filming them.

One video from Legoboy Productions, "My New LEGO Clone Army (2012)", highlights the creative and financial lengths to which fans go to build the biggest and most complete collections. Containing over 2,500 individual pieces (including figures, vehicles, weapons and repainted MOCs) Legoboy's display in the back-room of his house is illustrative of John Fiske's description of the fan collection as "a point where cultural and economic capital come together" (Fiske, 1992: 43). It is the material clue to a fan's financial and personal investment in a text and a symbol of their standing in the wider fan community: in this case, Lego *Star Wars*. Russell Belk suggests that collecting is normally done individually rather than in groups as it is "usually a competitive activity" (Belk, 1995: 68) and the collection itself can often emphasise fan competition where monetary value acts as "a way to 'keep score' or monitor growth and progress, even though [fans] may well have no intention or even a possibility of selling the collection" (Belk, 1995: 80). Displaying a successful collection to others collecting the same thing "brings the collector heightened status (within his or her collecting sphere) and feelings of pride and accomplishment" (Belk, 1995: 68).

Arguably, we can refer to Hills's concept of the "dialectic of value" here whereby Legoboy's collection displayed on YouTube is part of the normal "exchange value" of commodities but emerging "through *a process of localised (fan-based) use-valuations* (which are not entirely reducible to 'economic' models, being intensifications of personalised 'use-value')" (Hills, 2002: 35). Important components of this process are the "lived experiences of fandom" where personal memory becomes enmeshed with the physical artefacts. Belk argues that "most collectors see the items in their collection not as object identifying a cell in a taxonomy, but as packages of memories" (Belk, 1995: 92). Similarly, Tony Whincup (2004: 81) contends that "objects are established as unchanging vehicles for memory" reminding "us of who we are and of our differences from and associations with others". So, for example, in Legoboy's video he talks about where he got some of the figures, that they are not all store bought but many are bought from eBay individually in an effort to build a collection of multiple versions of the same figure. He also talks about how this 2012 army differs from previous armies he has collected in that he has fewer of certain vehicles in order to concentrate on buying and building others. This overarching personal narrative is also suggestive of how a "collection may provide its owner with an omnipotent sense of mastery" and "helps to explain why miniatures and toys are such popular collectibles" (Belk, 1995: 70). If, as I have argued, MOCs are mnemonic devices of fan memory, then the display of vast MOC collections also contributes to the sense of extended self.

In addition to the collector videos there are also fan-produced films on sites such as YouTube that recreate and add to the textual density of the *Star Wars* universe. MOCs and official figures are animated and given dialogue (more often comedic) thus making them even more real for the fans that collect and play with them. In the 7-minute video "Tales of the Savage, Blood-Thirsty, Rampaging, Out-of-Control Wampa!" by alnickelsfilms we are introduced to a Lego Wampa (a monster seen in *The Empire Strikes Back* [1980]) who walks into a fan recreation of Jabba's Palace with a Lego Jabba the Hutt eating. In anachronistic accents they converse with the Wampa moaning that he is misunderstood in the *Star Wars* universe and is therefore ostracised. Meant as an extratextual joke for fans, Jabba would never come face to face in a bar with a Wampa, and containing intertextual references to the physical limitations of fan MOCs this video plays with convention and subverts the *Star Wars* narrative. Relying on fan knowledge and memory it uses comedy to emphasise the constructed nature of the films, the fantasy worlds of Lucas's imagination and the malleability of Lego building and creativity.

As with many fan videos on YouTube it combines pre-established elements (in this case the Lego *Star Wars* figures) with original contributions (the fan story and dialogue) to create a mash up that speaks to fans (of both Lego and *Star Wars*). Both playful and intuitive, fan videos like this one do not simply add one element to another to make a new whole but they form what Shaun Wilson calls "a rupture of narrative" where "the weighted memory" of the original characters from the *Star Wars* universe are "repositioned through its facsimile" (Wilson, 2009: 192). For Garde-Hansen (2011: 116), the "repositioning of the memory of the original is important because we see the mediated past in a new light" (and in this case a totally new form, Lego). Therefore, this video plays, like many others on You-Tube, an important part in the retelling of the *Star Wars* story – it has been transformed. Barbara Klinger (2011: 210) argues that "once ephemeral productions are given exposure through mediatisation, their status as texts with some endurance amplifies their capacity to signify;" therefore, they create new meanings and new beginnings for future fan stories. Indeed, online videos give fans "more autonomy over their (multi)mediated portrayals" of personal identity, cultural capital and the text (van Dijck, 2007: 140). They are evidence of hard work and enjoyable play, visual reminders of the almost limitless potential of the use of Lego in reconstructing the self and the transformative use of nostalgia.

Playing with Narrative in *Lego Star Wars*

In 1997 the first Lego computer game was released, *Lego Island*, closely followed by *Lego Loco*, *Lego Chess* and *Lego Creator*. These early games offered digital freedom for even more creativity as players could use virtual bricks and accessories to create almost any vehicle, building or scenario they could imagine: for example, they could build their own island village with huts, people and vegetation. Customisation was the key to the increasing popularity of Lego on PC and game consoles. Paralleling the shift the company made in the 1970s, when it created systems to frame its various building sets, Lego introduced games that were based on certain themes or worlds: City, Knights' Kingdom, Racer, Bionicle, and Pirates. In 2005 Lego released the first *Star Wars* tie-in game, *Lego Star Wars: The Video Game*, closely followed by *Lego Star Wars II: The Original Trilogy* in 2006. As can be inferred by the titles the first game was very much linked to the prequels that had started in 1999 with *The Phantom Menace* where players could interact with all manner of characters, aliens and vehicles from all three films. The second game expanded the gameplay even more by giving gamers the opportunity to play through the original *Star Wars* saga as one of a number of famous characters: from Han Solo to Darth Vader. The success of these games, by 2009 the first had sold around 5.92 million copies across all platforms (Martell, 2009: 95), showed Lego the limitless potential and profit in making more tie-in games to promote alongside the toys. Titles to date are: *Indiana Jones: The Original Adventures* and *Indiana Jones 2: The Adventure Continues*, *Batman* and *Batman 2*, *Harry Potter: Years 1–4* and *5–7*, *Pirates of the Caribbean*, *Star Wars: The Complete Saga* and *Star Wars III: The Clone Wars*, *Marvel Super Heroes* and *Lord of the Rings*. More than 30 games have been released by Lego since *Island* in 1997 (Lipkowitz, 2009: 173).

Clearly, part of the attraction in these games is that gameplay is tied directly to the overarching narrative of the original source text. So, for example, in the *Indiana Jones* games gamers can play through scenes from all three films (latterly four films) and play as all the important and well-known characters to achieve the ultimate goal of either finding the Ark, destroying the Temple of Doom or securing the Holy Grail. In addition to this narrative play, gamers can also enjoy extra missions and tasks that are linked to the overall theme of the game/movie but are driven more by adventure than the limits of the original story. Across all Lego games this adventurous play, or "free play" as it is called, allows for greater experimentation. This freedom is greatly enhanced by the fact that while you play the story you earn points so that you can buy access to extra levels, new characters and abilities. Once all levels and abilities are open, gamers can then create their own characters and play as them within the story and "free play". Narrative and digital play thus become more personalised with your own Lego character (designed and named by you) engaging with the famous Lego versions of Luke Skywalker or Yoda. The MOC element of the games allows for the convergence of fan identity and fictional narrative, making the experience more individual, more real and more affective.

Fandom has been described by Matt Hills as a form of "affective play" in that fans "play" within and outside their favourite films or TV series by dressing up and performing, writing their own fan fiction, or simply attending conventions. What distinguishes any and all of these activities as "play" is that "it deals with the emotional attachment of the fan" and "it suggests that play is not always caught up in a pre-established 'boundedness' or set of cultural boundaries, but may instead imaginatively create its own set of boundaries and its own auto-'context'" (Hills, 2002: 112). Thus we can see the use of MOCs in the playing of *Lego Star Wars* as part of this fan "affective play" in that gamers can transform and go beyond the boundaries of the original game and story and insert their own self into the narrative. The software in all themed games also presents fans and gamers with the opportunity to transfer their physical MOCs into the digital world. As discussed earlier, MOC figures are created from the standard and themed body parts and accessories across the Lego world. So fans can create a MOC identity from the head of Indiana Jones and the torso of Princess Leia if they so wish. In the games these body parts exist in the game hub and so gamers can recreate their MOC figures, therefore themselves, and insert them into the context of the game world and thus create their own context for interacting with established characters, scenarios and gaming levels.

The transference of characters and narrative across different media platforms is emblematic of what media scholars call transmediality or transmedia storytelling. Henry Jenkins (2006a: 334) defines the latter as "stories that unfold across multiple media platforms, with each medium making distinctive contributions to our understanding of the world". In the context of the Lego games, each game version of the movie adds another level of meaning and story to the original. With MOCs also part of this transmedia process, gamers can move the story from the real world (physical toy) to the fictional world (virtual avatar) – and back again – playing through the narrative in ways not achievable by simply watching and rewatching the film, building the toy, or even being one of the main characters in the game. As gamers play through the levels as their MOC they can interact with original characters from the movies and literally place themselves on board the Death Star or Hoth and take part in the *Star Wars* universe. Dan Fleming recognises this shift in toy culture stating that they "are not the only mediatory objects in our lives; not the only objects to function transitionally for us" going on to argue that technological objects like video consoles are not so much "toys for big boys and girls" but "they generate a safe feeling when we give ourselves over to them" (Fleming, 1996: 195). Building on this, I would argue that *Lego Star Wars* is now as much a trans-media narrative as it is a toy brand or video game and the "affective play" of MOCs (making and collecting, playing with and as) brings that narrative to life for all fans, regardless of age or gender.

Work on computer games has long acknowledged the gender divisions that exist in who plays them, who designs them and who you can play as. As children's media, Jenkins (1998b: 275) argues, they "show strong continuities with the boyhood play fondly remembered by previous generations". Characters in computer games are predominantly male, females are rarely cast in the main role or as active. If they are present then female characters are optional "but when they are included, they are aggressive and have the physical attributes of a male-defined sex symbol" (Subrahmanyam and Greenfield, 1998: 59). I would not disagree with this assertion but I would argue that the "transmediality" and "affective play" in Lego video games give gamers greater freedom to play as either male or female – even a combination of both – and gender as a consequence becomes less important and noticeable than character and environment. Having to play as a female character to follow the narrative of the film in story play means players might wish to continue playing that character in "free play" or at least combine elements of that female character in the creation of their transgender MOC. Added to this, the MOC function in any of the themed Lego games means fans can bring in their own character that is solely determined by the player – and, if they have created a MOC figure already, their own identity can be inserted into the game world and story thus breaking down those gender barriers discussed and critiqued by game scholars.

Earlier I introduced the notions of "affective play" and transmedia narrative to argue that the Lego *Star Wars* brand, including games, MOCs and toys, creates a fictional universe that allows fans to create and play with identity – displaying these identities becomes an important part of the process of being a fan, collector and being a game player. This point can be further emphasised if we draw upon additional work on cult media and cult media fandom. For a media text to be defined as cult, intensely viewed and liked by a fan community, Matt Hills argues that it has to combine elements of what he terms three "family resemblances" which can either be found in a text (qualities and properties) or created by the viewer who sees it as sacred amongst other similar texts. The three "resemblances" are auteurism, endlessly deferred narrative (the story) and hyperdiegesis (the fictional universe/setting) (Hills, 2002: 131). While the first is not necessarily relevant to Lego *Star Wars* (although an argument can be clearly made about the source text being cult due to the creator's, George Lucas, vision for the *Star Wars* saga across six films, an animated series, books, comics, and merchandising) both deferred narrative and hyperdiegesis are important factors in the affective relationship fans share with their Lego MOCs, collections and gaming characters.

The "endlessly deferred narrative" in a cult text is centred on "a singular question or related set of questions" (Hills, 2002: 134) and thus can be seen to play a part in the interactive and goal-orientated gameplay of the Lego video games. Mapping onto the original narrative from the source films *Lego Star Wars* asks players to find Princess Leia, destroy the Death Star, confront Darth Vader and, at the end of each level, defeat the boss in order to progress and achieve their mission. Hyperdiegesis is "the creation of a vast and detailed narrative space, only a fraction of which is ever directly seen or encountered within the text" and operates "according to principles of internal logic and extension" (Hills, 2002: 137). As such, hyperdiegesis is the predominant way in which the Lego *Star Wars* brand attracts fans and players – George Lucas has created so many fictional planets, species and characters that fans have plenty to choose from to be their favourites. The game not only borrows from the source text – all the worlds, characters, alien species and vehicles exist and are accessible in Lego form – but it also extends the universe through the creation and inclusion of fan MOCs and gameplay. The narrative spaces offered by *Star Wars* and Lego coalesce to form an environment for fans that can be played in and played with and where notions of identity and community are malleable and continually changing. That fans and gamers can interact with the hyperdiegetic narrative and video environment makes Lego *Star Wars* an altogether unique and attractive media text.

Interactivity is crucial to Lego's success across all of its toy ranges, video games and online fan communities. As previously discussed, Lego fans, collectors and gamers interact with the physical toys and MOC figures, video game characters and narrative environments. To be able to physically feel part of the Lego *Star Wars* world is an important part of its attraction for fans and therefore needs to be examined in relation to the *Lego Star Wars* video game. Seth Giddings and Helen Kennedy, in their study of the game, point out its aesthetic and interactive qualities as reasons why it differs from other video games and why new methods for studying and talking about gaming need to be employed. In their study they recorded their experiences of, and reaction to, playing different characters through the levels and argue that gameplay "is characterized by a recombinatory *aesthesis*" allowing "moments for amplification of affect and effect within the game – generating extraordinary moments of visual and kinaesthetic pleasure" (Giddings and Kennedy, 2008: 31).

Rather like the examples of Lego *Star Wars* collecting I analysed earlier Giddings and Kennedy contend that "mastery" is part of the pleasure of playing the game but so are the "lack of agency, of being controlled, of being *acted upon*" when in two player mode (Giddings and Kennedy, 2008: 30). The authors specifically mention the multiplayer function in the game that forces players to work together and achieve a certain objective to advance the game rather than allowing individuals to explore the game world. When both of them played together, part of the enjoyment was the fact that the actions of one affected the other, so that in order to access a secret room and unlock a door one of them had to be a short character (like Yoda) and the other a droid (like R2-D2). Functionality combined with character ability was an important part of gameplay and forced the two of them to strategise and talk to each other in order to progress, as a consequence the game was teaching them as they went: "The learning player does not so much make choices as attempt to work out what the game is expecting them to do; the game trains the player" (18). I would argue that this aspect of *Lego Star Wars* is rooted in the history of Lego being seen as an educational toy intended to train children to be creative thinkers, builders and designers. In-game interaction and training through communal play and assuming a MOC identity encourages a more fulfilling playing experience. The game and the player's relationship with the *Star Wars* characters in the game transform as skills are developed and the self-created MOCs engage with levels and scenarios; again, as argued previously, the original object's use is transformed as part of what I call transformative nostalgia.

Conclusion

This chapter has examined how the popular children's toy Lego has become an important part of adult fan culture through the remediation of memory, nostalgia and identity. Through the various examples discussed I have argued that Lego fan play is itself a form of transformative nostalgia – nostalgia for childhood, nostalgia for the original qualities of the toy, nostalgia for the brand, and, in the case of *Star Wars* Lego collectors and gamers, nostalgia for the expansive potentials of the fictional universe created by George Lucas. As Lego adapted to an increasingly competitive toy market its use of new media technologies such as online fan clubs and games to maintain and attract both children and adults signalled an important shift in how memories of and nostalgia for childhood were mediated. Through the communal practices of Internet fan groups Lego fans were able to connect with others, display their own personal affection for the toy brand, and look back on properties of the toy and transform its use in the present. The remediation of an older toy brand, merging the physicality of play with the spectacle of display online, sustains fan nostalgia and allows for multiple connections with people, memories and emotions.

That Lego was able to respond to adult fan desire to reconnect with their childhood is due in most part to their own responses to the changing media landscape. As a modern toy company they have succeeded in moving into multiple "platforms" of entertainment, from sets to figures to franchise tie-ins to video games. The Internet has become their shop window to the world, displaying a variety of products that children and adult fans can use in their own individual ways and styles. For adult fans the Lego minifigure, just one of those products, is now an important commodity for purchase, trade, collection and personal identification. Fans take existing figures and remodel them to suit personal tastes and use them as avatars in an expanding online community and in the Lego video games. Here, the transformative nature of nostalgia for a childhood toy is manifested in the utilisation of a Lego minifigure to personify an individual adult fan's online identity and while gaming. My Own Creations are artefacts of fan nostalgia for a toy brand that has evolved and modernised over the past 50 years. Being physical objects, like any other, they "carry with them social and historical narratives ... [a]t the same time, they have the potential to evoke and carry with them autobiographical narratives" (Mitchell, 2011: 50). Moreover, they are emblematic of a contemporary fan practice that involves elements of collecting, competition and community while at the same time emphasising the importance of memory, identity and nostalgia for childhood transforming to adulthood. Fan collectors of Lego are representative of a breakdown in the distinction between adult and child but their "play" is not regressive or "childish". Lego fandom is both creative and playful, taking elements of childhood creativity (using Lego to build) and merging it with adult fan ingenuity (moulding Lego minifigures to reflect personal identity and even make some money).

This blurring of the line between adult and child is illustrated best by the Lego video games that have become popular with children and adults alike. Playing the game through interactive technology like the Nintendo Wii, fans of all ages can experiment with identity, subvert gender roles and again emphasise individuality through the inclusion of personalised minifigure avatars into the established narrative diegesis of the adapted *Star Wars* universe. The memories of and nostalgia for a childhood toy that was brought to life through the online activities of fans on the Lego website and the collecting habits and remodelling skills seen in fan videos are now remediated in the virtual world of computer gaming. Play has become interactive, Lego as a brand has become multifunctional, and nostalgic memories of childhood embodied by the fans' renewed affection for the physical toy have been remediated. This has meant Lego fandom is driven by nostalgia for one's own personal memories of childhood, the affective relationship fans share with the community, and the interaction between self and technology achieved through online videos and the games. While convergence culture allows for the remediation of childhood media such as cartoons, films and the toys of yesteryear it also allows adult fans to reconnect with their own youth and transform contemporary identities by including visible links with their past. Transformative nostalgia for toy products such as Lego discussed in this chapter is not inhibiting creativity but instead re-establishing the importance of identity in an increasingly technological and interactive global society. As such, transformative nostalgia for childhood should be viewed as an integral part of keeping in touch with the self and as an anchor to a personal history which can be remade, recreated and remoulded at the touch of a button or the purchase of a new toy.

CONCLUSION

Collecting History, Collecting the Self

This book has been an attempt on my part to address what I perceive as a general lack of appreciation within academic circles for the importance of collecting toys, memorabilia and other merchandise in fan culture. As is so often argued, fandom is active, it is participatory and it is creative. Therefore, the act of consumption (personified by the purchase of merchandise) is the antithesis of being a real fan because fans are not passive consumers – they are supposed to be producers, makers and doers. They are on the fringes, working to pick apart media texts and transform them to suit their own needs and the needs of the wider fan community. Collecting, as has been discussed in this book, is almost always done in isolation. The collector sets their own goals and targets particular items that might mean something very personal to them. The collecting of merchandise represents a long-term financial and emotional investment in a particular film or television series but it does not necessarily transform or change the text in ways that fandom is usually depicted as doing. However, for Henry Jenkins, fan culture is a "culture that is produced by fans and other amateurs for circulation through an underground economy and that draws much of its content from the commercial culture" (2006a: 325). Therefore, I would argue that collecting as a fan practice is at the very heart of what it means to be a fan as it clearly draws "content from the commercial culture" and in the circulation of second-hand and collectible items it represents "an underground economy" that creates and ascribes new meanings to the physical objects bought, sold and traded.

However, as I have also tried to establish in *Cult Collectors*, the impetus for this underground exchange is the attempt on behalf of the fan to reconnect with their own past through the interaction with memories and nostalgia embodied in the very objects they collect. Collecting toys, merchandise and other collectibles drawn from the popular entertainment industries enables fans to have a corporeal connection with a culture that is now almost all online, digital and inherently ephemeral. As new texts are produced and new fandoms created there is the potential for continual loss of old texts. Digital archives and fan sites allow for a certain level of preservation. New media platforms and sites like YouTube and TV Cream act as repositories for remediated content, but again these are ethereal in the sense that they appear on our screens but they cannot be extracted, manufactured and put on our shelves as items for display. In many ways fandom is about the display of one's passion for a media text – in the costume or clothes one wears at a convention or the images and blogs posted online – and from this comes a sense of distinction as fans accrue a level of cultural capital that sets them apart with the associated fan community. Collecting objects, keeping them, organising them and displaying them is then by its very nature about the process of distinction and accruing cultural capital. What you have in your collection identifies your level of fandom. Yet, as I have also argued in *Cult Collectors*, the collection does not make the person – they make the collection. The investment of personal memories in the creation of a collection results in the fact that each object means something, it is given significance by the collector.

As so often is the case, the memories that are inscribed onto each object in the collection are defined by certain experiences in the collector's life. That is why the importance of childhood memories and nostalgia felt for such times is a funda-mental aspect of cult collecting – it informs the processes of building a collection, provides personal meaning and situates each and every object in relation to others and to the collector. What is more, the relationship between objects and between collector and objects is often informed by the relationships formed within particular spaces and places. That is why a large proportion of *Cult Collectors* was devoted to understanding what goes on at conventions and how the practice of collecting is affected by issues relating to access, spatial design, physical layout, buildings, and even the city. In the case of the San Diego Comic-Con it is clear that physical objects in the form of merchandise, toys and other unique collectibles are highly sought after and are important aspects of the convention experience. The geography of the convention space creates a fan heterotopia that allows for the free flowing exchange of physical objects and, by extension, the continued development of a fan identity. Throughout this book identity has been an underlying theme, seen in my focus on the fan and collectors stereotypes that have had a direct influence on the public and media perceptions of fandom as well as in my analysis of fan collectors of Hollywood memorabilia, *Star Wars* figures, *Transformers*, and Lego.

As already intimated, collections do not completely make the fan but in their collecting fans create a sense of identity through the association of personal memories and nostalgia with particular objects they collect. Nostalgia then, as I argued in relation to Lego collecting, is a transformative process rather than an inhibiting and conservative emotion. It allows fans to breathe new life into old collectibles, giving them value through second-hand fandom, and creates new meanings for old texts that are remediated and brought back from childhood into adulthood. As I hoped this book would at least remind us, we are all products of our own past and the things we acquired in childhood and the texts we watched over time stay with us.

They often fade away only to come back, in different forms for sure, but my focus on collecting culture has shown that objects continue to mean something long after they have stopped being the popular thing they once were. This is perhaps best exemplified in the very recent fan phenomenon: Bronies.

Hasbro and Bronies: *My Little Pony* as Transformative Object

Bronies are male fans of *My Little Pony: Friendship is Magic* (2010–present), a reboot of the original *My Little Pony* (1984–7) series from the 1980s. In an article for *The Guardian*'s "Comment is Free" pages on their website Rebecca Angel discusses this new fan group, describing it as a form of rebellion:

> Bronies are a diverse group of adults that enjoy a show that makes them want to be nice to each other. Maybe the fact that any man gave *My Little Pony* a try is the most important point here. Having interests that go against what men are supposed to embrace is the sneakiest kind of rebellion.
>
> *(Angel, 2012)*

Bronies are archetypal fans in that they have taken a media text targeted at a different audience, transformed it through memes, videos, and websites, and ascribed new meanings to it through the personalisation of characters, images and narrative. In the spirit of contemporary media production the creators of the new series have responded to this fan enthusiasm and incorporated many elements from the fan culture; making the show more immediate, reverent and intertextual: "As the show progresses, themes of fan creation are written into it almost in a real-time manner. These can be anything from fans creating character names to full on cameos and sight gags within the show itself, and in one case, strange merchandising" (Shreve, 2012: 24). Thus, in Brony fandom, we can see many of the elements discussed in *Cult Collectors*: toys and other merchandise are central components in the creation of a fan community and an individual's identity as a fan is represented by physical objects that embody personal memories, often linked to the nostalgia felt for the childhood past. With Bronies we see this nostalgic celebration taken to new levels as a text originally aimed at girls from a previous generation is now being transformed by men of this generation. The core Brony demographic is teenagers not old enough to remember the 1980s series, so we are seeing here a nostalgic recollection of the past but one which is remediated through television and the Internet.

Hasbro has welcomed this interest from a different target audience and has replied in turn by producing merchandise to be collected by these new fans. At the 2011 Comic-Con the Hasbro booth launched a new series of Pony dolls, specifically for the Brony community. The Hub, Hasbro's cartoon network, has become a channel for nostalgic recollection as it screens both old and new versions of some of the 1980s' most popular toylines: *The Care Bears* (1985–8), *Strawberry Shortcake* (1980–5), *Transformers: Prime* (2010–present), *G.I. Joe: A Real American Hero*

(1983–7), alongside *My Little Pony: Friendship is Magic*. Hasbro has also licensed clothing aimed at both young girls and adult fans so that they can dress in the brand and exhibit their newfound pride at being a Brony. Gregory Schmidt (2013) cites how Hasbro now considers *My Little Pony* a "lifestyle brand", being able to traverse generations of fans and proving significant and valuable to individuals whether they are male or female, 10 or 30. As we have seen in *Cult Collectors*, multiple generations of *Transformers* fans are able to invest in the franchise and still get something out of it years later. Like Bronies, just because the product was originally conceived as a children's toy does not make it less applicable to them or their lives. However, as I have stressed throughout this work, the use of memory and nostalgia to inform one's fandom of a text from a generation past, or intended for a different audience or different interpretation, is crucial in creating a sense of meaning. From that meaning a sense of self identity is formed, organised and displayed through the accumulation of objects in a collection.

Within Brony fandom we can see familiar engagements with physical objects, media, and conventions that make it rather typical of fan culture. Indeed, part of what makes taking on a Brony identity so attractive is that it subverts many of those stereotypes that I discussed in the first two chapters of this book. Venetia Robertson argues "that the Brony community, through their consumption of 'girly' anthropomorphic animal media, engage in a playful re/construction of the largely masculine category of the geek" (2013: 3). Similarly, as I argued in relation to adult fans bringing back childhood texts to recollect and enjoy, Bronies are celebrating the very things that society dictates should be the preserve of one group over another. Their rebellion to do otherwise is the very essence of fandom and thus we can see fan collectors discussed in *Cult Collectors* as performing and practising the very nature of what it means to be a fan. The ponies in *My Little Pony* are "tools for personal meaning-making" argues Robertson (2013: 1) and thus they "provide an avenue for authentic self-expression and reification within the bosom of a community that supports and shares these goals. Bronies are not just among fellow fans, men, and geeks, but individuals turning to anthropomorphic animal media to seek an authentic experience of selfhood" (Robertson, 2013: 14). Since memories are employed to make that process more enjoyable and liberating suggests that fandom itself is a form of nostalgia: responsive to personal desire, informed by a sense of history and expressed in the creative work of fan activities. As a consequence, collecting as a fan activity reflects all the processes that make fandom what it is – a form of self identity – and nostalgia is the transformative inspiration that puts it into motion.

Towards the Media Archaeology of Fandom

The combination of old and new media with historical and physical objects within fan culture requires new directions in fan research. Indeed, this book was intended as a reconsideration of fan practices that have often been overlooked because they rely just as much on the materiality of media texts as they do on new digital communication technologies. A focus on the historical, physical and previously forgotten follows what is now a growing area of media studies, what Erkki Huhtamo and Jussi Parikka term "media archaeology" (2011). This involves uncovering discarded or forgotten materials in order to grasp a more nuanced sense of the past and how it has affected the present media environment. As new technologies continue to develop and frame our interaction with the media a sense of how forms, texts and cultures developed over time could be lost as we try to keep up with the flows of content and ideas across networks of social and global media. As such, we might lose sight of how history continues to affect our relationship with the media; particularly in terms of how we construct our identities through and across different media platforms: "The challenges posed by contemporary media culture are complex, but the past has been considered to have little to contribute toward their untangling. The new media have been treated as an all-encompassing and 'timeless' realm that can be explained from within" (Huhtamo and Parikka, 2011: 1).

A movement towards methods of media archaeology will necessarily require us to remain aware of how new media is not cut off from its history. There are continuities and crossovers, connections and contradictions that indicate we need to broaden our search to provide a more detailed and critical understanding of how audiences engage with the media. Similarly, in terms of fan studies, we need to look to history to identify the continuities and connections current fan culture has with the past. That is why *Cult Collectors* was so focused on notions of personal history and how memories embodied in collectible objects allow fans to reconnect with their childhood and other moments in their past. In this era of heightened media awareness and accessibility we must also consider what new media can offer fans in terms of looking back, as well as forward. All the while the Internet can provide fans with new spaces to build new networks and virtual communities, it can also allow fans and researchers a better insight into the real and material histories of fandom. Collecting the products of popular media texts is about celebrating the past through the uses of future media technologies in the present. As Huhtamo and Parikka assert, "Media archaeology rummages textual, visual, and auditory archives as well as collections of artifacts, emphasizing both the discursive and the material manifestations of culture" (2011: 3). Therefore, as intended in *Cult Collectors*, we must look to the material as well as the virtual to understand more fully the importance of particular fan practices, such as collecting, and evaluate what it means to be a fan in the first years of the twenty-first century.

It is encouraging to see other media scholars look to material culture to offer more nuanced and complex readings of popular media culture. Bob Rehak's 2013 study of the "object practices" of horror fans highlights the importance of physically making models for fans and how this extends the presence of certain historical media texts and franchises into contemporary culture. Similarly, work on Japanese media culture and its transmission to a global audience has revealed the importance of physical objects and collectibles in creating and sustaining Western fan cultures. Marc Steinberg's book on anime toys and characters (2012), Anne Allison's study of Japanese toys such as Pokémon (2006), and Christine Yano's (2004, 2006) and Brian McVeigh's (1996, 1997, 2000) work on Hello Kitty have all shown how toys, games and other merchandise act as cultural translators allowing transnational media texts to cross over international and local borders. Lastly, in the vein of media archaeology and preserving digital archives, James Newman's work on video game preservation (2012) suggests that we might better understand games and gaming culture if we consider their use within wider debates relating to fan identity and virtual collecting practices.

While I cannot profess that *Cult Collectors* has filled the fan studies gap in understanding collecting as fan practice completely; it certainly has revealed the importance of considering the historical and material when examining any particular fan culture. It should provide the first step for scholars who want to investigate and analyse the physical objects that make up fandom and the importance of memory and nostalgia in creating a fan identity. The toys we continue to buy and display, the collectibles we search for at conventions and shops, are reminders of the importance of material culture and the strong connections we still have with the past. For fans, collecting in all its forms is part of what makes feeling connected to favourite films and television series all the more personal and intimate. Fan communities share in their celebrations of media texts but the objects fans collect remind us that fandom is also a very personal activity. Memory and nostalgia are part of culture but they also allow us to connect with physical artefacts of popular culture in ways not originally intended by producers and manufacturers. *Cult Collectors* has shown that to be a collector is to be a fan, and to be a fan is to build a collection of objects and memories that shows just what it means to be you.

BIBLIOGRAPHY

Abercrombie, Nicholas and Brian Longhurst (1998), *Audiences: A Sociological Theory of Performance and Imagination*, London: Sage Publications.

Abraham, Kristin (2005, May), "TD Monthly's top 10 most wanted action figures," *TD Monthly: A Trade Magazine for the Toy, Hobby, Game & Gift Industry*. Retrieved from www.toydirectory.com/monthly/article.asp?id=1336.

"Action Comics Superman debut copy sells for $2.16m" (2011, December 1), *BBC News*. Retrieved from www.bbc.co.uk/news/entertainment-arts-15978677.

Aden, Roger C. (1999), *Popular Stories and Promised Lands: Fan Cultures and Symbolic Pilgrimages*, Tuscaloosa: The University of Alabama Press.

Allison, Anne (2006), *Millennial Monsters: Japanese Toys and the Global Imagination*, Berkeley: University of California Press.

Altman, Rick (1999), *Film/Genre*, London: BFI Publishing.

Alvarez, J.E. (2001a), *The Unofficial Guide to Transformers, 1980s Through 1990s: Revised & Expanded 2nd Edition*, Atglen, PA: Schiffer Publishing Ltd.

———. (2001b), *The Unofficial Guide to Japanese and International Transformers*, Atglen, PA: Schiffer Publishing Ltd.

Anderegg, David (2011), *Nerds: How Dorks, Dweebs, Techies and Trekkies Can Save America and Why They Might Be Our Last Hope*, New York: Tarcher/Penguin.

Angel, Rebecca (2012, 1 October), "Adult male My Little Pony fans? Bronies are true rebels," *The Guardian*. Retrieved from www.guardian.co.uk/commentisfree/2012/oct/01/my-little-pony-bronies-rebels.

Appadurai, Arjun (1986), "Introduction: Commodities and the politics of value," in *The Social Life of Things: Commodities in Cultural Perspective*, Arjun Appadurai, ed., Cambridge: Cambridge University Press, 3–63.

Attfield, Judy (1996), "Barbie and Action Man: Adult toys for girls and boys, 1959–93," in *The Gendered Object*, Pat Kirkham, ed., Manchester: Manchester University Press, 80–9.

Augé, Marc (1995), *Non-Places: Introduction to an Anthropology of Supermodernity*, John Howe, trans., London: Verso.

Augoustinos, Martha and Iain Walker (1995), *Social Cognition: An Integrated Introduction*, London: Sage Publications.

Auslander, Philip (1999), *Liveness: Performance in a Mediatized Culture*, London and New York: Routledge.

Backes, Nancy (1997), "Reading the Shopping Mall City," *Journal of Popular Culture* 31(3), 1–17.

Bainbridge, Jason (2012), "Fully articulated: The rise of the action figure and the changing face of 'children's' entertainment," in *Entertainment Industries: Entertainment as a Cultural System*, Alan McKee, Christy Collis and Ben Hamley, eds, London and New York: Routledge, 31–44.

Bal, Mieke (1994), "Telling objects: A narrative perspective on collecting," in *The Culture of Collecting*, John Elsner and Roger Cardinal, eds, London: Reaktion Books, 97–115.

Barbas, Samantha (2001), *Movie Crazy: Fans, Stars, and the Cult of Celebrity*, New York: Palgrave.

Barthes, Roland (1975), *S/Z*, Richard Miller, trans., London: Jonathan Cape.

Baudrillard, Jean (2005), *The System of Objects*, James Benedict, trans., London: Verso.

Beckett, Jeremy (2005), *The Official Price Guide to Star Wars Memorabilia*, New York: House of Collectibles.

Bednarek, Monika (2012), "Constructing 'nerdiess': Characterisation in *The Big Bang Theory*," *Multilingua: Journal of Interlanguage Communication* 31(2), 199–229.

Beecroft, Simon (2009), *Lego Star Wars: The Visual Dictionary*, London: Dorling Kindersley.

Belk, Russell W. (1995), *Collecting in a Consumer Society*, London and New York: Routledge.

Belk, Russell W. and Melanie Wallendorf (1994), "Of mice and men: Gender identity in collecting," in *Interpreting Objects and Collections*, Susan M. Pearce, ed., London: Routledge, 240–53.

Benjamin, Walter (2008), "The work of art in the age of mechanical reproduction," in *The Cult Film Reader*, Ernest Mathijs and Xavier Mandik, eds, Maidenhead: McGraw Hill, 29–40.

——. (2009), "Unpacking my library: A talk about book collecting," in *The Object Reader*, Fiona Candlin and Raiford Guins, eds, London and New York: Routledge, 257–62.

Berkowitz, Joe (2013, 7 March), "See the galaxy's biggest *Star Wars* Memorabilia Collection," *Co.Create*. Retrieved from www.fastcocreate.com/1682516/see-the-galaxys-biggest-star-wars-memorabilia-collection#1.

Berry, Steve (2007), *TV Cream Toys: Presents You Pestered Your Parents For*, London: Friday Books.

Bjarkman, Kim (2004), "To have and to hold: The video collector's relationship with an ethereal medium," *Television & New Media* 5(3), 217–46.

Bolin, Göran (2004), "Spaces of television: The structuring of consumers in a Swedish shopping mall," in *Mediaspace: Place, Scale and Culture in a Media Age*, Nick Couldry and Anna McCarthy, eds, London and New York: Routledge, 126–44.

Bolter, Jay David and Richard Grusin (1999), *Remediation: Understanding New Media*, Cambridge: The MIT Press.

Booth, Paul (2010), *Digital Fandom: New Media Studies*, New York: Peter Lang.

Bowles, Scott (2010, 27 July), "Has Comic-Con grown too big for its own good?" *USA Today*, 3D.

Boym, Svetlana (2001), *The Future of Nostalgia*, New York: Basic Books.

Brabazon, Tara (2005), *From Revolution to Revelation: Generation X, Popular Memory and Cultural Studies*, Aldershot, UK: Ashgate.

Bromley, Tom (2010), *All in the Best Possible Taste: Growing Up Watching Telly in the 1980s*, London: Simon & Schuster.

Brooker, Will (2002), *Using the Force: Creativity, Community and Star Wars Fandom*, London: Continuum.

——. (2005), "The *Blade Runner* experience: Pilgrimage and liminal space," in *The Blade Runner Experience: The Legacy of a Science Fiction Classic*, Will Brooker, ed., London: Wallflower, 11–30.

——. (2007a), "Everywhere and nowhere: Vancouver, fan pilgrimage and the urban imaginary," *International Journal of Cultural Studies* 10(4), 423–44.

——. (2007b), "A sort of homecoming: Fan viewing and symbolic pilgrimage," in *Fandom: Identities and Communities in a Mediated World*, Jonathan Gray, Cornel Sandvoss and C. Lee Harrington, eds, New York: New York University Press, 149–64.

Brown, Bill (2003), *A Sense of Things: The Object Matter of American Literature*, Chicago: The University of Chicago Press.

Brownfield, Troy (2008, 16 April), "*Wired's* geekster handbook: A field guide to the nerd underground," *Wired*. Retrieved from www.wired.com/culture/lifestyle/magazine/16-04/st_geekster.

Bucholtz, Mary (2001), "The whiteness of nerds: Superstandard English and racial markedness," *Journal of Linguistic Anthropology* 11(1), 84–100.

Buckingham, David (2011), *The Material Child: Growing Up in Consumer Culture*, Cambridge: Polity Press.

Buckingham, David and Julian Sefton-Green (2003), "Gotta catch'em all: Structure, agency and pedagogy in children's media culture," *Media, Culture, Society* 25(3), 379–99.

Burgess, Jean and Joshua Green (2009), *YouTube: Online Video and Participatory Culture*, Cambridge: Polity Press.

Burke, Timothy and Kevin Burke (1999), *Saturday Morning Fever: Growing Up with Cartoon Culture*, New York: St Martin's Griffin.

Cahill, James Leo (2006), "Between the archive and the image-repertoire: Amateur commercial still life photography on eBay," in *Everyday eBay: Culture, Collecting, and Desire*, Ken Hillis, Michael Petit and Nathan Scott Epley, eds, New York: Routledge, 185–200.

Candlin, Fiona and Raiford Guins (2009), "Introducing objects," in *The Object Reader*, Fiona Candlin and Raiford Guins, eds, London and New York: Routledge, 1–18.

Caputi, Mary (2005), *A Kinder, Gentler America: Melancholia and the Mythical 1950s*, Minneapolis: University of Minnesota Press.

Casey, Bernadette, Neil Casey, Ben Calvert, Liam French and Justin Lewis (2002), "Genre," in *Television Studies: The Key Concepts*, London: Routledge, 108–11.

Chvany, Peter A. (2003), "Do we look like Ferengi capitalists to you? *Star Trek*'s Klingons as emergent virtual American ethnics," in *Hop on Pop: The Politics and Pleasures of Popular Culture*, Henry Jenkins, Tara McPherson and Jane Shattuc, eds, Durham, NC: Duke University Press, 105–21.

Combs, James (1989), "Celebrations: Rituals of popular veneration," *Journal of Popular Culture* 22(4), 71–7.

Conner, Shawn (2012, 13 August), "Female geeks and gamers display girl power at gathering," *Vancouver Sun*, D9.

Coogan, Peter (2006), *Superhero: The Secret Origin of a Genre*, Austin: MonkeyBrain Books.

Couldry, Nick (2000), *The Place of Media Power: Pilgrims and Witnesses of the Media Age*, London: Routledge.

——. (2003), *Media Rituals: A Critical Approach*, London and New York: Routledge.

Crawford, Krysten (2005, 31 March), "The Jedi jackpot," *CNN/Money.com*. Retrieved from http://money.cnn.com/2005/03/31/news/newsmakers/starwars/.

Cross, Gary (1997), *Kid's Stuff: Toys and the Changing World of American Childhood*, Cambridge, MA: Harvard University Press.

——. (2004), *The Cute and the Cool: Wondrous Innocence and Modern American Children's Culture*, New York: Oxford University Press.

——. (2008), *Men to Boys: The Making of Modern Immaturity*, New York: Columbia University Press.

——. (2012), "Historical roots of consumption-base nostalgia for childhood in the US," paper presented at *The Multiple Life Cycles of Children's Media; Childhood Nostalgia Reconsidered*, PLACIM workshop, University of Reading, August 30–1.

Danet, Brenda and Tamar Katriel (1994), "No two alike: Play and aesthetics in collecting," in *Interpreting Objects and Collections*, Susan M. Pearce, ed., London: Routledge, 220–39.

de Certeau, Michel (1984), *The Practice of Everyday Life*, Berkeley: University of California Press.

de Groot, Jerome (2009), *Consuming History: Historians and Heritage in Contemporary Popular Culture*, London and New York: Routledge.

DiBlasio, Natalie (2013, 9 April), "We'd zap back to the '80s, if we could," *USA Today*, 1A.

Diffrient, David Scott (2010), "The cult imaginary: Fringe religions and fan cultures on American television," *Historical Journal of Film, Radio and Television* 30(4), 463–85.

Dixon, Bob (1990), *Playing Them False: A Study of Children's Toys, Games and Puzzles*, Stoke-On-Trent, UK: Trentham Book.

Dolan, Hannah with Elizabeth Dowsett, Shari Last and Victoria Taylor (2011), *Lego Star Wars Character Encyclopedia*, London: Dorling Kindersley.

Drake, Philip (2003), "'Mortgaged to music': New retro movies in 1990s Hollywood cinema," in *Memory and Popular Film*, Paul Grainge, ed., Manchester: Manchester University Press, 183–201.

DuCille, Ann (1996), *Skin Trade*, Cambridge, MA: Harvard University Press.

Dustin (2003, 14 July), "Star Wars Collectors Convention in Mexico City", Rebelscum. com. Retrieved from www.rebelscum.com/story/actionfigure/Star_Wars_Collectors_ Convention_In_Mexico_City_43924.asp.

Eco, Umberto (1998), *Faith in Fakes: Travels in Hyperreality*, William Weaver, trans., London: Vintage.

Egan, Kate (2007), *Trash or Treasure? Censorship and the Changing Meanings of the Video Nasties*, Manchester: Manchester University Press.

Eglash, Ron (2002), "Race, sex, and nerds: From Black geeks to Asian American hipsters," *Social Text* 20(2), 49–64.

Engelhardt, Tom (1995), *The End of Victory Culture: Cold War America and the Disillusioning of a Generation*, Amherst: University of Massachusetts Press.

Fawver, Kurt (2012), "We all go a little nerdy sometimes: Comic book conventions and the popularization of the unpopular," in *Cult Pop Culture: How the Fringe Became Mainstream, Vol. 3: Everyday Cult*, Bob Batchelor, ed., Santa Barbara, CA: Praeger/ABC-CLIO, 3–15.

Fiske, John (1992), "The cultural economy of fandom," in *The Adoring Audience: Fan Culture and Popular Media*, Lisa A. Lewis, ed., London: Routledge, 30–49.

Fitzherbert, Henry (2012, 26 February), "And the best supporting Oscar goes to … nostalgia," *Sunday Express*, 38.

Fleming, Dan (1996), *Powerplay: Toys as Popular Culture*, Manchester: Manchester University Press.

Fleming, Dan and Damion Sturm (2011), *Media, Masculinities, and the Machine: F1, Transformers, and Fantasizing Technology at its Limits*, New York: Continuum.

Foucault, Michel (1986), "Of other spaces," *Diacritics* 16(1), 22–7.

Galipeau, Steven A. (2001), *The Journey of Luke Skywalker: An Analysis of Modern Myth and Symbol*, Chicago, IL: Open Court.

Garde-Hansen, Joanne (2011), *Media and Memory*, Edinburgh: Edinburgh University Press.

Gauntlett, David (2007), *Creative Explorations: New Approaches to Identities and Audiences*, London: Routledge.

——. (2011), *Making is Connecting: The Social Meaning of Creativity, from DIY and Knitting to YouTube and Web 2.0*, Cambridge: Polity Press.

Gelder, Ken (2007), *Subcultures: Cultural Histories and Social Practice*, London: Routledge.

Geraghty, Lincoln (2003), "*Star Trek*: The Adventure," *Vector: The Critical Journal of the BSFA* 228 (March/April), 20–1.

——. (2006), "Aging toys and players: Fan identity and cultural capital," in *Finding the Force of the Star Wars Franchise: Fans, Merchandise and Critics*, Matthew Wilhelm Kapell and John Shelton Lawrence, eds, New York: Peter Lang, 209–23.

——. (2007), *Living with Star Trek: American Culture and the Star Trek Universe*, London: IB Tauris.

——. (2010), "Drawn to television: American animated SF series of the 1980s," *Science Film and Television* 3(2), 287–300.

——. (2011a), "Authenticity, popular aesthetics and the sub-cultural politics of an unwanted blockbuster: The case of *Transformers*," in *Valuing Films: Shifting Perceptions of Worth*, Laura Hubner, ed., London: Palgrave, 88–105.

——. (2011b), "'I've a feeling we're not in Kansas anymore': Examining *Smallville*'s Canadian cult geography," in *The Smallville Chronicles: Critical Essays on the Television Series*, Lincoln Geraghty, ed., Lanham, MD: Scarecrow Press, 129–52.

Gibian, Peter (1997), "The art of being off-center: Shopping center spaces and the spectacle of consumer culture," in *Mass Culture and Everyday Life*, Peter Gibian, ed., New York: Routledge, 238–91.

Giddens, Anthony (1991), *Modernity and Self-Identity: Self and Society in the Late Modern Age*, Cambridge: Polity Press.

Giddings, Seth and Helen W. Kennedy (2008), "Little Jesuses and *@#?-off robots: On cybernetics, aesthetics, and not being very good at *Lego Star Wars*," in *The Pleasures of Computer Gaming: Essays on Cultural History, Theory and Aesthetics*, Melanie Swalwell and Jason Wilson, eds, Jefferson, NC: McFarland Publishers, 13–32.

Goffman, Erving (1959), *The Presentation of Self in Everyday Life*, London: Penguin.

Gomery, Douglas (1992), *Shared Pleasures: A History of Movie Presentation in the United States*, Madison: University of Wisconsin Press.

Grainge, Paul (2002), *Monochrome Memories: Nostalgia and Style in Retro America*, Westport, CT: Praeger.

Gray, Jonathan (2003), "New audiences, new textualities: Anti-fans and non-fans," *International Journal of Cultural Studies* 6(1), 64–81.

——. (2010), *Show Sold Separately: Promos, Spoilers, and Other Media Paratexts*, New York: New York University Press.

Greene, Eric (1998), *Planet of the Apes as American Myth: Race, Politics, and Popular Culture*, Hanover, NH: University Press of New England.

Gregson, Nicky and Louise Crewe (2003), *Second-Hand Cultures*, Oxford: Berg.

Gross, Larry (1989), "Out of the mainstream: Sexual minorities and the mass media," in *Remote Control: Television, Audiences and Cultural Power*, Ellen Seiter, Hans Borchers, Gabriele Kreutzner and Eva-Maria Warth, eds, New York: Routledge, 130–49.

Gunning, Tom (1990), "The cinema of attractions: Early film, its spectator and the avant-garde," *Early Cinema: Space, Frame, Narrative*, Thomas Elsaesser, ed., London: BFI, 56–62.

Harvey, David (2007), "The Kantian roots of Foucault's dilemma," in *Space, Knowledge, and Power: Foucault and Geography*, Jeremy W. Crampton and Stuart Elden, eds, Aldershot: Ashgate, 41–7.

Hendershot, Heather (1996), "Dolls: Odour, disgust, femininity and toy design," in *The Gendered Object*, Pat Kirkham, ed., Manchester: Manchester University Press, 90–102.

Hesmondhalgh, David (2002), *The Cultural Industries*, London: Sage.

Hillis, Ken (2006), "Auctioning the authentic: eBay, Narrative effect, and the superfluity of memory," in *Everyday eBay: Culture, Collecting, and Desire*, Ken Hillis, Michael Petit and Nathan Scott Epley, eds, New York: Routledge, 167–84.

Hillis, Ken, Michael Petit and Nathan Scott Epley (2006), "Introducing everyday eBay," in *Everyday eBay: Culture, Collecting, and Desire*, Ken Hillis, Michael Petit and Nathan Scott Epley, eds, New York: Routledge, 1–17.

Hills, Matt (2002), *Fan Cultures*, London: Routledge.

——. (2003), "Putting away childish things: Jar Jar Binks and the 'virtual star' as an object of fan loathing," in *Contemporary Hollywood Stardom*, Thomas Austin and Martin Barker, eds, London: Arnold, 74–89.

——. (2009a), "Interview with Matt Hills, part 1," *doctorwhotoys.net*. Retrieved from http://doctorwhotoys.net/matthills.htm.

——. (2009b), "Interview with Matt Hills, part 2," *doctorwhotoys.net*. Retrieved from http://doctorwhotoys.net/matthills1.htm.

——. (2010a), "Attending horror film festivals and conventions: Liveness, subcultural capital and 'flesh-and-blood genre communities'," in *Horror Zone: The Cultural Experience of Contemporary Horror Cinema*, Ian Conrich, ed., London: IB Tauris, 87–101.

——. (2010b), "Mainstream cult," in *The Cult TV Book*, Stacey Abbott, ed., London: IB Tauris, 67–73.

Hilton-Morrow, Wendy and David T. McMahan (2003), "*The Flintstones* to *Futurama*: Networks and prime time animation," in *Prime Time Animation: Television Animation and American Culture*, Carol A. Stabile and Mark Harrison, eds, London: Routledge, 74–88.

"Holding out for telly's old heroes" (2013, 5 May), *The I*, 2.

Hollows, Joanne (2000), *Feminism, Femininity and Popular Culture*, Manchester: Manchester University Press.

——. (2003), "The masculinity of cult," in *Defining Cult Movies: The Cultural Politics of Oppositional Taste*, Mark Jancovich, Antonio Lázaro Reboll, Julian Stringer and Andy Willis, eds, Manchester: Manchester University Press, 35–53.

Honan, Mathew (2010, 27 September), "Inside ThinkGeek, where mythical meat can make millions," *Wired*. Retrieved from www.wired.com/magazine/2010/09/mf_think geek/all/.

Hoppenstand, Gary (2009), "Editorial: Revenge of the nerds," *The Journal of Popular Culture* 42(5), 809–10.

Hornby, Nick (1995), *High Fidelity*. London: Random House.

Hoskins, Janet (1998), *Biographical Objects: How Things Tell the Stories of People's Lives*, New York and London: Routledge.

Hubka, David (2002), "Globalization of cultural production: The transformation of children's animated television, 1980 to 1995," in *Global Culture: Media, Art, Policy, and Globalization*, Diane Crane, Nobuko Kawashima and Kenichi Kawasaki, eds, New York: Routledge, 233–55.

Huhtamo, Erkki and Jussi Parikka (2011), "Introduction: An archaeoloogy of media archaeology," in *Media Archaeology: Approaches, Applications, and Implications*, Erkki Huhtamo and Jussi Parikka, eds, Berkeley: University of California Press, 1–21.

Hunt, Nathan (2003), "The importance of trivia: Ownership, exclusion and authority in science fiction fandom," in *Defining Cult Movies: The Cultural Politics of Oppositional Taste*, Mark Jancovich, Antonio Lázaro Reboll, Julian Stringer and Andy Willis, eds, Manchester: Manchester University Press, 185–201.

Hutchings, Peter (2008), "Monster legacies: Memory, technology and horror history," in *The Shifting Definitions of Genre: Essays on Labeling Films, Television Shows and Media*, Lincoln Geraghty and Mark Jancovich, eds, Jefferson, NC: McFarland Publishers, 216–28.

Jamieson, Daz (2003), "Episode guide," in *The Transformers*, Season Two Part One DVD Box Set, Metrodome/Hasbro Inc./TV-Loonland Company.

Jancovich, Mark (2002), "Cult fictions: Cult movies, subcultural capital and the production of cultural distinctions," *Cultural Studies* 16(2), 306–22.

Jancovich, Mark and Nathan Hunt (2004), "The mainstream, distinction, and cult TV," in *Cult Television*, Sara Gwenllian-Jones and Roberta E. Pearson, eds, Minneapolis: University of Minnesota Press, 27–44.

Jenkins, Henry (1992), *Textual Poachers: Television Fans and Participatory Culture*, New York and London: Routledge.

——. (1998a), "Introduction: Childhood innocence and other modern myths," in *The Children's Culture Reader*, Henry Jenkins, ed., New York: New York University Press, 1–37.

——. (1998b), "'Complete freedom of movement': Video games as gendered play spaces," in *From Barbie to Mortal Kombat: Gender and Computer Games*, Justine Cassell and Henry Jenkins, eds, Cambridge, MA: MIT Press, 262–97.

——. (2002), "Interactive audiences?" in *The New Media Book*, Dan Harries, ed., London: BFI, 157–70.

——. (2006a), *Convergence Culture: Where Old and New Media Collide*, New York: New York University Press.

——. (2006b), *Fans, Bloggers and Gamers: Exploring Participatory Culture*, New York: New York University Press.

——. (2007), *The WOW Climax: Tracing the Emotional Impact of Popular Culture*, New York: New York University Press.

——. (2012), "Superpowered fans: The many worlds of San Diego's Comic-Con," *Boom: A Journal of California* 2(2), 22–36.

——. (2013), *Textual Poachers: Television Fans and Participatory Culture*, Updated twentieth anniversary edition, New York and London: Routledge.

Jenkins, Henry, Sam Ford and Joshua Green (2013), *Spreadable Media: Creating Value and Meaning in a Networked Culture*, New York: New York University Press.

Jenkins, Richard (2004), *Social Identity*, 2nd edn, London: Routledge.

Jenson, Joli (1992), "Fandom as pathology: The consequences of characterization," in *The Adoring Audience: Fan Culture and Popular Media*, Lisa A. Lewis, ed., London: Routledge, 9–29.

Jewett, Robert and John Shelton Lawrence (1977), *The American Monomyth*, Garden City, NY: Anchor Press.

Jindra, Michael (1994), "*Star Trek* fandom as a religious phenomenon," *Sociology of Religion* 55(1), 27–51.

——. (2005), "It's about faith in our future: *Star Trek* fandom as cultural religion," in *Religion and Popular Culture in America*, rev. edn, Bruce David Forbes and Jeffrey H. Mahan, eds, Berkeley: University of California Press, 159–73.

Jones, Mark (1994), "Why fakes?" in *Interpreting Objects and Collections*, Susan M. Pearce, ed., London: Routledge, 92–7.

Joseph-Witham, Heather R. (1996), *Star Trek Fans and Costume Art*, Jackson: University Press of Mississippi.

Kanfer, Stefan (1997), *Serious Business: The Art and Commerce of Animation in America from Betty Boop to "Toy Story"*, New York: Da Capo Press.

Karpovich, Angelina I. (2008), "Locating the 'Star Trek experience'," in *The Influence of Star Trek on Television, Film and Culture*, Lincoln Geraghty, ed., Jefferson, NC: McFarland Publishers, 199–217.

Kendall, Lori (1999a), "Nerd nation: Images of nerds in US popular culture," *International Journal of Cultural Studies* 2(2), 260–83.

——. (1999b), "'The nerd within': Mass media and the negotiation of identity among computer-using men," *Journal of Men's Studies* 7(3), 353–69.

——. (2000), "'OH NO! I'M A NERD!': Hegemonic masculinity on an online forum," *Gender & Society* 14(2), 256–74.

——. (2011), "'White and nerdy': Computers, race, and the nerd stereotype," *The Journal of Popular Culture* 44(3), 505–24.

Kirkham, Pat and Judy Attfield (1996), "Introduction," in *The Gendered Object*, Pat Kirkham, ed., Manchester: Manchester University Press, 1–11.

Kline, Stephen (1993), *Out of the Garden: Toys and Children's Culture in the Age of TV Marketing*, London: Verso.

——. (1995), "The empire of play: Emergent genres of product-based animations," in *In Front of the Children: Screen Entertainment and Young Audiences*, Cary Bazalgette and David Buckingham, eds, London: BFI, 151–65.

Klinger, Barbara (2006), *Beyond the Multiplex: Cinema, New Technologies, and the Home*, Berkeley: University of California Press.

——. (2011), "Re-enactment: Fans performing movie scenes from the stage to YouTube," in *Ephemeral Media: Transitory Screen Culture from Television to YouTube*, Paul Grainge, ed., London: BFI, 195–213.

Kompare, Derek (2006), "Publishing flow: DVD box sets and the reconception of television," *Television & New Media* 7(4), 335–60.

Kozinets, Robert V. (2001), "Utopian enterprise: Articulating the meanings of *Star Trek*'s culture of consumption," *Journal of Consumer Research* 28 (June), 67–88.

Krämer, Peter (2000), "*Star Wars*," in *The Movies as History: Visions of the Twentieth Century*, David W. Ellwood, ed., Stroud: Sutton Publishing, 44–53.

Kuhn, Annette (1999), "'That day *did* last me all my life': cinema memory and enduring fandom," in *Identifying Hollywood's Audiences: Cultural Identity and the Movies*, Melvyn Stokes and Richard Maltby, eds, London: BFI, 135–46.

——. (2002), *An Everyday Magic: Cinema and Cultural Memory*, London: IB Tauris.

Lancaster, Kurt (1996), "Travelling among the lands of the fantastic: The imaginary worlds and simulated environments of science fiction tourism," *Foundation: The Review of Science Fiction* 67 (Summer), 28–47.

Landsberg, Alison (2004), *Prosthetic Memory: The Transformation of American Remembrance in the Age of Mass Culture*, New York: Columbia University Press.

Leslie, Larry Z. (2012), "The disappearing bookstore rat," in *Cult Pop Culture: How the Fringe Became Mainstream, Vol. 3: Everyday Cult*, Bob Batchelor, ed., Santa Barbara, CA: Praeger/ABC-CLIO, 115–23.

Lipkowitz, Daniel (2009), *The Lego Book*, London: Dorling Kindersley.

Lundberg, Christine and Maria Lexhagen (2012), "Bitten by the Twilight saga: from pop culture consumer to pop culture tourist," in *Contemporary Tourist Experience: Concepts and Consequences*, Richard Sharpley and Philip R. Stone, eds, London: Routledge, 147–64.

MacDougall, J. Paige (2003), "Transnational commodities as local cultural icons: Barbie dolls in Mexico," *The Journal of Popular Culture* 37(2), 257–75.

Machin, David and Theo van Leeuwen (2009), "Toys as discourse: Children's war toys and the war on terror," *Critical Discourse Studies* 6(1), 51–63.

Marshall, P. David (2002), "The new intertextual commodity," in *The New Media Book*, Dan Harries, eds, London: BFI, 69–82.

Martell, Nevin (2009), *Standing Small: A Celebration of 30 Years of the Lego Minifigure*, London: Dorling Kindersley.

Martin, Paul (1999), *Popular Collecting and the Everyday Self: The Reinvention of Museums?* London and New York: Leicester University Press.

May, James (2009), *James May's Toy Stories*, London: Conway.

McArthur, J.A. (2009), "Digital subculture: A geek meaning of style," *Journal of Communication Inquiry* 33(1), 58–70.

McCracken, Grant (1988), *Culture & Consumption: New Approaches to the Symbolic Character of Consumer Goods and Activities*, Bloomington: Indiana University Press.

McVeigh, Brian J. (1996), "Commodifying affection, authority and gender in the everyday objects of Japan," *Journal of Material Culture* 1(3), 291–312.

——. (1997), "Reply to Kinsella (1997)," *Journal of Material Culture* 2(3), 385–7.

——. (2000), "How Hello Kitty commodifies the cute, cool and camp," *Journal of Material Culture* 5(2), 225–45.

Message, Kylie (2006), *New Museums and the Making of Culture*, Oxford: Berg.

Miles, Steven (2010), *Spaces for Consumption: Pleasure and Placelessness in the Post-Industrial City*, London: Sage.

Mitchell, Claudia (2011), *Doing Visual Research*, London: Sage.

Monaghan, Peter (2002, June 28), "Collected wisdom: A new wave of scholarship examines the centuries-old 'mental landscape' of collectors," in *Chronicle of Higher Education*, A17-A18.

Moody, Oliver (2013, June 10), "Nerds don't care that cool kids like them at last," *The Times*, 7.

Moores, Shaun (2012), *Media, Place & Mobility*, Basingstoke, UK: Palgrave Macmillan.

"My little collection" (2012, March 23), *Metro*, 34.

Newman, James (2012), *Best Before: Videogames, Supersession and Obsolescence*, London: Routledge.

Novick, Jed (2006), *Boys' Toys: An Illustrated History of Little Things that Pleased Big Minds*, London: New Burlington Books.

Noxon, Christopher (2006), *Rejuvenile: Kickball, Cartoons, Cupcakes, and the Reinvention of the American Grown-up*, New York: Three Rivers Press.

"One in five shops could close by 2018, warns study" (2013, May 28), *BBC News*. Retrieved from www.bbc.co.uk/news/business-22686180.

Oswalt, Patton (2011, January 19), "Wake up, geek culture. Time to die," *Wired*. Retrieved from www.wired.com/magazine/2010/12/ff_angrynerd_geekculture/.

Pearce, Susan M. (1994), "Objects as meaning; or narrating the past," in *Interpreting Objects and Collections*, Susan M. Pearce, ed., London: Routledge, 19–29.

——. (1995), *On Collecting: An Investigation into Collecting in the European Tradition*, London: Routledge.

Pearson, Roberta E. (2005), "The writer/producer in American television," in *The Contemporary Television Series*, Michael Hammond and Lucy Mazdon, eds, Edinburgh: Edinburgh University Press, 11–26.

Pinney, Christopher (2005), "Things happen: Or, from which moment does that object come?" in *Materiality*, Daniel Miller, ed., Durham, NC: Duke University Press, 256–72.

Pitzer, Juli Stone (2011), "Vids, vlogs, and blogs: The participatory culture of *Smallville's* digital fan," in *The Smallville Chronicles: Critical Essays on the Television Series*, Lincoln Geraghty, ed., Lanham, MD: Scarecrow Press, 109–28.

Porter, Jennifer E. (1999), "To boldly go: *Star Trek* convention attendance as pilgrimage," in *Star Trek and Sacred Ground: Explorations of Star Trek, Religion, and American Culture*, Jennifer E. Porter and Darcee L. McLaren, eds, Albany, NY: SUNY Press, 245–70.

Pustz, Matthew J. (1999), *Comic Book Culture: Fanboys and True Believers*, Jackson: University Press of Mississippi.

Quail, Christine (2011), "Nerds, geeks, and the hip/square dialectic on contemporary television," *Television & New Media* 12(5), 460–82.

Radnedge, Aidan (2010, 27 May), "These cars are all stars," *Metro*, 37.

Rehak, Bob (2013), "Materializing monsters: Aurora models, garage kits and the object practices of horror fandom," *Journal of Fandom Studies* 1(1), 27–45.

Reijnders, Stijn (2011), *Places of the Imagination: Media, tourism, Culture*, Farnham, UK: Ashgate.

Reynolds, Simon (2011), *Retromania: Pop Culture's Addiction to its Own Past*, London: Faber and Faber.

Richwine, Lisa (2012, 10 August), "Convention celebrates geek girl power," *Vancouver Sun*, D7.

Roberts, Robin (2001), "Performing science fiction: Television, theatre, and gender in *Star Trek: The Experience*," *Extrapolation* 42(4), 340–56.

Robertson, A.F. (2004), *Life Like Dolls: The Collector Doll Phenomenon and the Lives of the Women Who Love Them*, New York: Routledge.

Robertson, Venetia Laura Delano (2013), "Of ponies and men: *My Little Pony: Friendship is Magic* and the Brony fandom," *International Journal of Cultural Studies* (January), 1–17.

Ross, Karen and Virginia Nightingale (2003), *Media Audiences: New Perspectives*, Basingstoke, UK: Open University Press.

Sackett, Susan, ed. (1977), *Letters to Star Trek*, New York: Ballantine.

Saler, Michael T. (2004), "Modernity, disenchantment, and the ironic imagination," *Philosophy and Literature* 28(1), 137–49.

Sandvoss, Cornel (2005), *Fans: The Mirror of Consumption*, Cambridge: Polity Press.

Sansweet, Stephen J. (2012), *Star Wars: The Ultimate Action Figure Collection*, London: Titan Books.

Sansweet, Stephen J. with Anne Neumann (2009), *Star Wars, 1,000 Collectibles: Memorabilia and Stories from a Galaxy Far, Far Away*, New York: Abrams.

Sassaman, Gary and Jackie Estrada (2009), *Comic-Con: 40 Years of Artists, Writers, Fans and Friends*, San Francisco: Chronicle Books.

Schmidt, Gregory (2013, 2 March), "Classic toys redesigned to traverse generations," *The New York Times*. Retrieved from www.nytimes.com/2013/03/02/business/hasbro-expands-transformers-brand-into-new-media.html.

Scott, Suzanne (2013), "*Textual Poachers*, twenty years later: A conversation between Henry Jenkins and Suzanne Scott," in *Textual Poachers: Television Fans and Participatory Culture*, Updated twentieth anniversary edition, Henry Jenkins, New York and London: Routledge, vii–l.

Seiter, Ellen (1995), *Sold Separately: Parents and Children in Consumer Culture*, New Brunswick, NJ: Rutgers University Press.

Shackley, Myra (2001), *Managing Sacred Sites: Service Provision and Visitor Experience*, London: Thompson.

Shreve, Casey (2012), "My little fan culture: Ponies are epic," *Film Matters* 3(3), 22–6.

Shuker, Roy (2010), *Wax Trash and Vinyl Treasures: Record Collecting as a Social Practice*, Aldershot, UK: Ashgate.

Smith Feranec, Kelley C. (2008), "Collecting the Internet: How individually authored websites have generated nostalgia and a desire to collect the Internet," in *Collecting and the Internet: Essays on the Pursuit of Old Passions Through New Technologies*, Susan Koppelman and Alison Franks, eds, Jefferson, NC: McFarland, 9–22.

Smyth, Chris (2010, 24 February), "Slip inside and scare the kids: Dr Who fans offered a ramshackle piece of TV history," *The Times*, 11.

Sola, Tomislav (2004), "Redefining collecting," in *Museums and the Future of Collecting*, 2nd edn, Simon J. Knell, ed., Aldershot, UK: Ashgate, 250–60.

Spigel, Lynn (2001), *Welcome to the Dreamhouse: Popular Media and Postwar Suburbs*, Durham, NC, and London: Duke University Press.

Spurlock, Morgan (2011), *Comic-Con: Episode IV – A Fan's Hope*, New York: Dorling Kindersley.

Staiger, Janet (2005), "Cabinets of trangression: Collecting and arranging Hollywood images," *Particip@tions* 1(3).

Steinberg, Marc (2010), "A vinyl platform for dissent: Designer toys and character merchandising," *Journal of Visual Culture* 9(2), 209–28.

——. (2012), *Anime's Media Mix: Franchising Toys and Characters in Japan*, Minneapolis: University of Minnesota Press.

Stewart, Susan (1993), *On Longing: Narratives of the Miniature, the Gigantic, the Souvenir, the Collection*, Durham, NC: Duke University Press.

Straw, Will (1997), "Sizing up record collections: Gender and connoisseurship in rock music culture," in *Sexing the Groove: Popular Music and Gender*, Sheila Whiteley, ed., London: Routledge, 3–16.

——. (2007), "Embedded memories," in *Residual Media*, Charles R. Acland, ed., Minneapolis: University of Minnesota Press, 3–15.

Stromberg, Peter G. (1999), "The 'I' of enthrallment," *Ethos: Journal of the Society for Psychological Anthropology* 27(4), 490–504.

Subrahmanyam, Kaveri and Patricia M. Greenfield (1998), "Computer games for girls: What makes them play?" in *From Barbie to Mortal Kombat: Gender and Computer Games*, Justine Cassell and Henry Jenkins, eds, Cambridge, MA: MIT Press, 46–71.

Swafford, Brian (2012), "Critical ethnography: The comics shop as cultural clubhouse," in *Critical Approaches to Comics: Theories and Methods*, Matthew J. Smith and Randy Duncan, eds, New York: Routledge, 291–302.

Tankel, Jonathan David and Keith Murphy (1998), "Collecting comic books: A study of the fan and curatorial consumption," in *Theorizing Fandom: Fans, Subculture and Identity*, Cheryl Harris and Alison Alexander, eds, Cresskill: Hampton Press Inc., 55–68.

Tashiro, Charles (1991), "Videophilia: What happens when you wait for it on video," *Film Quarterly* 45(1), 7–17.

——. (1996), "The contradictions of video collecting," *Film Quarterly* 50(20), 11–18.

Thoma, Pamela (1999), "Of beauty pageants and Barbie: Theorizing consumption in Asian American transnational feminism," *Genders* 29 (April).

Thompson, Kristin and David Bordwell (2003), *Film History: An Introduction*, 2nd edn. Boston: McGraw Hill.

Tobin, Joseph, ed. (2004), *Pikachu's Global Adventure: The Rise and Fall of Pokémon*, Durham, NC: Duke University Press.

Todd, Zoe (2006), "Reading eBay: Hidden stories, subjective stories, and a people's history of the archive," in *Everyday eBay: Culture, Collecting, and Desire*, Ken Hillis, Michael Petit and Nathan Scott Epley, eds, New York: Routledge, 77–90.

Tuan, Yi-Fu (1977), *Space and Place: The Perspective of Experience*, Minneapolis: University of Minnesota Press.

Turkle, Sherry (2007a), "Introduction: The things that matter," in *Evocative Objects: Things we Think With*, Sherry Turkle, ed., Cambridge, MA: The MIT Press, 3–10.

——. (2007b), "What makes an object evocative?" in *Evocative Objects: Things we Think With*, Sherry Turkle, ed., Cambridge, MA: The MIT Press, 307–26.

Tyrrell, William Blake (1977), "*Star Trek* as myth and television as mythmaker," *Journal of Popular Culture* 10(4), 711–19.

van Dijck, José (2007), *Mediated Memories in the Digital Age*, Stanford: Stanford University Press.

———. (2009), "User like you? Theorizing agency in user-generated content," *Media, Culture & Society* 31(1), 41–58.

———. (2011), "Flickr and the culture of connectivity: Sharing views, experiences, memories," *Memory Studies* 4(4), 401–15.

Viner, Brian (2009), *Nice to See It, To See It, Nice: The 1970s in Front of the Telly*, London: Simon & Schuster.

Walton, Kendall L. (1990), *Mimesis as Make-Believe: On the Foundations of the Representational Arts*, Cambridge: Harvard University Press.

Wells, Paul (2002), *Animation and America*, Edinburgh: Edinburgh University Press.

Whincup, Tony (2004), "Imaging the intangible," in *Picturing the Social Landscape: Visual Methods and the Sociological Imagination*, Caroline Knowles and Paul Sweetman, eds, London: Routledge, 79–92.

White, Michele (2012), *Buy It Now: Lessons from eBay*, Durham, NC: Duke University Press.

Wilson, Shaun (2009), "Remixing memory in digital media," in *Save As … Digital Memories*, Joanne Garde-Hansen, Andrew Hoskins and Anna Reading, eds, Basingstoke, UK: Palgrave, 184–97.

Windsor, John (1994), "Identity parades," in *The Culture of Collecting*, John Elsner and Roger Cardinal, eds, London: Reaktion Books, 49–67.

Woo, Benjamin (2011), "The android's dungeon: Comic-bookstores, cultural spaces, and the social practices of audiences," *Journal of Graphic Novels and Comics* 2(2), 125–36.

Woodward, Kath (2002), *Understanding Identity*, London: Arnold.

Wyatt, Justin (1994), *High Concept: Movies and Marketing in Hollywood*, Austin: University of Texas Press.

Yano, Christine R. (2004), "Kitty litter: Japanese cute at home and abroad," in *Toys, Games, and Media*, Jeffrey Goldstein, David Buckingham and Gilles Brougère, eds, Mahwah, NJ: Lawrence Erlbaum Associates, 55–71.

———. (2006), "Monstering the Japanese cute: Pink globalization and its critics abroad," in *In Godzilla's Footsteps: Japanese Pop Culture Icons on the Global Stage*, William M. Tsutui and Michiko Ito, eds, New York: Palgrave, 153–66.

Young, S. Mark (2012), "Creating a sense of wonder: The glorious legacy of Space Opera toys of the 1950s," in *1950s "Rocketman" TV Series and their Fans: Cadets, Rangers, and Junior Space Men*, Cynthia J. Miller and A Bowdoin Van Riper, eds, New York: Palgrave, 149–62.

Zubernis, Lynn and Katherine Larsen (2012), *Fandom at the Crossroads: Celebration, Shame and Fan/Producer Relationships*, Newcastle upon Tyne: Cambridge Scholars Publishing.

Zukin, Sharon (2005), *Point of Purchase: How Shopping Changed American Culture*, London: Routledge.

FILMOGRAPHY

The Adventures of Tintin (2011), dir. Steven Spielberg, USA/New Zealand: Columbia/Paramount/Amblin Entertainment.

Angel (1999–2004), prod. David Greenwalt, Joss Whedon, USA: Mutant Enemy Productions/20th Century Fox Television.

Antiques Roadshow (1979–present), prod. Various, UK: BBC.

The Artist (2011), dir. Michael Hazanavicius, USA/France/Belgium: Studio 37/La Petite Reine/La Classe Américane.

Avatar (2009), dir. James Cameron, USA: Twentieth Century Fox/Dune Entertainment/Ingenious Film Partners.

The Avengers (2012), dir. Joss Whedon, USA: Marvel Studios/Paramount.

Babylon 5 (1993–8), prod. J. Michael Straczynski, USA: Warner Bros. Television/Babylonian Productions/Synthetic Works Ltd.

Back to the Future II (1989), dir. Robert Zemeckis, USA: Universal Pictures/Amblin Entertainment.

Battlestar Galactica (2003–9), prod. David Eick and Ronald D. Moore, USA/UK: NBC Universal/BSkyB/David Eick Productions.

Baywatch (1989–99), prod. Michael Berk, Douglas Schwartz, Gregory J. Bonann, USA: NBC.

Beauty and the Geek (2005–8), prod. Ashton Kutcher, Jason Goldberg, Nick Santora, USA: Fox 21.

Bedlam (2011–present), prod. David Allison, Neil Jones and Chris Parker, UK: Red Production/Sky Living.

Being Human (2008–present), prod. Toby Whithouse, UK: BBC.

The Big Bang Theory (2007–present), prod. Chuck Lorre and Bill Prady, USA: Warner Bros.

Blade Runner (1982), dir. Ridley Scott, USA/UK: The Ladd Company/Shaw Brothers/Warner Bros.

Buck Rogers (1950–1), prod. Joe Cates and Babette Henry, USA: ABC.

Buffy the Vampire Slayer (1997–2003), prod. Joss Whedon, USA: The WB/UPN/Mutant Enemy Productions.

Captain America: The First Avenger (2011), dir. Joe Johnston, USA: Paramount Studios/Marvel Studios.

Captain Video and his Video Rangers (1949–55), prod. Lawrence Menkin and James Caddigan, USA: DuMont Television.

Captain Z-Ro (1954–60), prod. Kathleen K. Rawlings, USA: W.A. Palmer Films Inc.

The Care Bears (1985–8), prod. Michael Hirsh, Canada/USA: DiC Enterprises/Nelvana Ltd./ Téléfilm Canada.

Clerks (1994), dir. Kevin Smith, USA: Miramax Films.

The Cleveland Show (2009–present), prod. Richard Appel, Mike Henry and Seth MacFarlane, USA: Persons Unknown Productions/Happy Jack Productions/Fuzzy Door Productions.

Close Encounters of the Third Kind (1977), dir. Steven Spielberg, USA: Columbia.

Community (2009–present), prod. Dan Harmon, USA: Krasnoff/Foster Entertainment/ NBC/Dan Harmon Production/Universal Television.

Coronation Street (1960–present), prod. Various, UK: Granada Television/ITV.

Doctor Who (1963–89 & 2005–present), prod. Various, UK: BBC.

Family Matters (1989–98), prod. Thomas L. Miller, Robert L. Boyett, William Bickley, USA: ABC/CBS/Miller-Boyett Productions.

Fanboys (2008), dir. Kyle Newman, USA: The Weinstein Company/Trigger Street/Picture Machine.

The 40-Year-Old Virgin (2005), dir. Judd Apatow, USA: Universal.

Free Enterprise (1999), dir. Robert Meyer Burnett, USA: Mindfire Entertainment.

Friday the 13th (1980), dir. Sean S. Cunningham, USA: Paramount Pictures/Georgetown Productions Inc.

Futurama (1999–present), prod. Matt Groening, USA: The Curiosity Company/Twentieth Century Fox Television.

Galaxy Quest (1999), dir. Dean Parisot, USA: DreamWorks.

Ghostbusters (1984), dir. Ivan Reitman, USA: Black Rhino Productions/ Columbia Pictures/ Delphi Films.

G.I. Joe: A Real American Hero (1983–7), prod. Joe Bacal, Tom Griffin, David H. DePatie and Don Jurwich, USA: Hasbro Inc./Marvel Productions/Sunbow.

Gilligan's Island (1964–7), prod. Sherwood Schwartz, USA: CBS.

Glee (2009–present), prod. Ian Brennan, Brad Falchuk and Ryan Murphy, USA: Brad Falchuk Teley-Vision/Ryan Murphy Productions/20th Century Fox Television.

Gremlins (1984), dir. Joe Dante, USA: Amblin Entertainment/Warner Bros.

Happy Days (1974–84), prod. Gary Marshall, USA: Paramount.

Hellboy (2004), dir. Guillermo del Toro, USA: Revolution Studios/Lawrence Gordon Productions.

Hellraiser (1987), dir. Clive Barker, UK: Cinemarque Entertainment BV/Film Futures/ Rivdel Films.

He-Man and the Masters of the Universe (1983–5), prod. Lou Scheimer, USA: Filmation Associates/Mattel Inc.

Heroes (2006–10), prod. Tim Kring, USA: Tailwind Productions/NBC Universal.

High Fidelity (2000), dir. Stephen Frears, UK/USA: Touchstone Pictures/Working Title.

The Hobbit: An Unexpected Journey (2012), dir. Peter Jackson, USA/New Zealand: New Line Cinema/MGM/WingNut Films.

Hollywood Treasure (2010–present), prod. Joe Maddelana, Gabriel Landau, Matt Weber, Avi Eshed, Scott Gurney and Deirdre Gurney, USA: Gurney Productions/Zupon Entertainment/ SyFy.

Hugo (2011), dir. Martin Scorsese, UK/USA: Paramount/GK Films.

The Hunger Games (2011), dir. Gary Ross, USA: Lionsgate.

Iron Man (2008), dir. Jon Favreau, USA: Paramount Pictures/Marvel Studios.

King of the Nerds (2013–present), prod. Ben Silverman, Craig Armstrong, Curtis Armstrong, Jimmy Fox, Rick Ringbakk and Robert Carradine, USA: TBS/Electus.

Jaws (1975), dir. Steven Spielberg, USA: Universal.

Jurassic Park (1993), dir. Steven Spielberg, USA: Amblin Entertainment/Universal Pictures.

Lara Croft: Tomb Raider (2001), dir. Simon West, USA/UK: Paramount/Mutual Film Company.

Life on Mars (2006–7), prod. Matthew Graham, Tony Jordan, Ashley Pharoah, UK: Kudos Film and Television/BBC.

Lost (2004–10), prod. J.J. Abrams, Jeffrey Lieber and Damon Lindelof, USA: ABC Studios/ Touchstone Television/Bad Robot.

Lost in Space (1965–8), prod. Irwin Allen, USA: CBS.

The Love Bug (1968), dir. Robert Stevenson, USA: Walt Disney Productions.

M.A.S.K. (1985–6), prod. Susan Cavan, Denis Héroux, Jean Chalopin, Andy Heyward and Tetsuo Katayama, USA/Japan: DiC Enterprises/Kenner/ICC TV Productions.

My Little Pony (1984–7), prod. Joe Bacal, Tom Griffin, USA: Marvel Productions/ Sunbow.

My Little Pony: Friendship is Magic (2010–present), prod. Lauren Faust, USA: Hasbro/The Hub.

Napoleon Dynamite (2004), dir. Jared Hess, USA: Fox Searchlight Pictures/Paramount/MTV Films.

Octopussy (1983), dir. John Glen, UK: United Artists/Eon Productions.

Pacific Rim (2013), dir. Guillermo del Toro, USA: Legendary Pictures.

Paul (2011), dir. Greg Mottola, UK/USA: Universal/Working Title/Relativity Media.

Pawn Stars (2009–present), prod. Brent Montgomery and Colby Gaines, USA: Leftfield Productions/History Channel.

Planet of the Apes (1968), dir. Franklin J. Schaffner, USA: Twentieth-Century Fox.

The Princess Bride (1987), dir. Ron Reiner, USA: Act III Communications/Buttercup Film Ltd.

The Real Ghostbusters (1986–91), prod. Michael C. Cross, USA: DiC Enterprises/Columbia Pictures Television.

Revenge of the Nerds (1984), dir. Jeff Kanew, USA: Interscope Communications/Twentieth-Century Fox.

Rocky (1976), dir. John G. Avildsen, USA: Chartoff-Winkler Productions/Universal.

Rocky Jones, Space Ranger (1954), prod. Roland Reed, Guy V. Thayer Jr. and Arthur Pierson, USA: Roland Reed Productions.

The Sarah Jane Adventures (2007–11), prod. Russell T. Davies, UK: BBC.

Shaun of the Dead (2004), dir. Edgar Wright, UK/USA: Universal.

She-Ra: Princess of Power (1985–7), prod. Lou Scheimer, USA: Filmation Associates/Mattel Inc.

The Simpsons (1989–present), prod. Matt Groening, USA: Gracie Films/Twentieth Century Fox Television.

Sin City (2005), dir. Frank Miller and Robert Rodriguez, USA: Dimension Films/Troublemaker Studios.

Skyline (2010), dir. The Brothers Strause, USA: Hydraulx Entertainment/Transmission/Rat Entertainment/Momentum Pictures.

South Park (1997–present), prod. Trey Parker and Matt Stone, USA: Comedy Central/Braniff.

Space Patrol (1950–5), prod. Dick Darley and Mike Moser, USA: ABC/Tower Productions.

Spaced (1999–2001), prod. Nira Park, UK: Channel Four.

Sphere (1998), dir. Barry Levinson, USA: Baltimore Pictures/Warner Bros.

Spider-Man (2002), dir. Sam Raimi, USA: Columbia Pictures/Marvel Enterprises.

The Spirit (2008), dir. Frank Miller, USA: Lionsgate/Dark Lot Entertainment/Oddlot Entertainment.

Star Trek: The Next Generation (1987–94), prod. Gene Roddenberry and Rick Berman, USA: Paramount.

Star Wars: Clone Wars (2003–5), prod. Genndy Tartakovsky, USA: Lucasfilm/Cartoon Network/Rough Draft Studios.

Star Wars: The Clone Wars (2008–present), prod. George Lucas and Carey Silver, USA: CGCG/Lucasfilm/Cartoon Network.

Star Wars: Episode I – The Phantom Menace (1999), dir. George Lucas, USA: Twentieth-Century Fox.

Star Wars: Episode II – Attack of the Clones (2002), dir. George Lucas, USA: Twentieth-Century Fox.

Star Wars: Episode III – Revenge of the Sith (2005), dir. George Lucas, USA: Twentieth-Century Fox.

Star Wars: Episode IV – A New Hope (1977), dir. George Lucas, USA: Twentieth-Century Fox.

Star Wars: Episode V – The Empire Strikes Back (1980), dir. Irvin Kershner, USA: Twentieth-Century Fox.

Star Wars: Episode VI – Return of the Jedi (1983), dir. Richard Marquand, USA: Twentieth-Century Fox.

Stargazing Live (2011–present), prod. Various, UK: BBC/BBC Two.

Starwoids (2001), dir. Dennis Przywara, USA: Wolverine Pictures.

Strawberry Shortcake (1980–5), prod. Romeo Muller and Robert L. Rosen, USA: LBS Communications.

Super Mario Bros. Super Show! (1989–91), prod. Steve Binder, John Grusd, USA/Canada: Dakota Pictures/DiC Entertainment/Nintendo.

Superman Returns (2006), dir. Bryan Singer, USA: Warner Bros./Legendary Pictures/Peters Entertainment.

Swingers (1996), dir. Doug Liman, USA: Miramax Films/Pathé.

Teenage Mutant Ninja Turtles (1987–96), prod. Fred Wolf, Kevin Eastman and Peter Laird, USA: Murakami Wolf Swenson/Fred Wolf Films/Mirage Studios.

Teenage Mutant Ninja Turtles (2003–9), prod. JoEllyn Marlow, USA: Mirage Studios/4Kids Entertainment/Dong Woo Animation.

The Terminator (1984), dir. James Cameron, USA: Hemdale Film/Pacific Western/Euro Film Funding/Orion Pictures.

Terminator 2: Judgment Day (1991), dir. James Cameron, USA/France: Carolco Pictures/ Pacific Western/Lightstorm Entertainment.

300 (2006), dir. Zack Snyder, USA: Warner Bros./Legendary Pictures/Virtual Studios.

Thundercats (1985–9), prod. Jules Bass, Arthur Rankin Jr, USA: Rankin/Bass/Warner Bros.

Tom Corbett, Space Cadet (1950–5), prod. Mort Abrahams, USA: Rockhill Productions/ CBS/ABC.

Top Gun (1986), dir. Tony Scott, USA: Paramount Pictures.

Torchwood (2006–present), prod. Russell T. Davies, UK/USA/Canada: BBC/CBC/Starz.

Toy Hunter (2012–present), prod. Ashley McFarlin Buie, Daniel A. Schwartz and Matt Sharp, USA: Travel Channel/Sharp Entertainment.

The Transformers (1984–7), prod. Gwen Wetzler, Nelson Shin, Joe Bacal, Margaret Loesch, Tom Griffin and Lee Gunther, USA/Japan: Hasbro Inc./Marvel Productions/ Sunbow/ Akom.

The Transformers (2007), dir. Michael Bay, USA: DreamWorks SKG/Paramount/TriStar Pictures/Hasbro Inc.

Transformers: Dark of the Moon (2011), dir. Michael Bay, USA: Paramount/Hasbro Productions.

Transformers: Prime (2010–present), prod. Alex Kurtzman, Roberto Orci and Jeff Kline, USA: Darby Pop Productions/Digitalscape Co. Ltd./Hasbro Studios.

The Transformers: The Movie (1986), dir. Nelson Shin, USA/Japan: Marvel Productions/ Sunbow Productions/Rank Film Distributors.

Trekkies (1999), dir. Roger Nygard, USA: Paramount.

Trekkies 2 (2004), dir. Roger Nygard, USA: Paramount.

Tron: Legacy (2010), dir. Joseph Kosinski, USA: Walt Disney Productions.

True Blood (2008–present), prod. Alan Ball, USA: HBO.

The Twilight Saga: Breaking Dawn Part 1 (2011), dir. Bill Condon, USA: Summit Entertainment/Sunswept Entertainment.

2001: A Space Odyssey (1968), dir. Stanley Kubrick, UK/USA: MGM/Stanley Kubrick Productions.

Vinyl (2000), dir. Alan Zweig, Canada: Ontario Arts Council/Canada Council.

The Walking Dead (2010–present), prod. Frank Darabont, Robert Kirkman and Tom Luse, USA: AMC/Circle of Confusion/Valhalla Motion Pictures.

Watchmen (2009), dir. Zack Snyder, USA: Warner Bros./Paramount Pictures/Legendary Pictures.

The Wizard of Oz (1939), dir. Victor Fleming, USA: MGM.

Xena: Warrior Princess (1995–2001), prod. John Schulian, Robert Tapert, USA/New Zealand: MCA Television/Renaissance Pictures.

The X-Files (1993–2002), prod. Chris Carter, USA: Ten Thirteen Productions/Twentieth-Century Fox Television.

X-Men (2000), dir. Bryan Singer, USA: Twentieth Century Fox/Marvel Enterprises.

INDEX

Note: Page numbers in italics refer to images.